# The Pragmatism and Prejudice of Oliver Wendell Holmes Jr.

# American Philosophy Series



The American Philosophy Series at Lexington Books features cutting-edge scholarship in the burgeoning field of American philosophy. Some of the volumes in this series are historically oriented and seek to reframe the American canon's primary figures: James, Peirce, Dewey, and Du Bois, among others. But the intellectual history done in this series also aims to reclaim and discover figures (particularly women and minorities) who worked on the outskirts of the American philosophical tradition. Other volumes in this series address contemporary issues—cultural, political, psychological, educational—using the resources of classical American pragmatism and neo-pragmatism. Still others engage in the most current conceptual debates in philosophy, explaining how American philosophy can still make meaningful interventions in contemporary epistemology, metaphysics, and ethical theory.

**Recent titles in the series:**

*The Pragmatism and Prejudice of Oliver Wendell Holmes Jr.*, edited by Seth Vannatta
*Richard Rorty and the Problem of Postmodern Experience: A Reconstruction*, by Tobias Timm
*Peirce and Religion: Knowledge, Transformation, and the Reality of God*, by Roger A. Ward
*William James, Moral Philosophy, and the Ethical Life*, edited by Jacob L. Goodson
*Epistemic Issues in Pragmatic Perspective*, by Nicholas Rescher
*Loving Immigrants in America: An Experiential Philosophy of Personal Interaction*, by Daniel G. Campos
*The Religious Dimension of Experience: Gabriel Marcel and American Philosophy*, by David W. Rodick
*Aesthetic Transcendentalism in Emerson, Peirce, and Nineteenth-Century American Landscape Painting*, by Nicholas L. Guardiano

# The Pragmatism and Prejudice of Oliver Wendell Holmes Jr.

Edited by Seth Vannatta

LEXINGTON BOOKS
Lanham • Boulder • New York • London

Published by Lexington Books
An imprint of The Rowman & Littlefield Publishing Group, Inc.
4501 Forbes Boulevard, Suite 200, Lanham, Maryland 20706
www.rowman.com

6 Tinworth Street, London SE11 5AL



British Library Cataloguing in Publication Information Available

**Library of Congress Cataloging-in-Publication Data Available**

ISBN: 978-1-4985-6124-2 (cloth)
ISBN: 978-1-4985-6126-6 (pbk)
ISBN: 978-1-4985-6125-9 (electronic)

# Contents

# Acknowledgments

I would first like to thank the contributors to this volume. I was honored that each of them agreed to contribute. Some have served as mentors to me. Collectively, to my mind, they have produced the very best scholarship on the work of Oliver Wendell Holmes Jr. Some have devoted their careers to this line of research. They were generous with their time and devoted to produce excellent chapters. I would also like to thank the Society for the Advancement of American Philosophy, the Atlantic Coast Pragmatist Workshop, the Law and Society Association, and the American Institute for Cultural and Philosophical Thought. Those institutions and associations provided valuable venues and occasions to receive helpful feedback on my work in this book. Individually, I would also like to thank Marilyn Fischer and Treavor Pearce for their helpful feedback on my chapter, and Sarah Woolwine, for agreeing to co-author it with me.

# Introduction

Seth Vannatta

Do I contradict myself?
Very well then I contradict myself,
(I am large, I contain multitudes.)
—Walt Whitman, "Song of Myself"[1]

Perhaps Whitman's poetic lines could be applied to Oliver Wendell Holmes. His legacy is a contested one. Holmes is hailed as the author of the greatest book on law by an American, *The Common Law*, and one of the best single essays on the law by an American, "The Path of the Law,"[2] which is the third most-cited law review article of all time, one from which *The Yale Book of Quotations* cites six passages.[3] Nicknamed the Great Dissenter, he is championed as a defender of the freedom of speech.[4] Richard Posner calls him "the most illustrious figure in the history of American law."[5] The rhetorical skill of some of his propositions in scholarly works and judicial opinions are so powerful and succinct that they have become engrained in the collective American legal consciousness: "The life of the law has not been logic; it has been experience";[6] "general propositions do not decide concrete cases";[7] and "it is the merit of the common law that it decides the case first and determines the principle afterwards."[8]

That said, Holmes is vilified by his critics. I imagine few scholars have presented papers on Holmes at academic conferences without hearing an audience member recite his infamous dictum, "Three generations of imbeciles are enough," from his reviled *Buck v. Bell* decision, as a premise in an argument whose implied conclusion is a rejection of the entire academic argument presented.[9] And as Susan Haack writes in this volume: "Holmes has been described as a great liberal,[10] a legal realist *avant la lettre*,[11] a precursor of the 'law and economics' movement,[12] a moral skeptic or nihilist,[13] and even as a proto-Nazi[14] and, by one exasperated critic, a 'cynical . . . brutalitarian';[15] Richard Posner called him "The American Nietzsche."[16] Grant Gilmore exclaimed: "Put out of your mind the picture of the tolerant aristocrat, the great liberal, the eloquent defender of our liberties, the Yankee from Olympus. All that was a myth, concocted principally by Harold Laski and Felix Frankfurter, about the time of World War I. The real Holmes was savage, harsh, and cruel, a bitter and lifelong pessimist who saw in the course of human life nothing but a continuing struggle in which the rich and powerful impose their will on the poor and weak."[17]

In addition to hyperbolic praise and blame, Holmes's scholarship eludes easy classification. His scholarly reputation and evaluations of him have evolved alongside the academic and political tastes of the times. Philosophy of law texts regularly include "The Path of the Law" in the section on legal realism. This is understandable since the realists were inspired by Holmes's essay and his prediction theory of law. But this is a bit like referring to Martin Luther as a Lutheran, an anachronism. Louis Menand indicated in *American Studies*, "Holmes has been called a formalist, a positivist, a utilitarian, a realist, a historicist, a pragmatist (not to mention a nihilist)."[18] Sheldon Novick characterized him as a materialist and structuralist,[19] and Michael Hoffheimer dedicated a book to showing that natural law and transcendentalist philosophy contributed to his mature legal theory.[20] Posner included among his contradictory labels, "atheist, Darwinian, eugenicist, moral relativist, aesthete, and man of the world."[21] Additionally, many have labeled Holmes a Social Darwinist, in large part because of the publication of his correspondences where it was discovered that he was quite skeptical of legislation redistributing wealth. And, along with his decision in *Buck v. Bell*, his reference to "taking in hand life and trying to build a race" suggest this label is appropriate.[22]

The authors in this volume seek to investigate the extent to which these labels are appropriate for Holmes's philosophy. Each chapter investigates one label, analyzes the secondary texts that support the use of the term to characterize Holmes's philosophy, and take a stand on whether or not the category is appropriate for Holmes in light of his career by assessing his judicial and non-judicial publications, including his books, articles, and posthumously published correspondences. The earlier chapters address Holmes's worldview in general in terms of his takes on sense of self and his social and moral philosophy. Each succeeding chapter focuses more on his jurisprudence specifically. As the title of this volume suggests, the arc of Holmes's career is long, but it bends toward pragmatism, and for this reason, each chapter builds to the final pay-off, the chapter by Susan Haack. That is, the thrust of the work as a whole leans toward the stand that Holmes's scholarship demonstrates significant pragmatist themes in the vein of Charles Sanders Peirce, William James, and John Dewey, despite the various ways

Holmes differs from these philosophers, and despite the occasionally disparaging remarks he made of them.

However, Holmes's philosophy is certainly tinted by prejudices of time and place, of his Boston upbringing, his Harvard education, his Civil War experience, and his many years on the Supreme Court during industrial change and world war. Holmes, in the spirit of Edmund Burke and later Hans-Georg Gadamer, is transparent that prejudice is a part of interpretation and adjudication and a part of Holmes's philosophy as a whole. As Holmes unpacks what constitutes "experience" in his first passage of *The Common Law*, he includes "the prejudices judges share with their fellow men."[23] To admit this is a part of the spirit of philosophical pragmatism itself.

The authors investigate these labels by looking to the past and write about Holmes's philosophy in light of the transformation of the law and legal scholarship since his death. This helps bring the scholarship on Holmes into the twenty-first century and enlighten readers as to the continued relevance of Holmes and of legal pragmatism.

In the opening chapter, Alexander Lian assumes most readers understand, given the last fifty years of scholarship especially after the publication of Holmes's correspondences, that Holmes was not a political "progressive" as he had once been described, as he repeatedly wrote to Harold Laski that he hated talk of uplift and reform. With this premise in mind, Lian assesses Louis Menand's response to the misguided project of capturing Holmes's political predilections with a nice-fitting label. Menand focuses on Holmes as the solitary thinker who makes manifest Ralph Waldo Emerson's "American Scholar" through his steadfast commitment to study the object of his profession—the law. Thus, Menand calls Holmes a "jobbist." Lian, by assessing Holmes's Emersonian spirit and those that inspired Holmes's philosophical passion, such as Sir Henry Maine, argues convincingly that Holmes, at his core, was a philosopher.

Albert Alschuler has referred to Holmes's "noble nihilism," that Holmes valued ends whose only foundation was that they were affirmed at all. Alschuler claims this is characteristic of a postmodern worldview, one which shares much in common with Friedrich Nietzsche.[24] In the second chapter, Raff Donelson investigates whether or not Holmes is a nihilist, a Nietzschean, or both. He argues that Holmes was neither a Nietzschean nihilist nor a nihilist at all. Donelson provides a definition of nihilism and offers textual support to explain why commentators have thought Holmes a nihilist and textual analysis in support of a non-nihilist reading of Holmes. Further, Donelson argues that the differences between Holmes and Nietzsche are many, the similarities few. Ultimately this opening chapter concludes that both Nietzsche and Holmes are anti-nihilists.

H. L. Pohlman has made the case that Holmes offered a utilitarian jurisprudence. This interpretation is understandable when the consequentialist features of his jurisprudence are highlighted. Holmes defined law, as well as legal rights and duties, in terms of the consequences of their transgression. Further, his remarks on adjudication and his skepticism of its relation to formal logic suggest a logic of consequents rather than merely one of antecedents, as John Dewey pointed out.[25] However, this interpretation ignores the experimentalism and pluralism in Holmes's theory of adjudication. In previous publications, Frederic Kellogg has used Holmes as a way to distinguish the philosophies of pragmatism and utilitarianism in general.[26] Here, in chapter 3, he looks at Holmes's original contribution to contemporary utilitarian theory and legal and ethical logic long dominated by the analytic canon. Asking how utility affects, or results from, the work of the law, Kellogg shows that Holmes illustrates how moral knowledge is generated in conflict of conduct and opinion, how Holmes's philosophy views law and ethical inquiry in a diachronic way, and the imperative of social transformation for resolving legal and moral conflicts. In contrast to the philosophical project of Derek Parfit, Kellogg's chapter argues that moral progress requires adaptation through democratic engagement, a pragmatist theme augmented by a Holmesean understanding of the nature of conflict and convergence.

Holmes's infamous statement in *Buck v. Bell*, that "three generations of imbeciles are enough,"[27] and his belief that force "is the *ultimata ratio*, and between two groups" have given rise to a discussion of Holmes's implicit or explicit Social Darwinism.[28] Some have even compared him to Hitler in this regard.[29] Many nineteenth-century theorists' ideas about race and evolution and fitness resound of Herbert Spencer's philosophy. Holmes is no exception, and he praised Spencer's work. In chapter 4, Seth Vannatta and Sarah Woolwine analyze how thoroughgoing his Social Darwinism was. Material for such an analysis includes a brief history of Social Darwinist thought, Holmes's application of evolutionary thinking to social phenomena, his preference for laissez-faire economics, his record on minority rights cases, and his decision in *Buck v. Bell*. Although the authors agree that Holmes is the first legal pragmatist, they find the label of Social Darwinist appropriate for Holmes.

One longstanding debate in jurisprudence is between the natural law theorists and the legal positivists on the relationship between law and morality. Generally speaking, natural law theorists hold that laws are just only insofar as they participate in the moral law, often defined in terms of divine law. Positivists hold that law emanates from some legitimately recognized authority, but its moral standing does not affect its standing as law. Holmes has been affiliated with both camps on this issue, although more so with the positivists. Chapters 5 and 6 examine whether Holmes fits neatly into either of these traditions. Michael Hoffheimer has argued that the prevailing scholarly assumptions that Holmes did not believe in natural law in any form were misguided. Hoffheimer claims that Emerson's transcendentalism was a form of natural law that influenced Holmes's philosophy throughout his career and that Holmes only rejected specific strands of natural law theory. In chapter 5, Allen Mendenhall exposes Holmes's skepticism of natural law in essays such as "Natural Law" and Holmes's general distaste for German and systematic treatments of the law in a Kantian and Hegelian vein. However, he too sees a permanent residue of Emersonian transcendentalism in Holmes's writing. Mendenhall situates Holmes's transcendentalist rhetoric and affinities within this literary tradition in a way that both illuminates the Emersonian characteristics of his oft-unnoticed natural-law tendencies and corrects misconceptions about the supposedly absolute divide between natural law and legal positivism.

Holmes's insistence that in order to understand the law, we need to distinguish law and morality has motivated many commentators to label him a legal positivist.[30] Others view this distinction as a heuristic device only and focus on Holmes's statements that the law is "the external deposit of our moral life" and that its practice "tends to make good citizens and good men."[31] In chapter 6, Catharine Wells compares Holmes's jurisprudence to legal positivism on the model of H. L. A. Hart's separation thesis. Wells recaps the criticism of Holmes's supposed positivism, examines legal positivism and its limitations as an analysis of law, and explains Holmes's position with respect to law and morality. The thread running through her chapter is the question of whether Holmes had the negative effect on the law his detractors, mentioned above, claim he did.

As mentioned above, many anthologies on the philosophy of law include Holmes in a section on legal realism. This is understandable in that many realists took Holmes's "The Path of the Law" to be the intellectual origin of legal realism.[32] Echoes of Holmes's philosophy resound in Benjamin Cardozo's *The Nature of the Judicial Process*, where Cardozo ultimately argues for the spirit of realism and the relaxation of adherence to precedent.[33] Legal realists build their program off of Holmes's prediction theory of the law and his anti-formalism. In chapter 7, Brian E. Butler traces these connections, but he also draws distinctions between Holmes and realism. In order to clarify the differences, Butler constructs an understanding of what the legal realists and Holmes generally stood for without attempting to offer a complete conceptual definition of either, as both the realists and Holmes were suspicious of the possibility or utility of such definitional approaches. Butler argues that the legal realists and Holmes had many aspects of commonality, including the anti-essentialism that make a complete definition of their positions wanting. They both critiqued the "classical" Langdellian concept-driven and rule-based version of legal theory, leaned toward a reliance on empirical data, and held a dynamic view of the law as a social institution. They were, however, engaged in different academic projects, and their divergent social and professional contexts account for the differences Butler discloses.

In the final chapter, Susan Haack provides clarification about many of the labels discussed in the first nine chapters, telling the reader "what's true but misleading, what's half-true, and what's just plain false in that litany of discrepant, one-dimensional classifications. . . ." She does so by way of a brief intellectual history of the origin and evolution of the pragmatist tradition, and Holmes's somewhat confused role in it. Haack provides an understanding of the pragmatist tradition not as a unified doctrine but as a family resemblance of several identifiable themes, attitudes, and intellectual preferences. She ends by showing how Holmes's work exemplifies these themes found in Peirce, James, and Dewey, despite all of their differences. This textual demonstration allows for an understanding of the contradictory nature of so many of the labels applied to Holmes in this chapter and in this volume as a whole.

Holmes was and is large. Whether or not his work provides sufficient evidence for the host of labels assigned to him and whether or not he contradicted himself will be left for the reader to decide, given our analyses herein.

## NOTES

1. Section 51 of Walt Whitman, "Song of Myself," in *The Portable Walt Whitman*, ed. Mark Van Doren (New York: Penguin Books, 1973), 96.

2. Oliver Wendell Holmes, "The Path of the Law," 10 *Harvard Law Review*, 457 (1897).

3. Fred R. Shapiro, "The Most-Cited Law Review Articles of All Time," *Michigan Law Review*, Vol. 110, Issue 8 (2012): 1483–520.

4. See *Schenck v. United States* 249 U.S. 47 (1919); *Abrams v. United States*, 250 U.S. 616 (1919); *Gitlow v. New York* 268 U.S. 652 (1925). In *Abrams* and *Gitlow*, Holmes wrote a dissent.

5. *The Essential Holmes: Selections from the Letters, Speeches, Judicial Opinions, and Other Writings of Oliver Wendell Holmes, Jr.*, edited by Richard Posner (Chicago: University of Chicago Press, 1992). ix.

6. Oliver Wendell Holmes, Jr., *The Collected Works of Justice Holmes*, edited by Sheldon M. Novick (Chicago: University of Chicago Press, 1995), Vol. 3, 115.

7. *Lochner v. New York* 198 U.S. 45 (1905).

8. *Collected Works*, edited by Sheldon Novick, 212. Also appears in chapter 2 of *The Common Law*.

9. *Buck v. Bell*, 274 U.S. 200 (1927).

10. John Dewey, "Justice Holmes and the Liberal Mind," in *Mr. Justice Holmes*, ed. Felix Frankfurter (New York: Coward McCann, 1931), 33. See also Benjamin Cardozo, introduction to *Mr. Justice Holmes*, 11.

11. See, e.g., Karl N. Llewellyn, "Some Realism about Realism: Responding to Dean Pound," *Harvard Law Review* 44, no. 8 (June 1931): 1222–64, 1227 n.18; Lon Fuller, "American Legal Realism," *University of Pennsylvania Law Review and American Law Register*, 82, no. 5 (1934): 429–62, 429; and, more recently, Louise Weinberg, "Holmes's Failure," *Michigan Law Review* 96 (December 1997): 691–723, 692. For a critical perspective, see Brian Z. Tamanaha, "Understanding Legal Realism," *Texas Law Review* 87 (2009): 731–85.

12. See, e.g., Robert Cooter, "Models of Morality in Law and Economics: Self-Control and Self-Improvement for the Bad Man of Holmes," *Boston University Law Review* 78 (1998): 903–30; Richard A. Posner, "Savigny, Holmes, and the Law and Economics of Possession," *Virginia Law Review* 535 (2000): 535–67.

13. See, e.g., Albert W. Alschuler, *Law without Values: The Life, Work, and Legacy of Justice Holmes* (Chicago: University of Chicago Press, 2000).

14. Francis E. Lucey, "Jurisprudence and the Future Social Order," *Social Science* 16 (1941): 211–17, 214.

15. Westbrook Pegler, "Fair Enough," *Boston American*, December 18, 1950, 34, 45.

16. Richard Posner, "Introduction," in *The Essential Holmes,* Richard Posner, ed. (Chicago: University of Chicago Press, 1992), xxviii.

17. Grant Gilmore, *The Ages of American Law* (New Haven, CT: Yale University Press, 1977), 48–49.

18. Louis Menand, *American Studies* (Farrar, Straus, and Giroux, 2003), 35.

19. *The Collected Works of Justice Holmes: Complete Public Writings and Selected Judicial Opinions of Oliver Wendell Holmes*, Vol. 1.

20. Michael Hoffheimer, *Justice Holmes and the Natural Law* (London: Routledge, 1992), xi.

21. Posner, *The Essential Holmes*, xvi.

22. Oliver Wendell Holmes Jr., "Ideals and Doubts" [1915], *The Collected Works of Justice Holmes*, Vol. 3, 443.

23. Oliver Wendell Holmes Jr., *The Common Law,* Lecture 1, in *Collected Works of Justice Holmes*, Vol. 3 (Chicago: University of Chicago Press, 1995), 115.

24. Albert Alschuler, *Law without Values: The Life, Work, and Legacy of Oliver Wendell Holmes, Jr.* (Chicago: University of Chicago Press, 2000), 20.

25. John Dewey, "Logical Method and Law," *The Philosophical Review*, Vol. 33, No. 6 (Nov. 1924), 560–72.

26. Frederic Kellogg, "Holmes, Pragmatism, and the Deconstruction of Utilitarianism," *Transactions of the Charles S. Peirce Society*, Vol. 23, No. 1 (Winter, 1987), 99–120.

27. 274 U.S. 200

28. Holmes to Frederick Pollock, February 1, 1920, *The Essential Holmes*, ed. Richard Posner (University of Chicago Press, 1992), 103.

29. Ben W. Palmer, "Hobbes, Holmes and Hitler," *American Bar Association Journal*, Vol. 31, No. 11 (Nov. 1945), 569–73.

30. See Patrick J. Kelly, "Was Holmes a Pragmatist? Reflections on a New Twist to an Old Argument," *Southern Illinois University Law Review*, 14, 427 (1989–1990).

31. "The Path of the Law," 10 *Harvard Law Review* 457 (1897).

32. L. L. Fuller, "American Legal Realism," *Proceedings of the American Philosophical Society*, Vol. 76, No. 2 (1936), 191.

33. Benjamin Cardozo, *The Nature of the Judicial Process* (New Haven, CT: Yale University Press, 2008), 7th ed., 149.

## *Chapter One*

# The Jobbist

Alexander Lian

Most people reading the pages of this collection know that Holmes was not a 'progressive' as historians and other writers typically use that term to describe actors in American political, social, or legal history. Holmes hated talk of uplift and reform. Similarly, most people would be wary of using the term 'liberal' to describe Holmes. The immense difficulty of defining liberal in a usefully precise and still historically accurate way aside, it just doesn't feel right. I know a few people who self-identify as liberals, and whom I tend to think of as liberals—even if they may not fully qualify as liberals under John Stuart Mill's usage—and hardly any of them (myself included) would, without hesitation, call Holmes a liberal.

The hesitation, the momentary doubt that this term liberal, either by itself or with the adjective progressive, fits what we know of this man, given what we know of these words' provenance, or their normal usage in political or academic discourse, arises, for the most part, from the perceived lack of suitable alternatives.

We feel confident that Holmes cannot be meaningfully described as a progressive. Why? Because so many writers have in so many ways interred the very idea. Whether he was a liberal must be handled with more finesse because of the free speech cases. Collectively they sustain a memorial to early twentieth-century American liberalism. Upon this carefully cemented pedestal of legal reasoning Holmes stands, a great Associate Justice of the United States Supreme Court, atop and aloof. Yet a slight turn of the head brings into view a much smaller monument, some distance away, no bigger from atop the pedestal's perspective than a very small tombstone. Inscribed with the name *Buck v. Bell*, it marks the grave of Carrie Buck's unborn children. It marks as well the reputation of a once widely touted liberal who once unforgettably said, in the now practically extinct trans-Atlantic accent of pre–Civil War Boston, "three generations of imbeciles are enough."[1]

Holmes the liberal may have died at least one death but Holmes the great legal thinker and literary persona lives on. We may agree that the man was no progressive—"and you, Justice Holmes, are no progressive!"—but the vehemence of that sawed-off declaration leads nowhere. It doesn't play a supporting role in the counter-thesis that Holmes was a reactionary. Nor does it contribute to a carefully wrought conviction that we have a masked conservative in our midst. We can run through the various other appellations that have affixed themselves to the man's name to describe his political or philosophical bent but at the end we are left with Holmes standing there alone, solitary. Perhaps in a not-so-strange twist of circumstance the only option left us is to see him as he seems to have seen himself: a solitary thinker.

But most members of the creative class have a hard time leaving things alone. We have to say *something*. We have to bring Holmes into our discussions, our discourse, somehow. We may all agree that describing him as a solitary thinker fits perfectly; but after a moment or two of silent meditation we begin again wondering, dialoging, whether this or that word or phrase reveals more about him, or to speak more precisely, reveals more about what entangles him in our lives, than another. Solitary thinker may be the best descriptor—likened to that magnificent jutting granite weathering both violent storms and the lapping surf on the New England coast—but it doesn't really move the plot along.

Louis Menand doesn't recognize the problem or its resolution in the same way. He thinks it a matter of misplaced essentialism. I'll explain what he means in a minute. For Menand the attempt to categorize Holmes's broader intellectual commitments is doomed to fail for the same reason that Newtonian mechanics cannot handle Einsteinian relativity, its frameworks for conceptualizing space and time are intentionally delimited, static, and therefore inadequate. Menand appears bemused by Sheldon Novick's suggestion that "Holmes was, in his thought, a structuralist." He calls that conclusion "unique."

> Novick's idea that Holmes was a structuralist belongs to a history that runs parallel to the history of efforts to define Holmes's politics [*e.g.*, progressive, liberal, civil libertarian democrat, aristocrat, reactionary]. This is the history of efforts to define Holmes's philosophy. Holmes has been called a formalist, a positivist, a utilitarian, a realist, a historicist, and a pragmatist (not to mention a nihilist). Commentators who cleave to one of these terms usually find themselves spending a good deal of time explaining why commentators who favor one of the other terms cannot possibly be right. This is generally an easier business than defending the term they prefer; and the reason is that none of these terms can possibly be right, because each singles out one aspect of law as

> the essential aspect, and it was Holmes's genius as a philosopher to see that law has no essential aspect.[2]

Essentialism, then, is taking a single characteristic or attribute or part and making it definitive of the whole. This is bad thinking. It brings to mind Jean-Paul Sartre's soul-shaking slogan, "existence precedes essence," and alerts us to the primacy of Holmes's native genius in seeing that the—what? reified thing? life activity? profession?—he most cared about had no essential, definitive trait.

To help non-lawyers understand what he means Menand describes a court of law as a "vortex of discursive imperatives."[3] Literary gnostics among the non-lawyers may get it, but the lawyers won't. Lawyers tend to be rather matter-of-fact, staid people, not whirling dervishes in pinstripe suits. They typically become disoriented and repetitive when abruptly asked to consider seriously the deeper signification of a tumult of words, whether spoken personally or by a colleague. Most of them accordingly won't be able to appreciate the intellectual finesse Menand brings to the task of describing the colligation of separate and competing juridical and political demands—he calls them imperatives—that through their repetitive, constant spin cohered into this country's prevailing legal system. In the power of the courts Holmes saw—as did his fellow lawyers John Chipman Gray and Nicholas St. John Green—the system's cynosure and its identifying marker as a *legal* system. So perhaps Menand's conclusion needs an important qualification: Holmes did consider a certain characteristic of law, the legitimacy it grants to the use of force, more important if not more essential than others.

Menand traces the source of the insight that law has no essential aspect to Holmes's masterwork, *The Common Law*. This book, which he describes as "bristling with pedantic details of legal antiquarianism and technical analyses of legal doctrine,"[4] develops the argument that law has no essential aspect—lawyers and judges work within a tradition that inculcates different analytical and rhetorical styles (formalist, utilitarian, moralist, historicist)—because the "active ingredient" (like yeast?) in law is experience. Experience makes law alive. To communicate the force of this perception Menand emphasizes three features of experience Holmes considered especially important: (1) it is not reducible to propositions; (2) it is not individual and internal but collective and consensual; and (3) it contains an inherent "imprecision factor," that is, "that experience is too amorphous, or too multiple, ever to dictate a single line of conduct."[5]

The third feature illuminates the first two. Experience as Menand explains it wars against essentialism; it sunders what the mind wants to cleave and keep cloven. The consequences for how one thinks about the problems life presents become evident in how those problems are framed (issues of imagination and conceptualization), the style of thinking used to explore proposed solutions and their ramifications (logic and rhetoric), and how one should best comport oneself (morals and ethics) given this basic mindfulness of experience's slippery character.

Given this take on Holmes's intellectual convictions and predilections, Menand may not be wholly unsympathetic with the notion that we do best to see Holmes as he saw himself, as a solitary thinker, but he would point out that this image fits within the ideal of the intellectual hero one finds in "The American Scholar." Holmes may have slightly altered the image to reflect his Civil War experience, modeling it after the exemplary devotion to military duty of his friend Henry Abbott, but the gravitational pull Holmes the historical figure exerts on the present lies mainly in how he personifies mature self-awareness in his utter conviction that certitude harbors violence.[6]

Essentialism thus becomes a watchword for danger. If law has no essential aspect it is because life has no essential aspect—other than, perhaps, to keep on keeping on.

Historians have it backwards, Menand says, when they use the phrase "loss of certainty" to describe a salient malformation in Holmes's cultural landscape. It was not the loss of certainty but the shocking discovery of uncertainty that galvanized thinkers and made them sensitive to what William James called the blooming, buzzing confusion,[7] even if for Holmes it was not the blooming but the booming, not the buzzing but the whizzing and ricocheting of bullets, that jolted him out of his abolitionist trance and made him awake to the shrouded threats to life and thought.[8] Forevermore he cleaved to the life-affirming disaffirmation best expressed in the words, "certainty is an illusion and repose is not the destiny of man."[9]

Holmes may have seen himself as a solitary thinker, and Menand seems willing to concede the point, but the truth is that Holmes no longer seems so solitary. Many, including Menand, have brought home the message that our lives are fated by circumstance and our opinions and outlooks will never escape the limitations of their birth. We are part and parcel of whatever prejudice or bias we can distinguish in ourselves or that others, ever so helpful, can find in us.

Menand resolves the descriptive and narrative problem by decentering the political and philosophical questions of how to best identify Holmes. Nor does he dwell on Holmes's self-image as a man of ideas. His Holmes is much more elemental. He is a man who has waded through a river of blood and come ashore baptized in a Vision of Individual Duty so profound that the word spiritual immediately comes to mind.[10] Menand notes Holmes's lifelong adherence to what Holmes called "jobbism," and punctuates the point by redirecting attention from what may be rather pedestrian concerns: "Calling Holmes a progressive or a reactionary is like calling, say, Wittgenstein a progressive or a reactionary."[11]

The comparison appears apt, even clever; it brings together the man who talked about the heroic duty of thinking thoughts in a "black gulf of solitude more isolating than that which surrounds the dying man,"[12] with the genius who uttered the most curious proposition in modern analytic philosophy: "What can be said at all can be said clearly; and whereof one cannot speak, thereof one must be silent."[13] What do thinkers like these have to do with political or philosophical labels?

But then Menand further explains his point: "It [the question] assumes that he [Holmes] was interested in the political consequences of his ideas. But one thing that can be said with certainty about Holmes as a judge is that he almost never cared, in the cases he decided, about outcomes. He didn't read the newspaper, and he was utterly, sometimes fantastically, indifferent to the real-world effects of his decisions. He saw the law as a series of minutely varied, frequently boring, but sometimes delightfully nasty intellectual problems."[14]

This assessment is difficult to understand. It blends known facts—that Holmes did not read newspapers or share Louis Brandeis's taste for data—with the surprising conclusion that he had no concern for the "real-world" effects of his decisions. It is almost beside the point that it's historically overdrawn. The first decision for which Holmes gained notoriety while on the Massachusetts Supreme Judicial Court was *Vegelahn v. Guntner*. In that 1896 case Holmes dissented from a majority opinion that overruled the permission that Holmes, sitting in equity, had temporarily granted strikers to picket in front of the establishment of their former employer after the lower court had ruled in favor of the employer and enjoined the strikers. He certainly understood the "real-world" effect of that decision.[15]

The real difficulty with Menand's assessment has to do with the unexpressed assumption that a man who pursued his own profession with such dedication, as befitting a jobbist, would be indifferent to the effects or consequences of his decisions—that is, of his legal work—because his concerns cannot be fitted into the progressive-reactionary political spectrum. Menand's view runs the risk of turning Holmes into an intellectual dandy who took to judging—as Wittgenstein took to teaching at a village school—to placate ambition and put a bit of bread on the table.

Calling Holmes, as does Menand, the "Emerson of professionalism,"[16] ultimately leads to the same interpretive quagmire as the solitary thinker gambit. If one does not step back and take a moment to consider the question of Holmes's main concern, of what he most cared about, the problem of fitting him into a cohesive narrative—one that takes into account both his concern and ours—remains intractable.

As do many other commentators, Menand makes a point to mention the cover letter Holmes wrote to Emerson in 1876 when he sent him a courtesy copy of his article, "Primitive Notions in Modern Law, No. 1."

> 10 Beacon St., Boston
> April 16/76
>
> My dear Mr. Emerson
>
> I send by this mail the article of mine of which I spoke. It is called "Primitive Notions in Modern Law." If the clothing of detail does not stand in the way I hope the ideas may not be uninteresting to you. It seems to me that I have learned, after a laborious and somewhat painful period of probation that the law opens a way to philosophy as well as anything else, if pressed far enough, and I hope to prove it before I die. Accept this little piece as written in that faith, and as a slight mark of the gratitude and respect I feel for you who more than anyone else first started the philosophical ferment in my mind.[17]

Menand interprets this short letter as a declaration of professional vocation; an early foreword to Holmes's message to his generation that "disinterested inquiry is the best way to crack the world's nut."[18] Novick sees it as marking the moment when Holmes realized that underlying the chaos and complexity of the common law lay a simple orderly "system of elements or structures of unconscious thought."[19] Frederic Kellogg views it as evidence of both the "incubus" that weighed on Holmes—his obsession with philosophy—and of Holmes's turn from an Austinian-inspired effort to categorize law toward a new "vision" of law that accepted the reality of historical change.[20] G. Edward White likewise sees it as marking the turn toward the historical that would characterize Holmes's mature scholarship. It signaled his integration (most evident in the still-to-come *The Common Law*) of historical awareness, analytic sophistication, and a keen sense of contemporary social policy concerns.[21] For Liva Baker it represents the euphoria of discovery—that in the law Holmes believed he found "one of the most articulate expressions of the underlying forces in human history[,]" one "evolutionary, responsive to the social and political environment."[22] It quelled his worry that an intelligent man could study law, be a lawyer (or a judge), and still keep his wits about him.[23] And in a closing counter-note, recent Holmes biographer Susan-Mary Grant thinks the importance of the letter overblown. Holmes had said the same thing to his friend William James almost a decade earlier.[24]

Of these choices I think Kellogg and Baker have the most relevant readings for our purpose of trying to understand the preoccupation that Holmes expresses to Emerson. Not knowing the comparisons Holmes had in mind makes it difficult to understand exactly what he was trying to say, however. That the law opens the way to philosophy as "well as anything else," sounds wondrous (especially to practicing lawyers!)—so long as we have some concrete idea of what he means by "anything else." The most likely candidates in the mid- to late nineteenth century—philosophical study proper (say, the Germans Kant and Hegel, the Scots Reid and Stewart, and the English Utilitarians or Idealists) and literature, broadly construed, or even mathematics—would be candidates precisely because they formed part of a recognized curriculum for improving a young mind (that is, endowing it with greater sensibility and fostering keener perceptions).

Let's hold on to that thought for a moment and consider how Holmes, many years after writing to Emerson, responded to Harold Laski's query regarding what set him on the path to *The Common Law*. Was it Henry Maine's *Ancient Law*? Laski asked.

> You ask me what started my book. Of course I can't answer for unconscious elements. I don't think Maine had anything to do with it except to feed the philosophic passion. I think the movement came from within — from the passionate demand that what sounded so arbitrary in Blackstone, for instance, should give some reasonable meaning — that the law should be proved, if it could be, to be worthy of the interest of an intelligent man — (that was the form the question took them). I went through much anguish of mind before I realized the answer to that question that I have often given since.[25]

The response to Laski adds much needed contrast to the letter to Emerson. Is the law worthy of the interest of an intelligent man? Can law—does it have the wherewithal, the capacity—feed the philosophic passion? And: what does it tell us about Holmes that he, for more than a decade before his Emersonian epiphany, chained himself to legal research and practice—including the grueling three-year task of editing *Kent's Commentaries*—even as the worry gnawed at his bones that he might be rendering himself unfit for the life of the mind?

Two decades after his cover letter to Emerson, and about a decade before the exchange with Laski, when Holmes was in his mid-fifties, he spoke at Brown University's commencement. In this short speech he provided a bit of autobiography. In speaking of the road he had travelled to reach the ideal Eternal City of thought he expressed many of the metaphors that subsequently gave rise to the solitary thinker meme. He speaks of law as an uncharted, unlit ocean. He depicts a thick fog of details, a night pitch black, frozen and conceptually bleak. He then recounts what undoubtedly would have made a strong impression upon a young man of his class, culture, and ambition: "Voices of authority warned that in the crush of that ice any craft might sink. One heard Burke saying that law sharpens the mind by narrowing it. One heard in Thackeray of a lawyer bending all the powers of a great mind to a mean profession. One saw that artists and poets shrank from it as from an alien world. One doubted oneself how it could be worthy of the interest of an intelligent mind."[26]

In these sentences we have a strong clue to the meaning of both Holmes's 1876 epiphany and Menand's characterization of Holmes as the Emerson of professionalism. The breakthrough for Holmes came in the realization that law "if pressed far enough" provided its own avenue to Emerson's ideal of oneness or all-encompassing unity. Everything is interconnected; one fact leads as well as any other to the ultimate consummation that is the whole.

Menand, in turn, recognizes how Holmes took the mundane, the mean, the practice of law, and transfigured it into a crucible of self-transformation. Though in Menand's rendition it partakes more of an aesthetic than an ethic. Menand's description brilliantly and seductively synthesizes the earlier Puritan or Calvinist God-driven ethic of work with a subsequent Deweyan faith in the inherent non-elitist virtues of individual inquiries and their reverberation. But does it do justice to the philosophic passion that Holmes felt? I don't think so.

Holmes is consistent in articulating the dominant passion of his life. He describes it as philosophic; in its ideal form it bears a strong familial resemblance to how Thomas Carlyle formulated the gist of the Victorian creed, "Truth, though the heavens crush me for following her."[27] But the two are not identical. One could sacrifice one's life in philosophic or philological or mathematical study; or in the study of rocks and their layered formations or of distinctive beaks of island birds or of unseen electro-magnetic forces present in the everyday, but law? And to make matters worse, not even the study of Roman law—which Cambridge and Oxford professors Maine and James Bryce argued had a strong claim to intrinsic intellectual value—but the chaotic Anglo-American common law?

Menand himself must certainly have some sense, however tenuous, of the intellectual desiccation legal study represented and, for many people, still represents. He finished the first year at Harvard Law before taking a leave of absence and completing a PhD in the English department at Columbia. He never went back to law school.

Some tenacity in Holmes kept him at it. Some commentators attribute it to his desire to distinguish himself from the tender-mindedness that his father exhibited. That explanation may be accurate. One still wonders whether the passion to break through the heavy fog, even if one only chances upon the twilight of reason, finds its raison d'être in the logic of non-identity between an eldest son and his father.

But to return to the main point. Under the canons of intellectual maturation operating at the time would the study of law, in and of itself, be sufficient means to greater sensibility and keener perceptions? Would the path of the law lead to some overarching truth of life or of existence? Would there be a revelation at hand? No one thought so. Burke cautioned young scholars to the dangers the legal profession and, implicitly, professionalism (though he did not use the word) posed to their intellectual well being. Legal study would deform their minds. Yet despite these warnings Holmes grimly persisted, in Wallace Stevens's classic phrase, "to make believe a starry *connaissance*."

Even after one has grasped the importance of self-reliance, "that one is safe in trusting to courage and to time," Holmes continues in his 1897 commencement address, one must take a final step. "[H]e must face the loneliness of original work."[28] One is tempted to interject that this is the point Holmes found himself when he wrote to Emerson in April 1876. He had no idea that *The Common Law* lay on the horizon, but the process had begun by which what had sounded "so arbitrary in Blackstone" would find its home, not in reason, but in experience. And experience as we all know is the life of the law, not logic.

Put into a sequence we have the following chain of events. Emerson catalyzes the philosophical ferment in Holmes's mind. After returning from the war Holmes decides, maybe even against his better judgment, to study law. Law takes hold of his life and, especially in those early years, begins to edge out strictly philosophical and literary materials. By 1873 he finishes editing *Kent's Commentaries* and now has the leisure time to devote attention to non-legal works. But for the most part he doesn't. He expands his readings to be sure yet they are mainly law related.[29] He returns to active scholarship enlivened and emboldened and reports to Emerson, upon the completion of "Primitive Notions In Modern Law," that the period of probation has ended. He has discovered that law, when pressed, yields to philosophic vision. We then infer from his much later letter to Laski that by law he means more like what one finds in Blackstone—a standard guide to the English common law—and less the law that is expertly codified or philosophically analyzed and systematized.

This derived sequence presents its own conundrum. *How* does the philosophic passion find its fulfillment in law? Or to put the question into the terms we have been using, how does one prove Burke wrong? How would one argue or show that the study of law does not narrow and deform student minds—or, to rework Emerson's colorful phrase, implant knives in their brains—but ultimately lead to a compendious realization that we are simply a working part of a stupendous ever-moving whole? Or more prosaically, by what means does legal study, a deep prolonged dive into legal materials and affiliated practices, materially expand the range and keenness of perception?

The answer has to do with recognizing law as a kind of pressure, the necessity of acting authoritatively in the moment in light of what appears most evident and pressing and true. If law is a specific kind of acting, then its study, pursued philosophically, creates its own pressure against the recalcitrant materials (the cases, statutes, treatises, for example) and forces them, if the pressure is great enough, to disclose the conditions of their existence. The philosophic passion ultimately takes root in the faith that the world is *knowable*. The next obvious step is to affirm that law is knowable and, less obviously, knowable in a way different than what had been habitually the case in common law jurisdictions.

What had been the case according to the author of "Primitive Conceptions in Modern Law" was largely supposition. The word should really be in the plural—suppositions—lots of them. We are so accustomed to hearing how Holmes used the power of historical analysis to unlock options and open the way for the release of intellectual energy[30] that we easily overlook that his early effort to project a remote conception, a primitive notion, as the source of many seemingly disconnected legal doctrines served the opposite and competing purpose of containing and sifting through a myriad of then present-day suppositions.

Suppositions are closely related to rationales. And in life they are plentiful and necessary, which is why Holmes sought to distinguish the "spontaneous action of the intelligence"[31] that led to perceptions of immediate advantage from the different kind of reasoning that characterized legal thinking. To this end he believed it vital to bring to his colleagues' attention "that the various considerations of policy which are not infrequently *supposed* [!] to have established these doctrines, have, in fact, been invented at a later period to account for what was already there,—a process familiar to all students of legal history."[32]

Our concern here is twofold. First, as to Holmes's intellectual breakthrough we suggest it happened when he realized that a historically alert and informed intelligence could winnow the various rationales and suppositions commonly used to explain legal doctrine. The recognition of historical contingency is really a secondary point. That same intelligence, at a more sophisticated level, could also begin to order and arrange the prevailing suppositions according to their continued viability. It would accomplish this task by coordinating them to the elements Holmes would later identify as prevailing in experience as it pertains to the activity or profession of law (felt necessities of the time, prevalent moral and political theories, avowed or unconscious intuitions of public policy, prejudices that judges share with others in their community).[33]

This explanation leads to the second point. If Holmes's philosophic passion expended itself in law, then law—the substantive doctrines, the integrated forms and procedures, the panoply of case, rule, statute, and decision—reacted in its own inimitable manner upon the passion, forcing it (Holmes) to be conscious of itself (himself) in a new way. When did Holmes come to realize that the movement by which suppositions become law and law turns into suppositions could not be delineated as simply and progressively logical without serious distortion? That question is hard to answer but evidently at some point—Frederic Kellogg suggests it probably began when he heard

Peirce lecture on logic[34]—it occurred to him that the philosophic passion (which posits the world as eminently knowable) had itself to be regulated. No more eye-opening dissent to the Victorian creed could be imagined that did not lead to its utter rejection.

Holmes's effort to recognize and regulate suppositions (more broadly: felt necessities, intuitions, policy convictions, etc.) worked out in its own way the fundamental insights of Malthus and Darwin. Holmes added to their scheme the precocious intuition that the unconscious sense of the present (understood expansively as a sense of actuality) frequently warred with as well as furthered and appeased the existing but dormant artifacts of the past (e.g., those which encapsulated primitive notions). Continuity with the past, Holmes famously said, is only a necessity not a duty. If history as a form of thought became the main vehicle by which embedded thought relativized the present (that is, by turning the present, ideationally speaking, into deracinated living suppositions), the present, in turn, had on its side of the equation the multitudinous seedlings of spontaneity and the intermittent, sometimes mesmerizing, hope of real novelty and change. The latter if unmanaged threatened to submerge the historic past in a welter of over-beliefs.

It may help clarify the argument of the previous section if we turn, briefly, to Henry Maine's *Ancient Law*. Holmes denied in response to Laski's query that Maine's book had much directly to do with *The Common Law*—a claim, incidentally, that has triggered repeated rounds of disbelief and much shaking of heads over Holmes's brazen unwillingness to acknowledge what seems obvious. But in saying that Maine fed the philosophic passion Holmes paid the man no small compliment in light of what Holmes held most dear.

Early in *Ancient Law* Maine describes in rough outline the stages societies undergo before instituting a legal code. The evident focus is on the Twelve Tables of ancient Rome. Maine points out the chief advantages of written legal codes over previous proto-law usages and customs. Maine argues that the Romans fortuitously instituted their code at an opportune time in their history, a time "when Roman society had barely emerged from that intellectual condition in which civil obligation and religious duty are inevitably confounded."[35] The timely institution of the Twelve Tables protected Rome from a danger common to barbarous societies, one usually "absolutely fatal" to their progress in civilization.

The danger is this. Prior to reaching the stage of instituting a legal code, a society in its infancy relies on usages to promote its physical and moral health. If these usages "are retained in their integrity until new social wants have taught new practices, the upward march of society is almost certain."[36]

> But unhappily there is a law of development which ever threatens to operate upon unwritten usage. The customs are of course obeyed by multitudes who

> are incapable of understanding the true ground of their expediency, and who are therefore left inevitably to *invent* superstitious reasons for their permanence. A process then commences which may be shortly described by saying that usage which is reasonable generates usage which is unreasonable.[37]

And by what mechanism does this occur?

> Analogy, the most valuable of instruments in the maturity of jurisprudence, is the most dangerous of snares in its infancy. Prohibitions and ordinances, originally confined, for good reasons, to a single description of acts, are made to apply to all acts of the same class, because a man menaced with the anger of the gods for doing one thing, feels a natural terror in doing any other thing which is remotely like it.[38]

Maine continues the argument with examples relating to diet, hygiene, and the social division of classes. The examples are drawn from early Indian law (Maine calls it "Hindoo law") and their cumulative rhetorical force arises from the contrast of Hindu law's development (or non-development as the case may be) to the Roman. The comparison gathers added saliency from Maine's assumption that the Romans and the Hindus arose from the same racial stock.

For reasons never entirely clear, Maine contends that the Roman code preserved the Roman people from the fate that attended most other primitive societies because "it was compiled while the usage was still wholesome, and a hundred years afterwards it might have been too late."[39]

Maine clearly wants us to extrapolate the inference that the Twelve Tables (as law) restrained and regulated a natural mode of thought. That mode, to describe it succinctly, is the natural tendency to produce a superfluity of suppositions. It is a mode of sheer human inventiveness, or in a more contemporary, less freighted word, play. At the extremes it leads to resourcefulness and ingenuity or to the unending multiplication of fears and paralyzing what-ifs. One may, of course, concoct scenarios where the mind is relatively quieted and uninventive, unenterprising and stupid. But the premise of the overflow of analogy and its control is one Maine used to develop the distinction between stationary societies and progressive ones.

He took as fundamental a human "superstitious disrelish for change."[40] Western Europeans, he added, did not fully comprehend or appreciate the distinctiveness of their societies in light of world history. "The tone of thought common among us, all our hopes, fears, and speculations, would be materially affected, if we had vividly before us the relation of the progressive races to the totality of human life."[41] What accounts for the difference between progressive and stationary societies remains largely opaque, Maine admitted. Yet one point stood out—and Maine developed it as a subsidiary theme in his book—law instituted on proper principles (Roman) enabled a society to progress through *how* it controlled and directed the superfluity of analogy when new situations arose. Broadly speaking, law provided the most intelligent social means for grafting new perceptions upon existing habits and camouflaging any real, substantive social change. This fundamental purpose of law remained unaffected even when Romans began to interpret their law in light of Stoic doctrine. The call to resist passion and to act according to Nature took on a similar coloration; an enjoinder to control and direct the profusion, proliferation of felt this-like-that thinking.[42]

Even in its internal procedures Roman law recognized the importance of harnessing the power of the natural tendency to produce a superfluity of suppositions. For example, when developing legal rules Roman jurists did not limit themselves to actual facts before them; they could use what we would call hypotheticals (in effect, analogies) to expand the scope of their decision-making process—"no combination of facts possessed any particular value more than another."[43]

Maine devoted major sections of *Ancient Law* to detailing how progressive societies advanced through various stages—he was not interested in the stationary societies except to use them as a photographic negative—and to underlining the necessary role law played in facilitating the movement from stage to stage.

Though the thought of Maine and Holmes may only intersect at various points, their endeavor to use a historically informed intelligence both to vet suppositions and to control their further formulation underscores the common inclination to emphasize the "gradual amelioration of a legal system."[44] This phrase, Maine's, characterized that "small section of the world" that the progressive societies constituted.[45] The ameliorative aspect of the legal system appeared to consist in the instituted ability to query, through suggested analogies, new social situations and new social wants and to maintain, simultaneously, a connection between new circumstances and existing habits. The fixity of a (written) legal code often provided these forays with the necessary ballast.

Though Holmes did not use the same language as Maine, he certainly possessed a well-developed intuition about the temporal aspects of law. Law not only existed in and through time; its most adept practitioners also recognized, in the process of quizzing new situations and new wants, that some analogies (suppositions) took much longer to suggest themselves than others.[46]

Maine recognized the potentially deleterious effects of what he called the "law of development" on a society's capacity to progress. Unbounded analogical thinking, unless guided through a written code (or, as in the case of England, a relatively fixed common law) and proper principles, would stymie social development. Holmes actually went one step further. He wondered about the deleterious effects of the philosophic passion on the law itself. This worry may explain a singularly odd passage in "Law in Science and Science in Law."

In that address, Holmes doubts "there is any more exalted form of life than that of the great abstract thinker, wrapt in the successful study of problems to which he devotes himself, for an end which is neither unselfish nor selfish in the common sense of those words, but is simply to feed the deepest hunger and to use the greatest gifts of his soul."[47] One can hardly imagine a more magnificent psalm of praise to the noetic urge.

Then Holmes abruptly says: "But after all the place for a man who is complete in all his powers is in the fight. The professor, the man of letters, gives up one-half of life that his protected talent may grow and flower in peace." He concludes, "But to make up your mind at your peril upon a living question, for purposes of action, calls upon your whole nature."[48]

In these words we again encounter the notion of pressure. The pressure of living in society, where ideas called forth by momentous questions are tested in action which then, as counter-movement, engenders its own—at times razor sharp—criticism. The mature Holmes primarily viewed law, in its active side, in this experimental mode. In its passive side it existed as a transcript of custom, habit, adventitious outcomes, dead or dormant modalities of consciousness. He recognized the importance of the "scientific study," but insisted that the "main ends of the subject are practical."[49] He even, in the same vein of thought, constricted the role of history in the study of law. One is not sure why but evidently Holmes felt that if pursued too persistently—to its logical extreme—the results of historical thinking or historical consciousness (both are implicated in Holmes's use of 'history') might make it inordinately difficult for thoughtful students of law to act with avowed legal purpose. "History," he said, "is only a means, and one of the least of means, of mastering a tool. . . . It's chief good is to burst inflated explanations."[50]

Bursting inflated explanations is no tiny feat, however. When we ask why explanations are "inflated" we are immediately led back to Holmes's epiphany in "Primitive Notions in Modern Law." He repeats the same insight over twenty years later: "[W]hen a lawyer sees a rule of law in force he is very apt to invent [most likely through analogy or supposition], if he does not find, some ground of policy for its base. But in fact some rules are mere survivals. Many might well be different, and history is the means by which we measure the power which the past has had to govern the present in spite of ourselves[.]"[51] In short, history, using the word compendiously, works well as a means to order and proportion current-day suppositions regarding the discernible grounds of existing law. It can help regulate our legal thinking. But Holmes did not believe it the best means for controlling the development of new legal thought. Other instruments of jurisprudence had to be perfected to fashion from the overarching prevalence of change in social beliefs and attitudes, those exacting articulations that find, or are destined to find, their expression in law.

What Holmes called the "law of fashion" limited the scope of history's usefulness in law.[52] On the other side of the coin, "felt necessities" and "intuitions of public policy," for example, limited the usefulness of traditional logic. These were all instances of a broader phenomenon, that certitude is not the test of certainty. In each mode certitude impelled an intensification of what Holmes called in another context delusive exactness, whether in thought, language, or the vivid two-dimensional imaginings of the beautiful, the good, and the putatively natural. "Certitude is not the test of certainty." That was how Holmes best expressed the insight that his own philosophic passion ultimately rested on a transcendental foundation as arbitrary—or as un-arbitrary—as his love for granite rocks and barberry bushes.[53]

Interpretive histories of the American identity traditionally devote much attention to the supposedly distinctive preference of these pioneering people for the practical. The rule of law, another favorite topic of chroniclers and expounders of the American experience, becomes slowly over time the favored repository of this bent; law is increasingly seen as an instrument for governing, regulating, and fashioning the needed social mechanisms for containing and directing indigenous American exploits, including exploitations. Robert Summers, for one, comes to the conclusion in the latter part of the twentieth century that this enhanced appreciation for law's pragmatic and instrumental use "represents a genuine and substantial contribution to Western legal thought."[54] It is, in his opinion, the fourth great tradition of Western legal theory, taking its place next to natural law philosophy, historical jurisprudence, and analytical positivism.[55]

Unsurprisingly, Summers identifies Holmes and *The Common Law* as the fountainhead of this tradition.[56] That is not to say that later participants did not react against Holmes, sometimes strongly. Yet in Holmes we find the most developed initial exposition of how both legal rules and practices are situated in the ongoing social stream and rendered purposeful, that is, declared or instituted to accomplish certain ends. But for Holmes it was not enough to present a grand tableau of living law. He also sought in his scholarship to chart its movements and evaluate its efficacy. Thus understanding law as an instrument or a tool had the net effect (Summers does not take this step) of revealing what seems more and more an intrinsic quality of law—law as a living mechanism.

Law becomes most evident as a living mechanism, almost indisputably so, once it has become well instituted in a society or ingrained in a culture. It acts as a membrane, filtering the new and expelling the old. Perhaps the quality we are insisting upon is better brought out in E. Donald Elliott's idea that in "Law in Science and Science in Law" Holmes is, in contemporary terms, describing law as a cybernetic system or as a form of social or artificial intelligence.[57]

This realization leads to two further points. First, it helps us understand better the claim by many commentators that Holmes employed specifically Darwinian methods in his legal analyses. For example, Perry Miller, the great American intellectual historian, regarded *The Common Law* as the "first and possibly still most impressive application to the façade of the law of that method of ascertaining forces at work which is the essential method of Darwin[.]"[58] Miller's insight is clarified and sharpened by philosopher Daniel Dennett's explication of Darwin's notion of natural selection: it is a mindless, mechanical, and algorithmic process. Dennett describes the essential features of an algorithmic process as steps or procedures for "sorting, winnowing, and building things." Dennett recognizes the algorithmic process as "substrate neutral," which means in this context that the notion is not tied down to its biological provenance.[59] One can apply it to other materials and areas of study, including, as Miller noted, law.

The second point takes us back to Menand calling Holmes the "Emerson of professionalism." Menand introduces the phrase in *The Metaphysical Club* to lead into a discussion of how Holmes reshaped the ideal of "The American Scholar." Holmes, Menand suggests, fused Emerson's archetypical portrayal with an image of the valiant Henry Abbott, whose devotion to military duty enabled him to prevent personal inhibitions and prejudices from twisting his loyalty or sapping his courage. A few pages earlier Menand had evocatively described Abbott's death; the description is sparse but somehow manages to convey movingly the pathos of the moment. The officer had ordered his men to drop to the ground but remained standing in full view better to direct gunfire at the enemy's positions. A bullet eventually got him. Menand believes this exemplar of military valor immensely impressed Holmes and, ultimately, found a second life in how Holmes comported himself as a jurist and a judge.[60]

Menand's take is beguiling because he skillfully integrates so much into the Holmes vignette. The Emersonian motif of sinking into one's own experience as the necessary first step for achieving intellectual independence; the transformative meaning of the Civil War for Holmes, especially when set against the Boston abolitionist backdrop; the drive toward professionalism in law that accelerated after the Civil War; the increased sophistication in how lawyers understood themselves and their practice, in terms of greater appreciation for law's history; the importance of procedures liberated from crusty tradition; the search for greater certainty, simplicity, and predictability in legal rules; the tremendous expansion of the American economy; the growing rift and attendant self-consciousness between capital and labor; the changing complexion and size of leading American cities, bulging with arrivals after arrivals from foreign lands; the initially almost imperceptible but increasingly obvious changes wrought by these economic and social dislocations; the ranging and increasingly rabid political enthusiasms; and, in the midst of it all, a judge who queried his own prejudices, looked askance at his fellow Americans who did not, and yet each workday went up the Capitol steps to play his designated part the best he knew how.[61]

Menand sees the core of the Holmesian aesthetic in the conviction that certitude leads to violence. But its nucleic composition lies at an even deeper orbit of perception—that of the futility of concern for individual value: "The key to Holmes's civil liberty opinions is the key to all his jurisprudence: it is that he thought only in terms of aggregate social forces; he had no concern for the individual."[62]

This opinion, one shared by many whom Holmes leaves cold, has had much to do with the continuing debate over Holmes and his legacy. It probably lies at the source of a cultural prejudice against Holmes, one that attempts at historical mitigation—the opinion expressed in *Buck v. Bell*, for instance, was widespread among card-carrying progressives—have done seemingly little to lessen.[63]

One does not expect a different result from the insight that Holmes reinterpreted Emerson—at least the Emerson of "The American Scholar"—in the language of modern professionalism, especially when the chosen profession is law. Menand's portrait effectively, and unfortunately, insulates Holmes in the aesthetic of modern self-creation. He does not emphasize Holmes's philosophic passion, his constant search for insight or aperçus. He does not stress Holmes's quest to find ways to transmute gained perception into knowledge and then convert knowledge into action. Menand's Holmes certainly represents an advance over those who use ambition as the organizing rubric for a Holmes biography; but the emphasis on professionalism or "jobbism" turns Holmes into an Abbott, an exemplar, a tribute to the dignity of duty, a tower of modern virtue that is, oddly, without any essential virtue (that is, leading to something beyond itself).

The defect in Menand's portrait is the same defect in the overall representation of Holmes in American culture. It fails to recognize the importance the philosophic passion held in Holmes's life and the equally important insight that that passion had to be contained and directed. In the context of law, in using law—in many of its different connotations—as the main vocabulary, the material and means to express the passion, to philosophize, Holmes recognized the pressure that law as a manifestation of the past, as an artificial social intelligence, exerts on the present. He took his stand in the present, in the live actuality of being as expressed in perception and thought. Yet he recognized this ever-pressing necessity of the past. To philosophize oftentimes one had to push back, to press against the materials; one had to recognize the existing living mechanisms of law that had a life of their own.

Through the constant, unremitting pressure of thinking he believed—he had faith—that a future better keyed to human wants and aspirations would arise.

The story of Holmes's changing reputation since the turn of the twentieth century has been told many times.[64] Menand notes how the fundamental proposition that one must doubt one's own conviction as far as that doubt will go and then take up what is left—Holmes's "can't help"—breaks in two directions. On the one side, it supports a bias toward the status quo. On the other, the status quo becomes restated as a social presumption that must prove itself.[65]

Yet Menand's emphasis on this strand of Holmes's thinking—the rejection of certitude—fails to appreciate the importance of the other half of the sentence: restating the test for certainty. The early legal realists—many of whom harbored progressive hopes—attempted to restate the tests for certainty in terms of the applicable social sciences. The results of that endeavor were mixed and contested. In time, and due to the course of events, people concerned with these matters began to emphasize more and more the virtues of uncertainty. This emphasis became more pronounced after certain Jesuit scholars launched their attack on Holmes.[66] And since then we have seen a seesaw between the two parts of the sentence, "Certitude is not the test for certainty." On the one end, scholars view Holmes as the paragon of modern relativism and, in Menand's hands, modern aestheticism; on the other, he represents the continuous search for the best tests to inform and improve lawmaking, whether arising from economics or behavioral psychology or cognitive science or some other area of human inquiry.

Holmes's uppermost interest lay in the philosophic passion. It led him to make a life in the law. Thus to understand Holmes we have to begin where his passion took deepest root. If that passion led him to a conclusion deeply unpalatable to the best of liberal opinion, in his day and in our own—that the human individual has no intrinsic, sacred value—then we must turn toward the law to which Holmes turned, the common law of his community, to understand its source. Once we grasp that law's living mechanisms we will also discover how to better focus his foremost concern—to improve their structures—through an affirmation of ends that is not exclusively disaffirmation of repose. By concentrating his concern and comparing it to our own we should in time discern the needed suppositions to fuse both concerns into a single, cohesive narrative.

## NOTES

1. *Buck v. Bell*, 274 U.S. 200, 207 (1927). The description of Holmes's accent as "trans-Atlantic" comes from G. Edward White, *Justice Oliver Wendell Holmes: Law and the Inner Self* (New York: Oxford University Press, 1995), 484.
2. Louis Menand, *American Studies* (New York: Farrar, 2003), 35.
3. Menand, *American Studies*, 35–36.

4. Menand, *American Studies*, 37.
5. Menand, *American Studies*, 38–46.
6. Louis Menand, *The Metaphysical Club: A Story of Ideas in America* (New York: Farrar, 2002), 57–61.
7. Menand, *American Studies*, 45.
8. Menand, *Metaphysical Club*, 38.
9. Oliver Wendell Holmes Jr., "The Path of the Law," in *The Collected Works of Justice Holmes* [hereafter CW], ed. Sheldon Novick (Chicago: University of Chicago Press, 1995), 3: 397.
10. Menand, *American Studies*, 49–69.
11. Menand, *American Studies*, 33.
12. Oliver Wendell Holmes Jr., "The Profession of Law," in CW 3: 472–473.
13. Ludwig Wittgenstein, *Tractatus Logico-Philosophicus*, trans. C. K. Ogden (1922; repr., New York: Dover, 1999), 27.
14. Menand, *American Studies*, 33.
15. See, e.g., Sheldon M. Novick, *Honorable Justice: The Life of Oliver Wendell Holmes* (Boston: Little, 1989), 221–223.
16. Menand, *Metaphysical Club*, 59.
17. Oliver Wendell Holmes Jr. to Ralph Waldo Emerson, 16 April 1876, Mark DeWolfe Howe Holmes research materials, Harvard University Library.
18. Menand, *Metaphysical Club*, 59.
19. Novick, *Honorable Justice*, 148.
20. Frederic R. Kellogg, *Oliver Wendell Holmes, Jr. and Legal Logic* (Chicago: University of Chicago Press, 2018), chs. 2–3.
21. White, *Justice Oliver Wendell Holmes*, 112–213.
22. Liva Baker, *The Justice from Beacon Hill: The Life and Times of Oliver Wendell Holmes* (New York: Harper, 1991), 249–251.
23. Baker, *Life and Times*, 249–251.
24. Susan-Mary Grant, *Oliver Wendell Holmes, Jr.: Civil War Soldier, Supreme Court Justice* (New York: Routledge, 2016), 88.
25. Oliver Wendell Holmes Jr., letter to Harold Laski, 1 June 1922, in *Holmes-Laski Letters: The Correspondence of Mr. Justice Holmes and Harold J. Laski, 1916–1935*, ed. Mark DeWolfe Howe (Cambridge, MA: Harvard University Press, 1953), 429–430.
26. Oliver Wendell Holmes Jr., "Address at Brown University Commencement," in CW 3: 517–518.
27. Thomas Carlyle, *Sartor Resartus*, ed. Archibald MacMechan (Boston: Ginn, 1897), 148; see also, Walter E. Houghton, *The Victorian Frame of Mind, 1830–1870* (New Haven, CT: Yale University Press, 1957), 94–96.
28. Oliver Wendell Holmes Jr., "Address at Brown University Commencement," CW 3: 518.
29. White, *Law and the Inner Self*, 128.
30. See e.g., James Willard Hurst, *Justice Holmes On Legal History* (New York: Macmillan, 1965), 9; Robert W. Gordon, *Taming the Past: Essays on Law in History and History in Law* (Cambridge: Cambridge University Press, 2017), 59–60.
31. Oliver Wendell Holmes Jr., "Primitive Notions in Modern Law, No. II," in CW 3: 21.
32. Oliver Wendell Holmes Jr., "Primitive Notions in Modern Law, No. I," in CW 3: 5 (emphasis added).
33. This argument is further developed in Alexander Lian, *Stereoscopic Law: Oliver Wendell Holmes and Legal Education* (Cambridge: Cambridge University Press, forthcoming), chs. 3 and 5.
34. Kellogg, *Legal Logic*, 44–47.
35. Henry Sumner Maine, *Ancient Law: Its Connection with the Early History of Society and Its Relation to Modern Ideas* (1861; repr., New York: Dorsett, 1986), 15.
36. Ibid.
37. Ibid., 15–16 (emphasis added).
38. Ibid., 16.

39. Ibid., 17; for perceptive commentary on this point of a "lucky legal mutation," see J. W. Burrow, *Evolution and Society: A Study in Victorian Social Theory* (Cambridge: Cambridge University Press, 1966), 164–167.
40. Maine, *Ancient Law*, 22.
41. Ibid., 18.
42. Ibid., 46–47.
43. Ibid., 32–33.
44. Ibid., 19.
45. Ibid.
46. On these elements in Holmes's thinking, see Hurst, *Justice Holmes On Legal History*, 19–86; Frederic R. Kellogg, *Oliver Wendell Holmes, Jr., Legal Theory, and Judicial Restraint* (Cambridge: Cambridge University Press, 2007), 1–9.
47. Oliver Wendell Holmes Jr., "Law in Science and Science in Law," in CW 3: 412.
48. Ibid.
49. Ibid.
50. Ibid.
51. Ibid.
52. Ibid., 406.
53. Oliver Wendell Holmes Jr., "Natural Law," in CW 3: 445–448.
54. Robert Samuel Summers, *Instrumentalism and American Legal Theory* (Ithaca, NY: Cornell University Press, 1982), 19.
55. Ibid.
56. Ibid.
57. E. Donald Elliott, "Legal Process as Artificial Intelligence," *The Journal of Legal Studies*, 13, no. 1 (1984): 113–146.
58. Perry Miller, ed., *American Thought: Civil War to World War I* (New York: Holt, Rinehart, and Winston, 1954), xxxvi.
59. Daniel C. Dennett, *Darwin's Dangerous Idea: Evolution and The Meanings of Life* (New York: Simon & Schuster, 1995), 48–60.
60. Menand, *Metaphysical Club*, 52–61.
61. Ibid., 49–69.
62. Ibid., 65.
63. Brad Snyder, *The House of Truth: A Washington Political Salon and the Foundations of American Liberalism* (New York: Oxford University Press, 2017), 450–452.
64. See, e.g., G. Edward White, "The Rise and Fall of Justice Holmes," *The University of Chicago Law Review*, 39, no. 1 (1971): 51–77.
65. Menand, *The Metaphysical Club*, 63–65.
66. The best telling of this story is in Edward A. Purcell Jr., *The Crisis of Democratic Theory: Scientific Naturalism & the Problem of Value* (Lexington, KY: University of Kentucky Press, 1973), 74–94, 197–217; see also, David A. Hollinger, *Morris R. Cohen and the Scientific Ideal* (Cambridge, MA: The MIT Press, 1975), 165–199.

## BIBLIOGRAPHY

*Buck v. Bell*, 274 U.S. 200 (1927).

Baker, Liva. *The Justice from Beacon Hill: The Life and Times of Oliver Wendell Holmes*. New York: Harper, 1991.

Burrow, J. W. *Evolution and Society: A Study in Victorian Social Theory*. Cambridge: Cambridge University Press, 1966.

Carlyle, Thomas. *Sartor Resartus*. Edited by Archibald MacMechan. Boston: Ginn, 1897.

Dennett, Daniel. *Darwin's Dangerous Idea: Evolution and the Meanings of Life*. New York: Simon & Schuster, 1995.

Elliott, E. Donald. "Legal Process as Artificial Intelligence." *The Journal of Legal Studies* 13, no. 1 (1984): 113–146.

Gordon, Robert. *Taming the Past: Essays on Law in History and History in Law*. Cambridge: Cambridge University Press, 2017.

Grant, Susan-Mary. *Oliver Wendell Holmes Jr.: Civil War Soldier, Supreme Court Justice*. New York: Routledge, 2016.

Hollinger, David A. *Morris R. Cohen and the Scientific Ideal*. Cambridge, MA: MIT Press, 1975.

Holmes, Jr., Oliver Wendell. "Address at Brown University Commencement." In *The Collected Works of Justice Holmes: Complete Public Writings and Selected Judicial Opinions of Oliver Wendell Holmes*, edited by Sheldon Novick, Vol. 3, 517–518. Chicago: University of Chicago Press, 1995.

———. "Law in Science and Science in Law." In *The Collected Works of Justice Holmes: Complete Public Writings and Selected Judicial Opinions of Oliver Wendell Holmes*, edited by Sheldon Novick, Vol. 3, 406–420. Chicago: University of Chicago Press, 1995.

———. "Natural Law." In *The Collected Works of Justice Holmes: Complete Public Writings and Selected Judicial Opinions of Oliver Wendell Holmes*, edited by Sheldon Novick, Vol. 3, 445–448. Chicago: University of Chicago Press, 1995.

———. "Primitive Notions in Modern Law, No. 1." In *The Collected Works of Justice Holmes: Complete Public Writings and Selected Judicial Opinions of Oliver Wendell Holmes*, edited by Sheldon Novick, Vol. 3, 4–16. Chicago: University of Chicago Press, 1995.

———. "Primitive Notions in Modern Law, No. 2." In *The Collected Works of Justice Holmes: Complete Public Writings and Selected Judicial Opinions of Oliver Wendell Holmes*, edited by Sheldon Novick, Vol. 3, 21–35. Chicago: University of Chicago Press, 1995.

———. "The Path of the Law." In *The Collected Works of Justice Holmes: Complete Public Writings and Selected Judicial Opinions of Oliver Wendell Holmes*, edited by Sheldon Novick, Vol. 3, 391–406. Chicago: University of Chicago Press, 1995.

———. "The Profession of the Law." In *The Collected Works of Justice Holmes: Complete Public Writings and Selected Judicial Opinions of Oliver Wendell Holmes*, edited by Sheldon Novick, Vol. 3, 471–473. Chicago: University of Chicago Press, 1995.

———. Oliver Wendell Holmes Jr. Letter to R. W. Emerson, 16 April 1876. Harvard University Holmes Digital Suite. Mark DeWolfe Howe's research materials relating to the life of Holmes, 1858–1968. General Correspondence, General, Group II: Box 14, Folder 32, Emerson, Ralph Waldo, correspondence, 1876.

Houghton, Walter E. *The Victorian Frame of Mind, 1830–1870*. New Haven, CT: Yale University Press, 1957.

Howe, Mark DeWolfe, ed. *Holmes-Laski Letters: The Correspondence of Mr. Justice Holmes and Harold J. Laski, 1916–1935, Volumes I and II*. Cambridge, MA: Harvard University Press, 1953.

Hurst, James Willard. *Justice Holmes On Legal History*. New York, Macmillan, 1964.

Kellogg, Frederic R. *Oliver Wendell Holmes Jr. and Legal Logic*. Chicago: University of Chicago Press, 2018.

———. *Oliver Wendell Holmes Jr., Legal Theory, and Judicial Restraint*. Cambridge: Cambridge University Press, 2007.

Lian, Alexander. *Stereoscopic Law: Oliver Wendell Holmes and Legal Education*. Cambridge: Cambridge University Press, Forthcoming.

Maine, Henry Sumner. *Ancient Law: Its Connection with the Early History of Society and Its Relation to Modern Ideas*. New York: Dorsett, 1986. Reprint of 1861 edition.

Menand, Louis. *American Studies*. New York: Farrar, 2003.

———. *The Metaphysical Club: A Story of Ideas in America*. New York: Farrar, 2002.

Miller, Perry, ed. *American Thought: Civil War to World War I*. New York: Holt, Rinehart, and Winston, 1954.

Novick, Sheldon M. *Honorable Justice: The Life of Oliver Wendell Holmes*. Boston: Little, 1989.

Purcell, Jr., Edward A. *The Crisis of Democratic Theory: Scientific Naturalism & the Problem of Value*. Lexington, KY: University of Kentucky Press, 1973.

Snyder, Brad. *The House of Truth: A Washington Political Salon and the Foundations of American Liberalism*. New York: Oxford University Press, 2017.

Summers, Robert Samuel. *Instrumentalism and American Legal Theory*. Ithaca, NY: Cornell University Press, 1982.

White, G. Edward. *Justice Oliver Wendell Holmes: Law and the Inner Self*. New York: Oxford University Press, 1995.

———. "The Rise and Fall of Justice Holmes." *The University of Chicago Law Review* 39, no. 1 (1971): 51–77.

Wittgenstein, Ludwig. *Tractatus Logico-Philosophicus*. Translated by C. K. Ogden. New York: Dover, 1999. Reprint of 1922 edition.

## *Chapter Two*

# The Nihilist

Raff Donelson

If nothing else is true about him, Justice Oliver Wendell Holmes Jr. was skeptical about morality.[1] In his most famous dissent, *Lochner v. New York*, Justice Holmes can be heard admonishing his colleagues for mistaking their views of political morality for a self-evident truth. He began his dissent saying, "This case is decided upon an economic theory which a large part of the country does not entertain."[2] The economic theory in question was laissez-faire economics. While his colleagues thought they knew that liberty, the liberty protected by the Fourteenth Amendment, required legislatures to adopt a laissez-faire approach to economic issues, Holmes was far less sure.[3] The fact that many people thought otherwise was even more reason for caution and judicial restraint. Though Holmes has largely been lauded for the *Lochner* dissent,[4] for his general skepticism, Holmes has drawn ire from many, and some have labeled him a "nihilist,"[5] a "Nietzschean,"[6] or both.[7]

This chapter demonstrates that Holmes was no Nietzschean nihilist. Such an accusation is triply mistaken. Holmes was no nihilist, nor was he a Nietzschean, and there is no such thing as a "Nietzschean nihilist" because Nietzsche was no nihilist either.

This chapter begins with offering a definition of "nihilism" that will serve as a touchstone for the proceeding discussion. Only with the definition of "nihilism" fixed can we have a productive conversation about who should have the label. After this preliminary work, I turn to the three main tasks of the chapter: showing that Holmes was no nihilist, that he was no Nietzschean, and that Nietzsche and Holmes are both anti-nihilists. On the first task, I not only offer textual support for a non-nihilist reading of Holmes, but I also try to explain why some commentators have erroneously called Holmes a nihilist. On the second task, I argue that the differences between Holmes and Nietzsche are too great—and the similarities too few and commonly found—for it to make sense to call Holmes a Nietzschean. The final task of this chapter aims to show that both Nietzsche and Holmes are anti-nihilists. As I show, those commentators who label Nietzsche a nihilist are making a similar kind of error as those who call Holmes a nihilist. Both kinds of critics miss the fact that both Holmes and Nietzsche are *in different ways* responding to nihilism. Thus, the final section of this chapter serves to underscore the message of the first two: Holmes is not a Nietzschean precisely because he is a different kind of anti-nihilist.

## DEFINING NIHILISM

Like "realism," "positivism," "pragmatism," and so many other philosophical terms, "nihilism" has come to refer to more than one idea. In what follows, I distinguish between two senses of the term: what I call *nihilism*$_1$ and *nihilism*$_2$. With the distinction drawn, we see what Holmes's commentators must have had in mind, for only one of these names a full-fledged philosophical position that can be the subject of agreement, disagreement, or scorn.

To grasp what it is to be a nihilist$_1$, consider the following. We are all nihilists$_1$ about witches, phlogiston, and the ether. What do those things have in common? We do not believe they exist. To deny that *x* exists is to be a nihilist$_1$ with respect to *x*. With that said, it should be clear that one cannot be a nihilist$_1$ *simpliciter*. One can be a moral nihilist$_1$ (denying the existence of moral properties), a theological nihilist$_1$ (denying the existence of deities), a doxastic nihilist$_1$ (denying the existence of beliefs), or a nihilist$_1$ about any other purported property or object, but to be a nihilist$_1$, one has to deny the existence of something in particular. Even if one denies the existence of everything, that is, even if one holds global nihilism$_1$, the *global* modifier is still needed.[8]

To be a nihilist$_2$ is to hold the view that life is somehow meaningless, hollow, or not worth living. Put this way, it would seem that nihilism$_2$ is just a form of nihilism$_1$, one on which the adherent denies the existence of "meaningfulness in life." This characterization of nihilism$_2$ misses something: nihilism$_2$ involves a negative practical attitude toward life.[9] In the cultural imagination, the melancholy nihilist$_2$ may arrive at her nihilist$_2$ stance because she holds a nihilist$_1$ view about morality or gods, but these kinds of nihilism are distinct. For instance, it is possible to reject theological nihilism$_1$ while continuing to deny that life is worth living; one might have this combination of views because one thinks life, as the plaything of an omnipotent being who expects one's obedience, is a hollow, worthless experience. Alternatively, it is possible to accept moral nihilism$_1$ while continuing to see life as fully worth living; one might have this combination of views because one finds the metaphysics of morality wholly irrelevant to our practical lives.[10]

It is widely believed that Holmes was a nihilist$_1$ about certain things, but, in calling him a *nihilist*, some of his various interpreters were saying more than that.[11] They thought he was a nihilist$_2$. This is the right reading of these interpreters for several reasons,[12] the most important of which is the grammatical reason suggested above. Interpreters write things like, "The filaments of [Holmes's] thought are astonishing in their variety. . . . One can find pragmatism, atheism . . . nihilism."[13] If we understand this commentator as claiming that Holmes was a nihilist$_1$, he has to be saying something too incomplete to be meaningful or something entirely trivial. Either commentator has left out the object of Holmes's denial, which leaves the reader entirely in the dark, or the commentator merely meant to say that there is *something* that Holmes does not believe in, which is trivial because everyone denies the existence of something.[14]

The preceding argument should be dispositive. Thus, our debate concerns whether Holmes (or Nietzsche) is rightly called a nihilist$_2$.[15]

## HOLMES IS NOT A NIHILIST

To see Holmes as a nihilist is to see him as a man who denies the existence of objective moral principles, who denies the existence of God, who denies that the Universe has any grand plan for human beings, and who, on the basis of these denials, detaches from life and becomes depressed. Such depression may express itself alternatively as melancholy or reckless abandon, but both attitudes stem from the practical stance that life is not worth living.

Albert Alschuler gives melodramatic voice to this understanding of Holmes. Alschuler reads Holmes as someone who found life meaningless and intermittently cared about nothing or advocated for reckless abandon. Alschuler draws attention to the fact that in Holmes's diary, he devoted one word to discuss his wedding that day: "Married."[16] Alschuler even points out that Holmes did not take a honeymoon as further proof that Holmes was a gloomy nihilist.[17] Other supposed proof is the fact that Holmes "rarely supported charities or political causes."[18] In one place, Alschuler writes, "Holmes had the courage of his nonconvictions."[19] On the reckless abandon variety of nihilism, Alschuler cites "[Holmes's] frequent glorification of the death of soldiers committed to causes they do not understand."[20]

Alschuler is not alone in seeing Holmes as a nihilist. While others avoid the specific term, they too read Holmes as a nihilist, whose skepticism went too far for his own good. One 1940s commentator summarized Holmes's thinking thus: "Mr. Justice Holmes pursued truth with vigor. . . . [T]here is something pathetic in the man's life-long search for . . . 'an echo of the infinite, a glimpse of its unfathomable process, a hint of the universal law.' It was a search that ended where it began, in the gloomy labyrinth of doubt and skepticism."[21] This same commentator wrote, "A dark sunless thing is Holmes' conception of man."[22]

Though I disagree with the "nihilist" label, Holmes's critics do get a few things right. He was no firm believer in deities or true moral values, but, as Holmes himself noted, "it does not follow that, without such absolute ideals we have nothing to do but to sit still and let time run over us."[23] In other words, Holmes saw his skepticism as no reason to become depressed. Holmes was not nihilistic. He greeted life with a good deal of optimism and energy, maybe even too much optimism, as some commentators have said.[24] In one place he wrote, "We all, the most unbelieving of us, walk by faith. We do our work and live our lives not merely to vent and realize our inner force, but with a blind and trembling hope that somehow the world will be a little better for our striving."[25] Holmes, like many of us, by turns chose to look away from our own inevitable demise and to think happy thoughts. As he once told a friend, "I dare say that the best way is not to bother about death until it comes, but just crack ahead."[26] Consider also how Holmes spoke about growing old: "as soon as a corner is turned the road stretches away again and ambition to go farther returns."[27] If he really were committed to the thought that life was not worth living, if he really thought that life was but a "gloomy labyrinth," what should we make of this ambition to go farther?

To sum up the discussion thus far, some critics of Holmes call him a nihilist because they make a certain inference. They infer nihilism from Holmes's skepticism, atheism, and supposed moral nihilism. Holmes outright said that this is a bad inference. Samples from Holmes's writings also reveal that he did not hold the relevant practical stance toward life that nihilism requires. I have not yet explained why Holmes found the inference bad, that is, why Holmes did not come to hold a negative practical stance toward life, given his other commitments. Below I explain this and, in the course of that explanation, demonstrate that Holmes was more than a non-nihilist, he was an anti-nihilist.[28] Before that discussion, however, I explain why Holmes is no Nietzschean.

## HOLMES IS NOT A NIETZSCHEAN

Several commentators compare Holmes and Nietzsche and conclude that these two shared quite a bit intellectually.[29] In this section, I consider two lists of supposed similarities between Holmes and Nietzsche. One list comes from Alschuler, the other from Richard Posner. Alschuler has an impressive list of similarities that is worth setting out in full:

> Holmes and Nietzsche were born three years apart and had much in common. [1] Both viewed life as a struggle for power; [2] both were antireligious [small qualification omitted]; [3] both saw ethics as lacking any external foundation; [4] both could fairly be regarded as existentialists; [5] both saw the suffering and exploitation of some as necessary to the creative work of others; [6] both were personally ambitious and had a strong work ethic (possibly reflecting their Protestant heritage); [7] both had a strong sense of personal destiny; both viewed the disciplined, creative life as an ideal; [8] both often seemed indifferent to the feelings of those around them; [9] both found in their wartime experiences a metaphor for the universe at large; and [10] both had military-style moustaches.[30]

Posner adds a few more items.[31] While I review Posner's list of similarities below, first I examine that of Alschuler.

Alschuler's ten points of comparison, when taken together, seem to make a strong case for Holmes being a Nietzschean (or Nietzsche a Holmesian). On closer inspection, of those points of comparison that are actually true, these traits are far too common to say anything significant. For instance, items (1), (2), and (3) on the list are true of Holmes and Nietzsche and arguably true of Marx, Darwin, and Freud as well. My point is not "therefore, we should conclude that Holmes is just as much a Nietzschean as he is a Marxist, Darwinian, or Freudian." Instead, I am pointing out that (1), (2), and (3) were *au courant* ideas among radicals during the latter half of the nineteenth century. Many of the most famous thinkers from that era espoused those things; thus, mentioning these similarities between Holmes and Nietzsche should not move us very far toward the thought that they shared a comprehensive philosophical outlook. Item (4) is false because Holmes is not an existentialist, but proving this will have to come later. Item (5) is true, but believing that some people's creative work depends on others' exploitation is commonplace. From the pyramids of Giza to the American transcontinental railroad, there are few great engineering feats that did not require many people's suffering, and everybody knows this.[32] Items (6) and (7) are true, but those traits characterize many highly successful people, and, regrettably, the same is true of the trait mentioned in (8). Item (9) is true of many who participate in war, and with (10), Alschuler is merely making a joke. In sum, if I can show that Alschuler is mistaken about (4), we have a very underwhelming case. Rather than having shown that Holmes was Nietzschean, Alschuler merely points out that Holmes was a nineteenth century *maître de soupçon* with some personality traits shared by other geniuses the world over.

Let us then examine the point about existentialism. Alschuler contends that Holmes was an existentialist. On a standard understanding of their view, existentialists first "maintain that there is no God of any sort, and no absolutes in the realms of value and morality. There are only men and things.

Men find themselves thrown into a cold and hostile world."[33] But the story does not end there, for the existentialist also maintains that humans create value.[34] Thus, according to the existentialist, the absence of gods and preexisting moral values should not be a cause of despair; rather, it is an opportunity to exercise one's freedom. If this common understanding of existentialism is the view Alschuler ascribes to Holmes,[35] he has made a poor interpretation of Holmes (and maybe Nietzsche too).[36]

It is true that Holmes doubts the existence of gods and objective moral values like existentialists do; however, Holmes differs from them in not accepting voluntarism. As I understand them, existentialists are eager to deny that values are "transcendent givens independent of human subjectivity," or in other words, they deny that values are "irreducible" to human wills.[37] On the existentialist view, values are really there, but some of us have wrongly understood them as things to be found instead of made. Holmes, on the other hand, had different things to say about value. In one place he wrote, "We all have cosmic destinies of which we cannot divine the end, if the unknown has ends."[38] Instead of repudiating the thought that there are values ontologically independent of human wills, Holmes admitted this possibility but denied that we know about such things. Holmes followed up that sentence with this: "Our business is to commit ourselves to life, to accept at once our functions and our ignorance and to offer our heart to fate."[39] While the beginning of this passage ("Our business is to commit ourselves to life") might remind one of an existentialist, imploring us to engage in radical choice and to create value, Holmes was saying something else. He instructed us to carry on in spite of "our *ignorance*" about the ontology of values. We should not be bothered with the ontology of values, claimed Holmes. This would prove to be a common refrain in his thought: "I think it futile to ask what does it all amount to. One may ask that about all human activities; and to one who thinks as I do, there is no answer except that it is not our business to enquire."[40] As I explain below, Holmes's indifference with respect to the ontology of morals is a central component of his pragmatism. Pragmatism and existentialism are, at bottom, different philosophical outlooks.[41]

The foregoing should make it clear that Holmes was no existentialist. Therefore, whatever one wants to say about Nietzsche, existentialism is not an outlook he shared with Holmes. With that, it should be clear that Alschuler has not offered much to substantiate the claim that Holmes is Nietzschean. Next, I turn to Posner's list of similarities between Holmes and Nietzsche.[42]

For Posner, the points of similarity are: (a) use of genealogy; (b) exposing contingent systems of values for the contingencies they are; (c) skepticism about reason; (d) anti-mentalism; (e) illiberalism; and (f) non-nihilism. This list is far more interesting than that of Alschuler because the items on Posner's list are idiosyncratic. If Holmes and Nietzsche did share a number of idiosyncratic traits, there is a better case to be made that Holmes was, as Posner put it, "the American Nietzsche."

On (a), Posner is largely right. Nietzsche employed genealogy as did Holmes, though Holmes used it to a lesser extent. Genealogy seeks to show that the causes for a phenomenon (e.g., that a population has a particular set of moral beliefs or that a social institution has particular features) sharply diverge from the rationales moderns give for that phenomenon.[43] For example, "genealogical analysis shows that the concept of liberty is an 'invention of the ruling classes' and not fundamental to man's nature or at the root of his attachment to being and truth."[44] One can accept this supposed showing about the concept of liberty or not. The general point remains, namely that genealogical analysis seeks to uncover the true existence and persistence conditions for "those things that continue to exist and have value for us."[45] The genealogist sets out the real reasons for our convictions and ways of life, not the post-hoc rationalizations we settle on later. Nietzsche famously provided a genealogy of morality.[46] In his book, *The Common Law*, Holmes aimed to do much the same for law. As he wrote,

> A very common phenomenon, and one very familiar for the student of history, is this. The customs, beliefs, or needs of a primitive time establish a rule or a formula. In the course of centuries the custom, belief, or necessity disappears, but the rule remains. The reason which gave rise to the rule has been forgotten, and ingenious minds set themselves to inquire how it is to be accounted for. Some ground of policy is thought of, which seems to explain it and to reconcile it with the present state of things; and then the rule adapts itself to the new reasons which have been found for it, and enters on a new career.[47]

In this long passage from Holmes, we see him making two genealogy-friendly points, first that our legal rules have backstories of which we are unaware and second that our modern justifications for our rules are not the reasons for which we follow them. Posner is thus right about (a) and about (b) too. However, Holmes does not employ genealogical methods in much of his work outside of *The Common Law*. Genealogy figures in two of Nietzsche's major works, but in Holmes's other works, genealogy does not make an appearance. For instance, in his great essay, "The Path of the Law," Holmes provided an ahistorical theory about the nature of the law and about several doctrinal areas of law.[48] In Holmes's opinions as an appellate judge in Massachusetts and on the United States Supreme Court, his decisions are known to be pithy and not great pieces of historical scholarship. This is to say, while Nietzsche was *the* genealogist, Holmes was just an occasional fellow-traveler.

What should one make of this supposedly shared skepticism about reason, the trait mentioned in (c)? It is true that both Holmes and Nietzsche were humbler about what reason could achieve than others. Nietzsche, for instance, was skeptical of those philosophers who "wanted to supply a rational foundation for morality."[49] He seems to have thought that all we could do is describe the mores of particular peoples or stump for mores that we like. Rational reflection will not enable us to discover the *right* mores. Holmes thought similarly about morality and about 'natural' legal duties. He ultimately held these were preferences and that "[d]eep-seated preferences can not be argued about."[50] Holmes is also famous for having said, "The life of the law has not been logic: it has been experience."[51] Relatedly, he called a fallacy "the notion that the only force at work in the development of the law is logic."[52] Again, we hear that *logic*, or rational reflection, will not enable us to discover much about morality or the law. So far, this skepticism about reason is just another way of stating (3) from Alschuler's list, namely that Holmes and Nietzsche are skeptical about foundations for values. Do Holmes and Nietzsche go further in decrying reason? This is doubtful. Nietzsche, insofar as he engaged in genealogical critique, employed and presumed that others would employ reason. Genealogical critiques are arguments that seek to undermine one's conviction by showing that the process by which one came to hold the conviction was not responsive to the reasons that would validate that conviction. To make such critiques is to reason, and to expect others to appreciate such critiques is to believe that they too can reason. Nietzsche thus had a *limited* skepticism about reason. Much the same is true of Holmes. Holmes, while denying that reason could help us discover the right laws or mores, thought that reason helped elsewhere. For instance, Holmes once wrote, "Reason working on experience does tell us, no doubt, that if our wish to live continues, we can do it only [by obeying society's standards]."[53] In this passage, Holmes was saying that reason can help one to make good inductive inferences for one's personal benefit. He had other roles for reason to play too, for he happily noted that "the man of the future is the man of statistics and the master of economics."[54] Here Holmes claimed that reason facilitates good inductive inferences for societal benefit. It is thus an overstatement to allege that Holmes and Nietzsche were reason skeptics. They saw a more modest role for reason than their excessively rationalist contemporaries.

Let us now turn to (d). Specifically, Posner writes that "both are sub- or antimentalists."[55] In claiming that both Holmes and Nietzsche were antimentalists,[56] Posner puts forward something that is technically correct but highly misleading. Posner's neologism is an umbrella term, wide enough to cover two very different positions. Holmes discouraged using mental states as elements for certain legal causes of action. For instance, he thought that we should not understand contracts as requiring a meeting of the minds; rather he thought that we should require some non-mental-state objective criterion. Holmes argued for this way of arranging the law because it would lead to more predictable legal outcomes. While it is hard to prove that someone had a particular mental state, it is far easier to prove that someone took a particular action. If one understands *mentalism* as a commitment to using mental states as elements of legal causes of action (which is not an unreasonable understanding of the term), then, sure, Holmes is an anti-mentalist. This understanding has nothing to do with Nietzsche though. Nietzsche thought that conscious mental states do little or nothing to explain action. If one understands *mentalism* as a commitment to explaining lots of phenomena by reference to individuals' conscious mental states (which is not an unreasonable understanding), then, sure Nietzsche is an anti-mentalist. In a sense, Posner is making an equivocation. Formally speaking, we can interpret away the formal problem of equivocation, for, if anti-mentalism is a disjunctive view that includes the positions of both Holmes and Nietzsche, there is no equivocation. But any such fix makes Posner's comparison weak. Instead of showing that Holmes and Nietzsche shared some significant, idiosyncratic view, he will have shown that they held different views that we can lump together in an entirely *ad hoc* way, which affords no explanatory gains.

On (e), Posner is right that Holmes and Nietzsche are both illiberal, but this commonality is less interesting than it appears. In fact, that this attribution looks like an interesting point says more about us than it says about Holmes or Nietzsche. Being illiberal is far stranger now that it was before. Plato, Aristotle, Aquinas, Machiavelli, Hobbes, Marx, and Schmitt are all illiberal. It is only now with the modern ascendancy of liberalism that someone's illiberalism is an oddity. In the time of Holmes and Nietzsche, this ascendancy was not yet complete. Vestiges of feudalism and aristocratic values still had place, and these Holmes and Nietzsche both embraced.

Discussing Holmes's and Nietzsche's reactions to nihilism takes up the space of the next section, so I defer thinking about point (f) until then. Even with that task deferred, it is worth taking stock of the long and meandering conversation, comparing Nietzsche and Holmes. I have sought to closely consider two commentaries, which claim that Holmes is a Nietzschean. Alschuler had a ten-point list of similarities, and I argued that this list contained too many commonplaces to sustain the notion that Holmes and Nietzsche shared anything too deep. The only substantial and idiosyncratic trait on Alschuler's list, namely existentialism, is not shared after all. Posner had a shorter list, but one with more promise because of its idiosyncratic traits. I argued that while none of the supposed commonalities proved to be flat-out wrong, they ultimately showed less than they promised. The foregoing should lead one to think that calling Holmes a Nietzschean is not so much incorrect as unhelpful.

## NIETZSCHE AND HOLMES AS ANTI-NIHILISTS

In this last substantive section of the chapter, I show that Holmes and Nietzsche were anti-nihilists but of different stripes. Holmes was a pragmatist, and this led him to take issue with the reasons for which people adopt nihilism. Nietzsche actually approved of the reasons for people to adopt nihilism but still thought it presented a problem. Organizationally, first I explain what it would mean to call Holmes a pragmatist. Next, I offer evidence that Holmes endorsed pragmatism. Then, I show how pragmatism functions as a kind of anti-nihilism. Finally, I contrast this kind of anti-nihilism with the variety on offer from Nietzsche.

To show that Holmes was a pragmatist, first I must make clear what will and will not suffice as a showing. Some who are convinced that Holmes was *not* a pragmatist are happy to rest their hats on the fact that Holmes had few kind words to say about William James, one of the classical pragmatists.[57] Others are content to note that Holmes eschewed the label *pragmatist.*[58] These points, however, will not suffice. Charles Sanders Peirce, the founder of pragmatism, also disliked James's philosophy and also eschewed the label. We have to dig a little deeper.

One might think that espousing the pragmatist theory of truth is the *sine qua non* of pragmatism, but espousing that thesis is sufficient but not necessary. Peirce denied it,[59] and so have many other famous pragmatists.[60] As I explain below, Holmes denied it too, but that should not count him out.

For our purposes, Holmes will count as a pragmatist if he holds that the goal of inquiry is practical. More precisely, Holmes was a pragmatist, if he thought that we should test various propositions against practical criteria—such as whether accepting a given proposition will help us to cope with the world or whether accepting the proposition satisfies certain desires we have. Someone is a pragmatist if she tests propositions by such practical criteria and not by purely descriptive criteria, such as whether we are accurately tracking mind-independent facts.

Having set a standard for how to tell if Holmes was a pragmatist, let us examine the evidence. It is well known that Holmes made critical remarks about Williams James. On one occasion, he wryly summed up James as having claimed that "by yearning we can modify the multiplication table."[61] Holmes was caricaturing James, but Holmes the lampoonist himself once wrote that "Thinking is an instrument of adjustment to the conditions of life."[62] This sounds mighty pragmatist, for it suggests that the criteria by which to appraise our thinking are by how well they enable us to adjust to the conditions of life, not by how accurately thought represents the world as it is.[63] If this interpretation is right, the ridicule of James can appear in new light. Perhaps Holmes was saying the following: we should not modify the multiplication tables just because we so yearn; we will not be well-adjusted to the conditions of life, if we act like that.

I am suggesting that Holmes adopted an instrumentalist understanding of inquiry, which is sufficient (but perhaps not necessary)[64] for pragmatism. This instrumentalist understanding of inquiry is not identical to holding the pragmatist theory of truth. According to the pragmatist theory of truth, a proposition is true if and only if believing or accepting that proposition satisfies some practical end of some set of agents. The instrumentalist understanding of inquiry differs from the pragmatist theory of truth in that the former tells us how to inquire while the latter tells us about the metaphysics of truth. One might adopt the former because one already adopts the latter, but these are conceptually distinct. Holmes, contrary to what some commentators contend,[65] did not espouse the pragmatist theory of truth. In fact, he likely espoused a more traditional correspondence theory of truth, which claims that a proposition is true if and only if that proposition corresponds to how the world is. Holmes's skepticism can be summed up as the idea that "truth serves as an unattainable ideal."[66] Why is truth unattainable? Holmes thought both that we cannot capture the world as it is and that the truth means capturing of the world as it is. Therefore, his skepticism presupposes the correspondence theory.

Looking to Holmes's most famous pronouncement on truth, we find no contradiction with my reading. Famously and frequently, Holmes proclaimed, "all I mean by truth is what I can't help thinking."[67] Despite appearances, this is no claim about the metaphysics of truth. This claim is epistemic. Holmes was voicing his familiar skepticism. He claimed that those propositions he called true were just those that he could not help believing. Holmes was thus admitting that he had no justification for those beliefs other than that he had come to hold them and hold them so strongly that he could not believe otherwise. Holmes thought we are all in this epistemic situation. He thereby opposed two kinds of anti-skeptics. He opposed the typical anti-skeptic, the person who claims an ability to fit her beliefs to the cosmos. As he said, "the universe has in it more than we understand."[68] Holmes also opposed the idealist anti-skeptic, the person who thinks that the cosmos must fit her beliefs. Holmes explicitly denied that the limits of his scheme of beliefs are "necessarily limits to [the cosmos]."[69]

Once we see Holmes's pragmatism, his anti-nihilism becomes more discernible too. Holmes was skeptical about moral truth and the existence of gods, but he did not succumb to nihilism due to his pragmatism about morality and other matters. Nihilism, marked by a negative attitude toward life, is an inference people draw from moral nihilism (or skepticism, atheism, some other lack that can frustrate someone's hopes). For Holmes, such hopes are the seeds of nihilism. The proto-nihilist aims to discover, *inter alia*, the true moral values, but, according to Holmes, when we are trying to determine what to do, our task is *not* to track such values but rather to settle on a course of action that works, that helps us to adjust to the conditions of life. After we deliberate and arrive at our best answers to practical questions, it is "unnecessary to demand of the Cosmos an assurance that to *it also* our best is superlative," said Holmes.[70] The proto-nihilist wants such assurance and becomes a full-fledged, depressed nihilist when she judges that the cosmos will not give it to her. It is likely his skepticism that led Holmes to suggest that we give up on the task of tracking moral (and other) truths, but whatever his reasons, once we do abandon that task, we must abandon it completely and no longer worry about moral ontology and epistemology writ large. This is why Holmes kept saying that it was not our business to inquire about the source and true nature of morality or to wonder whether our values are the true ones. We have seen how Holmes avoided nihilism for himself, why the absence of moral values did not lead *him* to infer that "we have nothing to do but to sit still and let time run over us."[71] We can also see that Holmes went further. He was someone who decried nihilism. He thought that falling into nihilism was to make an important mistake, to think that our task as humans is something that it isn't.[72] As he once put it, "Having made up your mind that you are not God don't lie awake nights with cosmic worries."[73] Ultimately, Holmes thought nihilism was a foolish, arrogant misapprehension of the point of human life.

Nietzsche, like Holmes, went beyond non-nihilism and adopted a kind of anti-nihilism. However, Nietzsche had a different complaint to lodge against nihilism. By turns, he called it "the danger of dangers"[74] and "pathological."[75] Because nihilism is an equivocal term, one might wonder whether, in making these claims, Nietzsche relied on the same understanding as I have in our discussion. Indeed, he did. He not only understood the phenomenon in the same sense, but he also understood the etiology the same. For Nietzsche, nihilism is a negative attitude toward life brought on by a recognition that morality and divinity are not as one has long suspected. Nietzsche hoped that we would supersede this attitude. In one place, he wrote longingly, "This man of the future, who will redeem us not only from the hitherto reigning ideal [Christianity and its attendant focus on God and absolute moral values] but also from that which was bound to grow out of it, the great nausea, the will to nothingness, nihilism . . . *he must come one day*."[76]

Nietzsche claimed that nihilism is dangerous. To my knowledge, he does not define this danger. In calling nihilism pathological and by analogizing it to nausea, he seems to have suggested that nihilism is painful for its adherent. Whatever the precise danger, danger is the heart of Nietzsche's worry. This differs markedly from Holmes. Holmes, again, held that the nihilist is a fool who misunderstands the purpose of human life. While Nietzsche would likely agree with that sentiment, his worry centers on the danger that nihilism presents. The misunderstanding that nihilism entails was just not as worrisome for Nietzsche. In fact, Nietzsche, unlike Holmes, thought that nihilism was a necessary, transitory stage toward enlightenment.[77] Nihilism "was bound to grow out of" the collapse of the "reigning ideal." Holmes, by contrast, did not think nihilism was necessary. For him, nihilism is an unforced error.

## CONCLUSION

This chapter has sought to show that Holmes was not a "Nietzschean nihilist." When they accused him of nihilism, Holmes's commentators were claiming that Holmes adopted a negative attitude toward the project of life, brought on by finding out that the world lacks something that he wished were there, such as absolute moral values or deities. Holmes was not a nihilist so understood because he was a fairly optimistic man who thought that the presence or absence of moral values and deities should have no effect on one's spirits. Holmes was also not a Nietzschean. The differences between the two are several, and the commonalities are ultimately too commonplace to draw any interesting inferences. One commonality between the two is that they both were anti-nihilists, that is, they both thought that nihilism is a grave error. But even in this similarity, Holmes and Nietzsche differed. Holmes was a pragmatist, someone who understood our task as humans to be one of striving, coping, adjusting ourselves to the conditions of the world. As a result, Holmes thought we should be unconcerned with the metaphysical questions that occasion nihilism. Nietzsche, on the other hand, saw no problem with having metaphysical concerns. He even thought that nihilism was an inevitability, if one paid attention to the world and noticed its deficits (e.g., that there is no God). Nietzsche's problem with the nihilist is that she poses a danger. Nietzsche hoped that those of us who recognize the death of God will move on and supersede the dangerous state of mind that nihilism is. Nietzsche thought he had, and thus 'Nietzschean nihilist' is an oxymoron. All the more reason why Holmes was no such thing.

## NOTES

1. I thank Seth Vannatta and Steven Heyman for reading drafts of this chapter and offering insightful feedback.

2. *Lochner v. New York*, 198 U.S. 45, 75 (1905) (Holmes, J., dissenting).

3. I mean that literally. Holmes was personally quite opposed to anything that sounded like socialism. In one place he wrote, "I see no right in my neighbor to share my bread. I mean moral right of course." "23 July 1925 Letter to Harold Laski," in *The Essential Holmes*, ed. Richard A. Posner (Chicago: University of Chicago Press, 1992), 141. Again: "I may add that class for class I think the one that communism would abolish is more valuable—contributes more, a great deal more, than those whom communism exalts." Holmes, "21 May 1927 Letter to Harold Laski," in *The Essential Holmes*, 144. However, he denied that he knew what would be best or if there were a fact of the matter of that kind.

4. For praise of the *Lochner* dissent, see Roscoe Pound, "Liberty of Contract," *Yale Law Journal* 18, no. 7 (1909): 464; Felix Frankfurter, "The Constitutional Opinions of Justice Holmes," *Harvard Law Review* 29, no. 6 (1916); Richard Posner, introduction to *The Essential Holmes*, by Oliver Wendell Holmes, ed. Richard Posner (Chicago: University of Chicago Press,1992), xvii. But see Cass Sunstein for criticism. Sunstein agrees with the reading offered here that Holmes's "skepticism about normative argument [is one of] the very personal building blocks for his enthusiasm for judicial deference" in *Lochner*, but Sunstein goes on to defend the *Lochner* majority against Holmes. "Lochner's Legacy," *Columbia Law Review* 87, no. 5 (1987): 880.

5. Posner claims that one can find traces of nihilism in Holmes. Posner, introduction, xix. However, Posner does not think that Holmes is a nihilist full-stop. "Holmes is not a nihilist after all, at least not a consistent one." *The Problems of Jurisprudence* (Cambridge, MA: Harvard University Press, 1990), 242.

6. Burrow claims that Holmes's "celebrations of war, intensity of life, heroism, and will" are "Nietzschean." "Holmes in His Intellectual Milieu," in *The Legacy of Oliver Wendell Holmes, Jr.*, ed. Robert W. Gordon (Palo Alto, CA: Stanford University Press, 1992), 29. Posner calls Holmes "the American Nietzsche." Introduction, xxviii. Elsewhere, Posner stresses some similarities between Holmes and Nietzsche. *The Problems of Jurisprudence*, 239–244. For some pushback, see Seth Vannatta and Allen Mendenhall, "The American Nietzsche? Fate and Power in the Pragmatism of Justice Holmes," *UMKC Law Review* 85, no. 1 (2016): 187–205.

7. On the very same page, Albert Alschuler calls Holmes both a Nietzschean and an adherent of "noble nihilism." *Law without Values: The Life, Work, and Legacy of Justice Holmes* (Chicago: University of Chicago Press, 2000), 20.

8. Of course, in a conversation, a modifier might be understood (in the grammatical sense).

9. See Tracy Llanera, "The Deep Personal Resonance of Nihilism," *Journal of Philosophy of Life* 7, no. 1 (2017).

10. For an explicit statement of such a view, see Raff Donelson, "Ethical Pragmatism," *Metaphilosophy* 48, no. 4 (2017): 383–403. As we see below, Holmes also endorsed a view like this.

11. See, e.g., John Ford who claimed that Holmes denied the existence of God, moral values, and truth. "Fundamentals of Holmes' Juristic Philosophy," *Fordham Law Review* 11 no. 3 (1942): 255–78. Paul Gregg said much the same about Holmes: "Truth, man, the common good, even God, are nothing." "Pragmatism of Mr. Justice Holmes," *Georgetown Law Journal* 31, no. 3 (1943): 294. These statements explicitly aim to paint a melancholy picture of Holmes, which indicate that they view Holmes as a $nihilist_2$. But see Steven J. Heyman, "The Dark Side of the Force: The Legacy of Justice Holmes for First Amendment Jurisprudence," *William & Mary Bill of Rights Journal* 19, no. 3 (2011): 661–723, for a theorist whose main disagreement with Holmes is his moral nihilism1.

12. We might also think that those interpreters who call Holmes a nihilist are referring to $nihilism_2$ because of how they support the nihilism accusation. I explain this further below when I rebut the charge of $nihilism_2$.

13. Posner, introduction, xix.

14. Moreover, this would be redundant because the commentator already said that Holmes is an atheist.

15. For economy, I henceforth abandon the subscripts; generally, nihilist (and its cognates) will mean $nihilist_2$ (and its cognates) unless context indicates otherwise.

16. Alschuler, *Law without Values*, 34.

17. Alschuler, *Law without Values*, 34.

18. Alschuler, *Law without Values*, 38.

19. Alschuler, *Law without Values*, 30.

20. Alschuler, *Law without Values*, 20.

21. Gregg, "Pragmatism of Mr. Justice Holmes," 263 (second ellipsis in the original).

22. Gregg, "Pragmatism of Mr. Justice Holmes," 274.

23. Holmes, *The Essential Holmes*, 118.

24. Susan Haack, "On Legal Pragmatism: Where Does 'The Path of the Law' Lead Us?" *The American Journal of Jurisprudence* 50, no. 1 (2005): 92.

25. Holmes, "Address at Ipswich," *The Essential Holmes*, 74.

26. Holmes, "14 October 1911 Letter to Alice Stopford Green," in *The Essential Holmes*, 3.

27. Holmes, "30 January 1921 Letter to Morris Cohen," in *The Essential Holmes*, 34.

28. If the contrast between the non-nihilist and the anti-nihilist is unclear, consider a similar contrast between the non-smoker and the anti-smoker. While the non-smoker simply does not smoke cigarettes, the anti-smoker campaigns against the use of cigarettes.

29. These scholars include Alschuler, Posner, Vannatta and Mendenhall, as well as David Luban. For reasons of space, I focus on the remarks of Posner and Alschuler.

30. Alschuler, *Law without Values*, 19.

31. See Posner, *The Problems of Jurisprudence*, 239–244.

32. Perhaps Alschuler wanted to make the following stronger point. Not only did both Holmes and Nietzsche think that exploitation made certain creative work possible but they also approved of such exploitation on that basis. This is a less commonly held belief. Hurka claims that Nietzsche held that view in his "Nietzsche: Perfectionist," in *Nietzsche and Morality*, eds. Brian Leiter and Neil Sinhababu (Oxford: Oxford University Press, 2007), 17–20. It is possible that Holmes did as well.

33. Richard Schacht, "On 'Existentialism,' Existenz-Philosophy and Philosophical Anthropology," *American Philosophical Quarterly* 11, no. 4 (1974): 291.

34. As Sartre put it, "human reality is that by which value arrives in the world." *Being and Nothingness: A Phenomenological Essay on Ontology*, trans. Hazel Barnes. (New York: Washington Square Press, 1956), 144.

35. And it looks like it is. Alschuler writes, "existentialism can be regarded as the belief that human life is meaningless except insofar as it is invested with meaning through personal acts of will." *Law without Values,* 19.

36. For the claim that existentialism as I have described it does not apply to Nietzsche, see Schacht, "On 'Existentialism,'" 292.

37. Sartre, *Being and Nothingness*, 796.

38. Holmes, "Reflections on the Past and the Future," in *The Essential Holmes*, 6.

39. Holmes, "Reflections on the Past and the Future," 6.

40. Holmes, "6 May 1925 Letter to Marguerite Einstein, 11th Marchioness of Tweeddale," in *The Essential Holmes*, 75.

41. Even Alschuler admits this. He thinks we have to choose between seeing Holmes as a pragmatist or as an existentialist. *Law without Values*, 20.

42. See Posner, *The Problems of Jurisprudence*, 239–244.

43. I take this characterization to be completely in line with the one given by Brian Leiter in his *Nietzsche on Morality* (New York: Routledge, 2002), 166–170.

44. Michel Foucault, "Nietzsche, Genealogy, History," in *The Foucault Reader*, ed. Paul Rainbow. Trans. Donald F. Bouchard and Sherry Simon (New York: Pantheon Books, 1984), 78–79.

45. Foucault, "Nietzsche, Genealogy, History," 81.

46. See Friedrich Nietzsche, "Part Five: Natural History of Morals," in *Beyond Good and Evil: Prelude to a Philosophy of the Future*, trans. Walter Kaufmann (New York: Vintage Books, 1966); Friedrich Nietzsche, *On the Genealogy of Morals*, trans. Walter Kaufmann and R. J. Hollingdale (New York: Vintage Books, 1967).

47. Oliver Wendell Holmes, *The Common Law* (Boston: Little, Brown, and Company, 1881), 50.

48. Oliver Wendell Holmes, "The Path of the Law," *Harvard Law Review* 10, no. 8 (1897): 457–78.

49. Nietzsche, "Natural History of Morals," 97.

50. Oliver Wendell Holmes, "Natural Law," *Harvard Law Review* 32, no. 1 (1918): 41.

51. Holmes, *The Common Law*, 1.

52. Holmes, "The Path of the Law," 465.

53. Holmes, "Natural Law," 42.

54. Holmes, "The Path of the Law," 469.

55. Posner, *The Problems of Jurisprudence*, 240.

56. "Anti-mentalist" is my shorthand for Posner's more tortured phrase "sub- or antimentalists."

57. See, e.g., Alschuler, *Law without Values*, 18.

58. See, e.g., Ford, "Fundamentals," 266.

59. On Peirce's theory of truth, *p* is true if and only if *p* would be believed at the end of inquiry. Charles Sanders Peirce, "How to Make Our Ideas Clear" in *Charles Peirce: Selected Writings (Values in a Universe of Chance)*, ed. Philip P. Wiener (New York: Dover, 1958), 133.

60. For instance, Richard Rorty, the late twentieth-century pragmatist, was a deflationist about truth, a view that is inconsistent with the inflationary pragmatist theory of truth. Rorty wrote that truth "is just the nominalization of an approbative adjective." "Feminism and Pragmatism," in *Truth and Progress* (Cambridge: Cambridge University Press, 1998), 226.

61. Holmes, "29 March 1917 Letter to Harold Laski," in *The Essential Holmes*, 37.

62. Holmes, "6 September 1920 Letter to Morris Cohen" in *The Essential Holmes*, 105.

63. Of course, one might think that only by making accurate representations of the world will one be effective in adjusting to the conditions of the world. That might be the case, but these two criteria would still be conceptually distinct. And the latter condition, which is practical, is the one Holmes in fact invoked.

64. Grey, who shares my instrumentalist reading of Holmes, contends that that instrumentalism is a necessary component of pragmatism. See his "Holmes and Legal Pragmatism," *Stanford Law Review* 41, no. 4 (1989): 787–870. I errantly endorsed that view in the past; I see little reason to argue about this now.

65. Vannatta and Mendenhall, "The American Nietzsche?" 191; Ben W. Palmer, "Hobbes, Holmes, Hitler," *American Bar Association Journal* 31, no. 11 (1945): 571.

66. Vannatta and Mendenhall, "The American Nietzsche?" 191.

67. Holmes, "17 June 1908 Letter to Lewis Einstein," in *The Essential Holmes*, 70.

68. Holmes, "Natural Law," 43.

69. Holmes, "17 June 1908 Letter to Lewis Einstein," 70.

70. Holmes, "6 May 1925 Letter to Marguerite Einstein, 11th Marchioness of Tweeddale," 75–76. Emphasis added.

71. Holmes, "Ideals and Doubts," in *The Essential Holmes*, 118.

72. This imputation of mistake resembles how Llanera understands Richard Rorty's opposition to nihilism. See her "Rethinking nihilism," 941–45.

73. Holmes, "8 February 1931 Letter to Lewis Einstein," in *The Essential Holmes*, 17.

74. Friedrich Nietzsche, *The Will to Power*, ed. Walter Kaufmann, trans. Walter Kaufmann and R. J. Hollingdale (New York: Vintage Books, 1968), §69n39. I was relatively unfamiliar with Nietzsche's *nachlass* before writing this chapter. I was helped immeasurably by reading Schacht's "Nietzsche and Nihilism," *Journal of the History of Philosophy* 11, no. 1 (1973): 65–90.

75. Nietzsche, *The Will to Power*, §13.

76. Nietzsche, *Genealogy of Morals*, 96.

77. Nietzsche, *The Will to Power*, §13.

## BIBLIOGRAPHY

Alschuler, Albert W. *Law without Values: The Life, Work, and Legacy of Justice Holmes*. Chicago: University of Chicago Press, 2000.

Burrow, J. W. "Holmes in His Intellectual Milieu." In *The Legacy of Oliver Wendell Holmes, Jr.*, edited by Robert W. Gordon, 17–30. Palo Alto, CA: Stanford University Press, 1992.

Donelson, Raff. "Ethical Pragmatism." *Metaphilosophy* 48, no. 4 (2017): 383–403.

Ford, John C. "Fundamentals of Holmes Juristic Philosophy." *Fordham Law Review* 11, no. 3 (1942): 255–78.

Foucault, Michel. "Nietzsche, Genealogy, History." In *The Foucault Reader*, 76–100. Edited by Paul Rainbow. Translated by Donald F. Bouchard and Sherry Simon. New York: Pantheon Books, 1984.

Frankfurter, Felix. "The Constitutional Opinions of Justice Holmes." *Harvard Law Review* 29, no. 6 (1916): 683–702.

Gregg, Paul L. "Pragmatism of Mr. Justice Holmes." *Georgetown Law Journal* 31, no. 3 (1943): 262–95.

Grey, Thomas. "Holmes and Legal Pragmatism." *Stanford Law Review* 41, no. 4 (1989): 787–870.

Haack, Susan. "On Legal Pragmatism: Where Does 'The Path of the Law' Lead Us?" *The American Journal of Jurisprudence* 50, no. 1 (2005): 71–105.

Heyman, Steven J. "The Dark Side of the Force: The Legacy of Justice Holmes for First Amendment Jurisprudence." *William & Mary Bill of Rights Journal* 19, no. 3 (2011): 661–723.

Holmes, Oliver Wendell. "Natural Law." *Harvard Law Review* 32, no. 1 (1918): 40–44.

———. *The Common Law*. Boston: Little, Brown, and Company, 1881.

———. *The Essential Holmes*. Edited by Richard A. Posner. Chicago: University of Chicago Press, 1992.

———. "The Path of the Law." *Harvard Law Review* 10, no. 8 (1897): 457–78.

Hurka, Thomas. "Nietzsche: Perfectionist." In *Nietzsche and Morality*, edited by Brian Leiter and Neil Sinhababu, 9–31. Oxford: Oxford University Press, 2007.

Leiter, Brian. *Nietzsche on Morality*. New York: Routledge, 2002.

Llanera, Tracy. "Rethinking Nihilism: Rorty vs Taylor, Dreyfus and Kelly." *Philosophy and Social Criticism* 42, no. 9 (2016): 937–50.

———. "The Deep Personal Resonance of Nihilism." *Journal of Philosophy of Life* 7, no. 1 (2017): 81–91.

Luban, David. "Justice Holmes and the Metaphysics of Judicial Restraint." *Duke Law Journal* 44, no. 3 (1994): 449–523.

Nietzsche, Friedrich. *On the Genealogy of Morals*. Translated by Walter Kaufmann and R. J. Hollingdale. New York: Vintage Books, 1967.

———. "Part Five: Natural History of Morals." In *Beyond Good and Evil: Prelude to a Philosophy of the Future*, 95–118. Translated by Walter Kaufmann. New York: Vintage Books, 1966.

———. *The Will to Power*. Edited by Walter Kaufmann. Translated by Walter Kaufmann and R. J. Hollingdale. New York: Vintage Books, 1968.

Palmer, Ben W. "Hobbes, Holmes, Hitler." *American Bar Association Journal* 31, no. 11 (1945): 569–73.

Peirce, Charles Sanders. "How to Make Our Ideas Clear." In *Charles Peirce: Selected Writings (Values in a Universe of Chance)*, 113–36. Edited by Philip P. Wiener. New York: Dover, 1958.

Posner, Richard A. Introduction to *The Essential Holmes*, by Oliver Wendell Holmes, edited by Richard A. Posner. Chicago: University of Chicago Press, 1992.

———. *The Problems of Jurisprudence*. Cambridge, MA: Harvard University Press, 1990.

Pound, Roscoe. "Liberty of Contract." *Yale Law Journal* 18, no. 7 (1909): 454–86.

Rorty, Richard. "Feminism and Pragmatism." In *Truth and Progress*, 202–27. Cambridge: Cambridge University Press, 1998.

Sartre, Jean-Paul. *Being and Nothingness: A Phenomenological Essay on Ontology*. Translated by Hazel Barnes. New York: Washington Square Press, 1956.

Schacht, Richard. "Nietzsche and Nihilism." *Journal of the History of Philosophy* 11, no. 1 (1973): 65–90.

———. "On 'Existentialism,' Existenz-Philosophy and Philosophical Anthropology." *American Philosophical Quarterly* 11, no. 4 (1974): 291–305.

Sunstein, Cass R. "Lochner's Legacy." *Columbia Law Review* 87, no. 5 (1987): 873–919.

Vannatta, Seth and Allen Mendenhall. "The American Nietzsche? Fate and Power in the Pragmatism of Justice Holmes." *UMKC Law Review* 85, no. 1 (2016): 187–205.

*Chapter Three*

# The Utilitarian

Frederic Kellogg

"Law provides a way to philosophy and I hope to prove it before I die."
—Oliver Wendell Holmes Jr. to Ralph Waldo Emerson, April 16, 1876

How should we assess this sentence, written 142 years ago by Holmes to Emerson? A casual quip? Not according to the historical context: Holmes was driven by intense ambition for an enduring place in the pantheon of jurisprudence, and at age thirty-four, he was not given to light-hearted remarks to the seventy-two-year-old Emerson.[1]

This suggests a larger question: is Holmes relevant for contemporary legal or moral philosophy? To most scholars of Holmes, or of philosophy, that claim will seem so ludicrous that we might equally well imagine him as a maverick graduate student at Harvard in the 1970s, submitting foundationally critical papers to John Rawls. That counterfactual image actually works for me; I have recently claimed in some detail that his intensive studies of law, informed by a critical response to early modern philosophy, led to an original logical theory, called social inductivism, that (when updated) challenges the contemporary analytical canon not just in law but in logic and ethics.[2]

In this chapter I will argue that Holmes's logical theory reveals an underlying blindness in the utilitarian tradition, as it has developed from Henry Sidgwick to the contemporary consequentialists of today. It is a blindness to the reality of constant, endemic conflict in society over utility itself, and the necessity of the revision of reasoning, and transformation of practices, for its resolution.

Back to Holmes's 1876 comment to Emerson: What did the word "philosophy" mean in the Cambridge (Massachusetts) of 1876? Not what it means today: it implied a strong historicist Millian empiricism. Holmes's equivalent of a "PhD advisor" in the 1860s was Chauncey Wright, whose own models were Francis Bacon, John Stuart Mill, and Charles Darwin. Holmes's "graduate curriculum" consisted of exhaustively revising the entire legal encyclopedia *Kent's Commentaries on American Law*, plus readings on recent English science and philosophy and discussions with Wright, William James, Charles Peirce, and others (originating well before the Metaphysical Club). The outcome was a social-constructivist philosophy of legal logic, naturalizing themes drawn from Hume, Kant, and Hegel.[3]

His view fits with "classical" pragmatism, as a continuum of inquiry, deeply incompatible with the tide of analysis and formal logic that would sweep through philosophy in the twentieth century.[4] Even the ever-collegial Rawls would have resisted his vision, just as Rawls consistently ignored John Dewey, who is given virtually no consideration in *A Theory of Justice* (1971) or in his *Lectures on Moral Philosophy* (2000).[5]

Take utilitarianism, or (as now more popularly known) consequentialism, in which interest has been revived since Rawls substantially redefined rule utilitarianism in 1951. Does Holmes's law provide any insight into this complex issue?

## UTILITY AND INQUIRY

How does utility affect, or result from, the work of the law? That is quite another question from how *utilitarianism* might affect or result from it. I want to keep both questions in play, in order to address Holmes's indirect contribution, not just to utilitarian theory, but to legal and ethical logic, a contribution I claim is original to the analytical canon that has so long dominated moral theory. It will engage three themes: (1) moral knowledge as generated in conflict, of *conduct* as well as opinion; (2) the extension in time and space (in the sense of the extension in *society*) of ethical inquiry; and (3) the imperative of social transformation (of conduct as well as of discourse and persuasion) for resolving serious conflicts, if they are to be finally resolved at all. Answers to these questions are drawn, *mutatis mutandis*, from legal history, which serves as an empirical context for understanding normative inquiry.

The very nature of utility is constantly disputed in everyday life, and disputes must generally be resolved for civil society to survive. Holmes developed his overall perspective in the years immediately following the American Civil War, and the specter of that conflict (dare I say involving very different views of "utility") hangs over it. His diaries of reading during that period include Jeremy Bentham, John Austin, and John Stuart Mill, three classical utilitarians. He was also reading about natural science and recent controversies over scientific and logical method and attending lectures by

Charles Peirce on "The Logic of Science, or, Induction and Hypothesis." His reading and many discussions with James, Wright, and others shaped his early essays on law, which in 1870 and 1873 produced the approach to legal logic that I have called social inductivism.[6]

That phrase simply means that inductive inference is social in actual practice; it is not always and only performed, as commonly portrayed, all at once by an individual or idealized objective mind. It is fundamentally pragmatist, in the tradition now recognized as stemming from Charles Peirce and William James, and contributes (in retrospect) to Dewey's own ethical thinking.[7] Holmes's socialized normative induction is an extended process of inquiry, and as such deserves association with classical pragmatism. But it is unique in its emphasis on endemic dispute and often outright conflict driving the continuum of social inquiry, the necessity of convergence of opposing positions to produce a consensual view of the world (you might call it a Holmesean realism), and the transformative necessity of any successful inductive process. By transformative, I mean the necessity of the convergence (albeit piecemeal) of conduct and practice as well as of opposing viewpoints.

Elements and precursors of these factors are evident in the early meetings of the Cambridge intellectuals in the 1860s and '70s, but it was Holmes who fleshed them out through an account of the history of hard-fought transformations in law. Here a sharp contrast lies with the utilitarian tradition, parallel to the broader contrast between analytical and pragmatist philosophy. Utilitarians acknowledge that utility may be disputed, but ultimately assume that conflicts can and must be commensurated through a "utilitarian calculus," originally an accounting of pleasure and pain. The idea of omniscient measurement has always been problematic from the lack of anything but a purely speculative omniscient *measurer*.[8] Yet actual normative life is replete with constantly changing *standards of measurement*.

Measurement must and does indeed take place; the challenge is understanding how. As I hope to demonstrate, the context of calculation, the environment of normative reasons, is hardly static, and along with transformation of normative practice comes transformation of *meanings* defining expected utility. Opposing views or expectations of utility are not reconciled by constant tallying and balancing, but by and through adaptation, with the adjustment of habits and practices. Society does not always work out conflict through an uber-legislative calculus imposed by utilitarian fiat, but often, and perhaps mostly, by redefining or replacing the terms and forms of calculation in disputed problematic contexts.

To paraphrase Charles Peirce (writing in 1866), our fate depends on understanding the logic of transformation.[9] How does civilization survive constant conflict? It requires the *retirement* of incommensurable reasons, not the forcing of choices among them. Our fate depends upon the piecemeal transformation of what might be called the "reasons environment," doing so with particular controversial moral questions, such as those surrounding medically assisted death. This could never be resolved by the original standoff between murder or suicide, but has given way to the identification and application of numerous detailed practical issues like improved medical technology, living wills, and ultimately local legislation. Other examples of subtle transformation in legal conflict are rife; I will later deploy a simple example, used by Holmes, of traffic regulation.

Within the insight of transformation lies Holmes's original contribution to *normative induction*—the process through which society either hammers out consensual resolutions to opposing views of utility or descends into civil violence as it did in 1861. This will affect our assessment of both utilitarianism and mainstream contemporary ethical theory, and indeed of pragmatist ethics as it is understood by contemporary writers. I first examine contemporary utilitarian theory, then the contribution of Holmes's thought, and then how it suggests further research.

## UTILITARIAN THEORY TODAY

It is easy to confuse a basic utilitarianism with a conception of pragmatism as applying a consequentialist test to generalizing. What is the difference, in addressing moral questions, between balancing utility and applying Peirce's 1878 pragmatic maxim, determining meanings by "conceivable effects" and their "practical bearings"?[10] If there is not a significant difference, pragmatism gets placed in roughly the same position as utilitarianism in the putative assessment of statements assessing acts, rules, and practices. Both, then, readily imply a momentary, or "camera-flash," model of normative reality, picturing all expected consequences in society as if visible at once, to a camera with a lens displaying prospective or expected utility. Existing rules and the practices that underlie them are viewed as "de facto," already established, always already inherent in the context of moral inquiry.[11]

Let's approach this through another distinction: utilitarianism as a form of synchronic moral analysis, and pragmatism as the study of convergent change and adaptation. Analytical normative theory assumes a static conceptual universe for the purpose of utility analysis.[12] Pragmatism as here understood, rather than applying an instantaneous consequentialism, assumes that analysis of any given difficult moral question may be influenced by its relative position or stage in the discovery and completion of a broader and more general question. In other words, inquiry into the specific ethical question *q* (what is right in this case to do *now*) often comes *within* an extended continuum *Q*, representing inquiry into what will be viewed as right after exploration of the more general question, in which *q* may be early or late in the larger and longer extended social inquiry.

When a particular *q* first arrives, the full nature of a possibly extended *Q* remains yet unspecified. An example is assisted death, which began as a standoff between suicide and homicide. Dr. Jack Kevorkian sought to raise a broader question (and jump-start a continuum of inquiry) by devising a device for minimal medical assistance accessing mortality to a severely ill patient, for which he was prosecuted and imprisoned in 1999. His case was thus an early "*q*." A generation later, after extended social inquiry into many instances of what is now the complex question of assisted death forced open by Kevorkian's extraordinary career, the larger issue (the "*Q*") has acquired a new utility analysis on both sides. Suicide and homicide no longer dominate the conversation. A specific inquiry *today* (yet another *q*) will take place within a transformed reasons environment. Earlier reasons regarding expected utility have been retired and replaced.

Hence any original *q*, or indeed any given particular inquiry during the extended period, may be an *inquiry within an inquiry*, a point that is critical to understanding social inductivism and its bearing on utilitarian theory. This has an important impact on the notion of rules and rule formation. The retrospective utility calculus for *Q* will be different from the earlier reasons calculus of *q*, in ways yet invisible at the earlier camera-flash moment. Adaptation and the revision of practices will occur during the social continuum of inquiry, in some matters more readily than in others.[13] Yet the stages of inquiry and transformation are invisible to the hypothetical instant utility camera.

I dare say such an extension through time has already transformed a *Q* underlying this chapter: the standoff between act-utilitarian and rule-utilitarian models of thinking. Utilitarianism is commonly broken down into act and rule utilitarianism, but its categories have evolved, in particular since the criticism of David Lyons and others, and of John Rawls's early essays and his eventual social contract theory, raising and addressing problems with the very concept of rule utilitarianism.

Act utilitarianism (AU) holds that an act is morally right if and only if it would produce at least as much utility, or expected utility, as any other available act. Rule utilitarianism (RU) holds that moral agents should follow whatever rules would produce the most utility or expected utility. Sheer act utilitarianism has the problem of "justifying too much," warranting bad acts for the general good, like hanging the innocent to please an angry mob or to stop a wave of crime. But hanging the innocent is clearly contrary to a utilitarian system of rules.[14]

John Rawls in 1951 offered an interpretation preventing utilitarianism from justifying too much, "by stating utilitarianism in a way which accounts for the distinction between the justification of an institution [establishing accepted practice] and the justification of a particular act falling under it."[15] He did so by distinguishing two concepts of rules, the summary and practice views. In the former, "rules are pictured as summaries of past decisions arrived at by the *direct* application of the utilitarian principle to particular cases."[16] In this view, particular cases are logically prior to rules, whereas in the latter view, institutions and practices are prior. Punishment, for example, would be assessed within the concept of an institutionalized practice, within the justice system, itself adopted for overriding utilitarian considerations. So also with practices like promising.[17]

However, as David Lyons argued in 1965, the question would still arise whether and how *exceptions* should be evaluated by the utilitarian calculus. The issue of exceptions to a utilitarian rule is critical to understanding the nature of rule formation, particularly in the *continuum* that is implicit in Holmes's theory. Rawls, according to Lyons, understood exceptions by using an "escape clause" for the problem raised by a possible act which is opposed to an accepted practice, but which would *still* bring about greater overall utility.

To illustrate, Rawls notes that an answer to "why should I keep my promise" is that "doing so in *this* case will have the best consequences."[18] Rawls concedes that "it is always necessary to take into account the effect which our action will have on the practice of making promises."[19] He recognized that the strict act utilitarian may yet observe that there might be a case where the promisor could argue that, even calculating the utility of the practice, "breaking the promise would lead to a better state of affairs on the whole [. . .] no matter how slight the advantage won by breaking the promise."[20] Hence the non-conforming action would be best in view of all utilitarian considerations *including* the importance of the practice.[21]

Rawls's "escape" *defended* RU from this objection, by arguing "One is inclined to think it would either turn out that such a case came under an exception defined by the practice itself, [. . .] or it would happen that the circumstances were so peculiar that the conditions which the practice presupposes no longer obtained."[22] But Lyons in 1965 pressed his objection further, arguing that this still failed to save a rule from collapsing into act utilitarianism. Lyons called Rawls's escape a fragile "ceteris paribus" (other things being equal) argument: rules like "do not break promises" could instead be viewed as "elliptical formulations of *ceteris paribus* rules [. . .] the suppressed *ceteris paribus* condition can in each and every case be taken in terms of the [AU] *escape clause*: 'except when you know or are quite certain that the effects of not following the main body of the rule would be better.'"[23] He explained:

> The considerations which justify using the de facto moral rules to begin with, and those which determine justifiable exceptions to them, are all of one piece. If one accepts Act-Utilitarianism one can view the de facto moral rules as if they have the (AU) escape clause as an implicit qualification.[24]

Thus, Lyons's argument challenged the very foundation of rule utilitarianism, claiming that there is no *extensional* difference between act and rule utilitarianism.

This extensionalist challenge to the utilitarian tradition can hardly be underestimated (though it is a problem only for analytical theory, not, as I will argue, for pragmatism). Brad Hooker recently summarized it as follows: "In other words, for every situation where compliance with some rule would not produce the greatest expected good, rule-consequentialism seems driven to favor instead compliance with some amended rule that does not miss out on producing the greatest expected good in the case at hand. But if rule-consequentialism operates this way, then in practice it will end up requiring the very same acts that act-consequentialism requires."[25]

I will refer to this point as "extensional equivalence," or simply "extensionalism." It would appear to be highly dangerous, if not fatal, to any utilitarian account of a rule-based regime of law or morals:

> If rule-consequentialism ends up requiring the very same acts that act-consequentialism requires, then rule-consequentialism is indeed in terrible trouble. Rule-consequentialism is the more complicated of the two theories. This leads to the following objection. What is the point of rule-consequentialism with its infinitely amended rules if we can get the same practical result much more efficiently with the simpler act-consequentialism?[26]

The above is a condensed summary of an important recent turning point in the history of utilitarianism. It has energized a new school of academic writers, notably Brad Hooker and Michael Ridge, who are revising rule utilitarianism following Lyons's extensionalist challenge. This is exciting for the field, as they are probing the basic assumptions underlying moral theory and its relation to the work of general moral theorists such as Derek Parfit. I need not delve further into the new views of utilitarianism here, as my brief summary of the extensionalist challenge already provides an opening for better understanding the pragmatist critique, its continuum of inquiry, and the fundamentally diachronic character of normative inquiry. My task is to show that a *pragmatic* moral philosophy, with its own distinctive account of grounding rules on utility, requires abandoning the momentary, camera-flash model of normative reality.

## HOLMES

The foregoing summary is designed to sketch very briefly the main challenge that utilitarianism encounters today in defending the very basis of a system of rules. It sets the stage for an explanation of the alternative account drawn from Holmes, who was not concerned with utilitarian theory per se, but rather with addressing the actual process of rule formation in discrete areas like tort, crime, possession, and so on.[27]

The insight to be emphasized is that, in an actively disputed legal context, any rule resolving a given dispute is indeed (as Rawls saw in 1951) rooted in a *practice*; but the practice in effect *replaces* an earlier unsettled calculus of opposing reasons—and this only happens upon successful *adaptation*. That is, a *real and often intractable conflict* is at stake, and a potentially continuing one. As noted above, the background of broader conflicts (many yet unresolved) is unrecognized by the instantaneous analytical model of extensionalism. The varied and emergent nature of utility conflicts is simply invisible to, and unseen by, the momentary utility camera. What does this mean for Lyons's argument about Rawls's "escape clause"?

Lyons, Hooker, and other writers wrestling with the extensionalist RU problem simply fail to see that *previously settled* conflicts underlie and explain both *acceptance* of, and *compliance* with, what extensionalism sees as "de facto" rules. Thus, for Holmes, any "exception to the rule" (which extensionalism still assumes to be based on the original calculus) requires *further* convergence through resolution of *further conflict.*[28] In other words, Lyons's objection to the "escape clause" assumes that the reasons environment is static throughout the often extended process of dispute resolution, which itself has contributed, and continues to contribute, to the existence and redefinition of relevant practice. As I hope to demonstrate, this is not as intricate as it may sound.

How does a practice emerge amidst conflict, and how is it affected by further conflict? Take a simple example that Holmes mentions in an 1873 paper, the emergence of English "rule[s] of the road." Holmes observes that rules of the road are practices that have been "worked out" after a "sufficient amount of fighting."[29] This suggests that we imagine disputes over vehicular collisions for which at first there is no settled rule.

I will try to flesh this out from personal experience, as both a driver and former trial lawyer. In America we drive on the right; in Britain they drive on the left. Even so, I am reasonably familiar with the rules that relate to driving a rental car on English streets and highways, for example in those confusing clockwise "roundabouts." Let's ask what might have happened when drivers first entered what might have been an *early* English roundabout.

Going back to that hypothetical time, I imagine myself as the trial counsel representing Ms. Quickly, who was struck by a lorry when she blithely dashed into that primitive roundabout (assuming, if you will, that there was a complete absence of accepted driver conduct). I will naturally engage in exhaustive discovery to bring up everything in the utilitarian calculus favorable to her case, including her being late to church (and the fact that the lorry was carrying a cargo of scandalous literature), anything to sway the judge or jury. Counsel for the lorry driver will raise countervailing arguments such as his need for income and his duty as a professional driver to advance the interests of commerce.

This rather absurd caricature serves nevertheless to illustrate the early *q*, a new conflict over competing utilities. In the early or novel case, the list of properties relevant to the utilitarian calculus is long. There are aggravating and mitigating factors everywhere you look, on both sides.[30] Holmes's point is that rules begin to be formed from within an environment of yet unregulated disputes. Once a remedial practice, and then a reinforcing rule, establishes a presumptive right of way for any vehicle *already* in the roundabout, none of the earlier drivers' (or their lawyers') reasons will be relevant; they will have been progressively overruled as the general issue is judicially explored and resolved.[31] Generalism in law is a product of establishing a commitment to finite expectations in a given problematic situation. It often occurs at a later stage of inquiry, if and when the relevant properties can be winnowed down to a formula.[32]

So what about Lyons's claim that "The considerations which justify using the de facto moral rules to begin with, and those which determine justifiable exceptions to them, are all of one piece"? I suggest that they are *not at all* part of the same extensionalist "picture," as the private considerations of individual drivers, presumably argued in a succession of cases (in the continuum of inquiry), leading toward adoption of the practice and eventual rule, have progressively been dismissed and are ultimately no longer relevant to the adopted practice.

Convergence of opposing purposes is implicit in working out the rules of the road. So then, I ask, is an exception always already covered? According to Lyons, "If one accepts Act-Utilitarianism one can view the de facto moral rules as if they have the (AU) escape clause as an implicit qualification."[33] Let us assume that an early claim of exception comes from the local fire department. Of course, the rule must adapt to allow a general exception for fire equipment, but a conditional one, only when displaying lights and sirens. Here too Holmes's remark suggests the prospect of further "fighting." Assume that the first fire department vehicles enter the roundabout *without* lights and sirens. Collisions will occur, the dispute will re-engage the continuum of inquiry, and the conditional exception will be worked out in a further convergence.

This ongoing process, which Holmes called specification (of course always possible through legislation), is pervasive throughout the law, detailed in his 1870 and 1873 articles.[34] Specification, through repetition of disputes and particular judgments, creates patterns of conduct that can be judicially recognized, as prophylactic practices are adopted and approved, and as broader standards of conduct emerge from retrospective judicial findings of similarity, in what Edward Levi in 1949 called a "moving classification system," resolving disputes and guiding public conduct.[35]

Extensionalism, on the other hand, posits a sweeping and fatal (but woefully unexamined) challenge to any utilitarian regime of rules, recently summarized as follows by Hooker:

> Here is why some have thought rule-consequentialism collapses into practical equivalence with act-consequentialism. Consider a rule that rule-consequentialism purports to favor—e.g., "don't steal." Now suppose an agent is in some situation where stealing would produce more good than not stealing. If rule-consequentialism selects rules on the basis of their expected good, rule-consequentialism seems driven to admit that compliance with the rule "don't steal except when . . . or . . . or . . ." is better than compliance with the simpler "don't steal." This point generalizes. In other words, for every situation where compliance with some rule would not produce the greatest expected good, rule-consequentialism seems driven to favor instead compliance with some amended rule that does not miss out on producing the greatest expected good in the case at hand. But if rule-consequentialism operates this way, then in practice it will end up requiring the very same acts that act-consequentialism requires.[36]

Hooker's tacit acceptance of extensionalism, that "don't steal" is (in Lyons's phrase) an "elliptical formulation of a ceteris paribus rule" and therefore cannot be distinguished from an act-utilitarian scheme, misses the crucial point of Holmes's *specification.* The overbroad "don't steal" generalization fails to reflect and define an actual specified rule-based practice. Stealing is constantly being specified; take the historic problem of legally defining the term "theft." Early cases of bailment, before the adoption of common practices for tradesmen, remained unsettled until practices were adopted through specification.[37] The problem of redefining theft continues today in disputes over newly digitalized intellectual property, requiring specified practices. So also with Lyons's claim that "keeping promises" is another *ceteris paribus*; specification of "promising" lies at the core of thickly specified contract doctrine.[38]

Holmes's heavily researched account of rule formation implies an environment of constant development and revision, rather than an always static landscape of clear and detailed utilitarian permissibility and impermissibility. Holmesean rules emerge from extended normative inquiry and convergent practices that depend in detail on feedback from society into the resolution of recurring disputes. Multiple opposing arguments from utility will apply to early novel cases, before eventual classification makes them irrelevant, as similarities of conduct are established and accepted. Various "*q*"s are transformed by the adaptive convergent definitions of larger "*Q*"s.[39]

For a pragmatist model of inquiry, the impingement of experience on moral knowledge begins with the necessity of a common need: resolution of particular disputes that (when unresolved) threaten the social order. The new dispute is often first conceived as either novel or original, or as situated in a gray area equidistant from opposing prior precedents. Over time, further experience establishes both similarities and differences in the emerging sense of a core problem. While the original dispute may *suggest* a general problem, it must be more precisely determined, or "specified," before a general rule can be adopted through accepted practice.

Resolution of the uncertain case requires revising an *actual* context, not just an immediate conceptual *sense* of context, because a complex larger problem may be implicated in the specific dispute. A *pragmatic* grounding of rules on utility requires abandoning the momentary, camera-flash model of normative reality. The camera cannot detect the broader *Q*s in different stages of completion. One might say that Holmes's normative ontology does not imply a fixed landscape, but something more like a variable and constantly changing seascape, with areas of settled calm, and other areas of turbulence, a "dappled world," to borrow Nancy Cartwright's metaphor for the conceptual environment of natural science.[40]

Holmes's position is drawn from a study of law, but it translates into a general normative theory, more empirically based than abstract utilitarianism. Holmes's process of convergence implies more than a purely cognitive dimension to the analyzing and reconciling process. There must also be a convergence of communal practice and *action.* This means that *compliance*, the incentivized tendency of actors to follow the particular rule, and *acceptance*, the belief that a given rule is necessary and correct, are generated locally on a piecemeal basis, rather than globally and uniformly, from reliance on a presumptive utility calculus, majestic Kantian or Rawlsian principle or principles, or an "ideal code," as Brad Hooker has recently proposed.[41]

## ACCEPTANCE AND COMPLIANCE IN THE CONTINUUM

So what would Holmes have written in 1970, as a graduate student in Rawls's philosophy department? On rule utilitarianism, addressing Rawls's 1951 contribution and Lyons's critique, he would have set forth examples from legal inquiry. He would have accepted and endorsed Rawls's practice-based conception of rules, but emphasized the extended process of their *adoption* as a prelude to rule formation, emphasizing dependence on convergence through conflict, management, and eventual entrenchment, of prophylactic practices in all areas of law, contract, tort, criminal law, even extending to the interpretation of constitutional rights.[42] He would have applied the continuum of inquiry even to statutory interpretation, in cases where legislated terms are yet unspecified. And he would have elaborated on his suggestion (in an 1899 lecture) that the extended social inductive process applies not just to law but to ethics and indeed other areas of uncertainty in human knowledge.[43]

We know of course that by 1970 Rawls had forsaken rule utilitarianism for the social contract tradition, updating it with his theory of justice as fairness, advancing the hypothesis of an original contract formed under a "veil of ignorance."[44] How might Holmes have viewed this turn by Rawls toward Kantian contractualism? Does Holmes's social inductivism also imply a critique extending to other strains of contemporary analytical moral philosophy?

I think it clearly does. Here he would emphasize his radically different account of *acceptance* and *compliance* in the normative domain. For analytical moral theory, these two critical components—how and why humans adopt and follow the normative order—are understood as requiring a universal explanation. They must either exist conceptually, uniformly (or univocally) throughout the (properly conceived) Kantian (or utilitarian, or contractual) regime—or *not at all*. That is, the analytical philosopher examines and adjusts Rawls's conceptual system for its overall theoretical *global* bearing on problems of acceptance and compliance, whereas for Holmes the two elements stand or fall *locally*, only (or mainly) insofar as they are established in the resolution of particular disputes.

Let me stretch my earlier counterfactual to its outer limit, and ask what Holmes might be writing today at Oxford University, in the wake of Derek Parfit's major contributions to analytical moral theory. Imagine Holmes focusing on a recent paper on Parfit by Michael Ridge, one of the newly energized rule utilitarians mentioned at the end of section II of this chapter.[45] Ridge's 2017 article locates recent utilitarian theory within the context of analytical moral theory in general. His commentary on Derek Parfit's *On What Matters* (2014–2017) opens with the following observation:

> The central thesis of Derek Parfit's *On What Matters* is that three of the most important secular moral traditions—Kantianism, contractualism, and consequentialism—all actually converge in a way onto the same view. It is in this sense that he suggests that we may all be "climbing the same mountain, but from different sides."[46]

Ridge's paper challenges Parfit's bold claim, and in a manner that provides a further clue to where and how Holmes would articulate the importance of a transformative continuum. This has to do with the failure of analytical theory to recognize endemic social conflict, driving the need for revision of practices and the adoption of consensual rules. For Holmes's pragmatism, all three "secular moral traditions" of mainstream philosophy, if indeed they are "climbing" at all, are situated nevertheless on a stationary conceptual landscape, attempting to perform what Parfit calls "moral mathematics" from a synchronic viewpoint, through their separate (but putatively reconcilable) instantaneous and contemporary global *cameras*. All three analytical lenses are blind to the real world of particular, active continua of inquiry, from each of which public acceptance and compliance must constantly and separately be wrought.

Ridge's rule-utilitarian challenge highlights this failure by putting Parfit's project to a realistic operational test. Parfit had already noted that Kantian contractualism falls prey to the "ideal world objection":

> The basic idea is that Kantian moral principles are designed for an ideal world of perfect moral virtue, but that to follow such principles in our very non-ideal world could, and often would, have horrible consequences.[47]

What are these "horrible consequences"? A notable example is Kantian pacifism, blindly maintained in the presence of a totalitarian aggressor, in an *actual* "non-ideal world." The result can be the rapid demise of the Kantian ideal world itself. This is an extreme example of the fact that humans cannot be expected always and uniformly to *comply* (or reject leaders who do not comply) with ideal schemes or principles. Hence for Parfit the analytical solution is to *revise* the global principles accordingly. To reach the mountaintop, all three "secular moral traditions" have to be revised. First utilitarianism:

> Parfit argues that the solution is to redefine rule-consequentialism so that it is defined not in terms of universal acceptance, but in terms of universal acceptance *and* any level of acceptance short of universal acceptance apart from no acceptance whatsoever.[48]

Also revised is Kant's formula of the universal law, the supreme principle of morality: "I ought never to act except in such a way that I could also will that my maxim should become a universal law."[49] Parfit arrives at a version that seems to combine the best elements of Kantianism and contractualism: "Everyone ought to follow the principles whose universal *acceptance* everyone could rationally will"[50] (my italics).

Parfit's task was to show that Kantianism, contractualism, and consequentialism are mutually revisable and reconcilable to avoid internal conceptual conflict. He argued that, with sufficient broad consideration by the entire community of analytical thinkers, the jointly revised set of principles would converge. Then the world of analytical philosophy would be in a position to advance a formula by which all theorists were clearly moving upward on the same "mountain," toward what Parfit summarized as the "Triple Theory":

*Triple Theory*: An act is wrong just when such acts are disallowed by some principle that is optimific, uniquely universally willable, and not reasonably rejectable.[51]

The theory's principles will be *consequentialist* because they would lead to the best results (optimific); *Kantian* because they are universally willable; and *contractualist* because no person could reasonably reject them. In the end, Parfit hoped, philosophers could conceivably celebrate the ultimate prospect of moral progress.

Vigorous debate, engaging analytical writers across the globe, continues over the implications of Parfit's large body of work.[52] It has opened up a broader discussion, one that pragmatism must engage to more fully be understood. At stake is the very definition of moral progress. Does it come through the search for a global scheme, or an understanding of the social dimension driving malleable reasons in the resolution of disputes? Pragmatism does not replace Parfit's "three secular traditions," but addresses the particularized and changing aspects of them that constantly shape and reshape conceptions of utility, as well as moral and contractual principles.

My purpose in this chapter is to suggest to pragmatists that the dominant analytical worldview stands as a challenge to advance their response to analytical moral philosophy in greater detail. Parfit's goal of "moral progress" should motivate them to show that analytical philosophers confuse armchair theory with contingent reality. Real moral progress requires constant adaptation through democratic engagement, revisiting Dewey's own vision, but with a Holmesean understanding of the nature of conflict and convergence.

## NOTES

1. In his letter to Emerson, Holmes enclosed an article he had published in the *American Law Review*, of which he was co-editor with Arthur Sedgwick. Three years later Holmes would write to Sedgwick, "My object in writing these articles is to take up from time to time the cardinal principles and conceptions of the law and make a new and more fundamental analysis of them—For the purpose of constructing a new Jurisprudence or New First Book of the law." Holmes to Sedgwick, July 12, 1879 (Harvard Law School Library).

2. See Frederic Kellogg, *Oliver Wendell Holmes Jr and Legal Logic* (Chicago: University of Chicago Press, 2018).

3. Kellogg, *Holmes and Legal Logic*, chs. 1–2, 10.

4. Kellogg, *Holmes and Legal Logic*, ch. 10; Ralph Sleeper, *The Necessity of Pragmatism: John Dewey's Conception of Philosophy* (New Haven, CT: Yale University Press, 1986), 134–61, explaining why John Dewey's *Logic: The Theory of Inquiry* was misunderstood and ignored by mainstream analytical philosophers.

5. Although Rawls's views on Dewey's pragmatism have not been assessed in comprehensive detail, Eric Thomas Weber's *Rawls, Dewey and Constructivism* offers critical insight. Further hints are suggested by Rawls's marginal notes in a copy of Dewey's *Theory of Valuation* purchased by Prof. Brian Butler of UNC Ashfield after being transferred for sale after Rawls's death to a local bookstore. The notes suggest that Rawls preferred the approach to value of his colleague Ralph Barton Perry in *General Theory of Value* (Cambridge, MA: Harvard University Press, 1967). (Rawls comments "unfair to Perry who recognized this" next

to Dewey's comment "The chief weakness of current theories of valuation which relate the latter to desire and interest is due to failure to make an empirical analysis of concrete desires and interests as they actually exist." Rawls also comments "who would support this?" next to a passage explicating Dewey's view of "The Continuum of Ends-Means.") When offered for sale the library appeared to have included no other Dewey works. Copy of Rawls's copy of Dewey's *Theory of Valuation*, 19, 29, 44, library of Brian Butler.

6. Kellogg, *Holmes and Legal Logic*, chs. 1–3.

7. Kellogg, *Holmes and Legal Logic*, ch. 10.

8. See, e.g., J. L. Mackie, *Ethics: Inventing Right and Wrong* (New York: Penguin Books, 1977), fn. 125.

9. Charles S. Peirce, *Writings of Charles S. Peirce: A Chronological Edition* 1: 393. "Upon the correct answer to that question [of inductive inference] much depends. Our fate hangs upon it. All difficult questions require an understanding of the reason of our faith in experience as a witness to the future and unexperienced."

10. The pragmatic maxim "Consider what effects, which might conceivably have practical bearings, we conceive the object of our conception to have. Then, our conception of these effects is the whole of our conception of the object." As found in Peirce's 1878 article "How to Keep Our Ideas Clear," *Writings* 3: 266. I am not suggesting that Peirce took a static consequentialist position, only that some readers tend to apply this pithy definition of pragmatism as more comprehensive than intended.

11. David Lyons, *Forms and Limits of Utilitarianism* (Oxford: Clarendon Press, 1965), 194.

12. Derek Parfit calls this "moral mathematics." *Reasons and Persons* (Oxford: Clarendon Press, 1984), 67.

13. See Kellogg, *Holmes and Legal Logic*, ch. 5; Edward H. Levi, *Introduction to Legal Reasoning* (Chicago and London: University of Chicago Press, 1949), describing the century-long continuum of inquiry into the concept of "dangerous instrumentality."

14. Rawls, "Two Concepts of Rules," in *Theories of Ethics*, Foot, ed. (Oxford: Oxford University Press, 1967), 149.

15. Rawls, "Two Concepts," 156.

16. Rawls, "Two Concepts," 158.

17. Rawls, "Two Concepts," 163. As will be seen, the sweeping term "promising" is unhelpful in defining actual practices.

18. Rawls, "Two Concepts," 153.

19. Rawls, "Two Concepts," 153.

20. Rawls, "Two Concepts," 154.

21. Rawls, "Two Concepts," 153–54.

22. Rawls, "Two Concepts," 154.

23. David Lyons, *Forms and Limits of Utilitarianism* (Oxford: Carendon Press, 1965), 180.

24. Lyons, *Forms and Limits of Utilitarianism*, 180.

25. Brad Hooker, "Rule Consequentialism," in *Stanford Encyclopedia of Philosophy*, 2018, 18.

26. Brad Hooker, "Rule Consequentialism."

27. Holmes used many examples, and a fuller account of his development is found in Kellogg (2007 and 2018). An early Holmes example (the 1866 English case of *Beadel v. Perry*, L. R. 3 Eq. 465) involved neighboring landowners disputing construction near a property line affecting the neighboring property, an issue then not yet covered by local regulation. Another example was the application of the standard of negligence in tort adjudications. "The Theory of Torts," *Collected Works* 1: 328.

28. My use of the term "conflict" implies any form of dialectic interaction leading to alteration of opposing reasons that initially appeared intractable, including matters settled by dialogue or negotiated through legislation.

29. Holmes, "The Theory of Torts," *The Collected Works of Justice Holmes: Complete Public Writings and Selected Opinions of Oliver Wendell Holmes*, edited by Sheldon M. Novick (Chicago and London: University of Chicago Press, 1995) 1: 329.

30. I have recently noted and discussed an analogy with Jonathan Dancy's ethical particularism in "The Snake and the Roundabout."

31. Readers familiar with Holmes will recall that he used the figure of "Mrs. Quickly" to illustrate the same point in "The Path of the Law": "The reason why a lawyer does not mention that his client wore a white hat when he made a contract, while Mrs. Quickly would be sure to dwell upon it along with the parcel gilt goblet and the sea-coal fire, is that he foresees that the public force will act in the same way whatever his client had upon his head." Holmes, *Collected Works* 3: 391.

32. Holmes referred to *Beadel v. Perry* as reaching a "mathematical" formula. "To leave the question to the jury forever, is simply to leave the law uncertain. Accordingly, we read in a recent equity case that what was left at large to the jury fifty years ago has now become a mathematical rule; that a building cannot be complained of unless its height exceeds the distance of its base from the base of the ancient windows." *Collected Works* 1: 328. Compare Edward Levi's account of the rise and fall of the concept of dangerous instrumentality. Levi, *An Introduction to Legal Reasoning* (Chicago & London: Chicago University Press, 1949), 9–27.

33. Lyons, *Forms and Limits of Utilitarianism*, 180.

34. Holmes, *Collected Works* 1: 212, 326.

35. Levi, *Introduction*, 4.

36. Hooker, "Rule Consequentialism," 18.

37. Holmes, *The Common Law*, *Collected Works* 3: 198 ff.

38. Holmes, *Collected Works* 3: 241 ff.

39. In the process of comparison, consideration is increasingly given to the nature and requirements of competing purposive activities, to what Lon Fuller called the "intermeshing anticipations" (or expectations) of those involved in the affected activities. Lon Fuller, *The Law in Quest of Itself.* See generally, Kenneth Winston, ed., *Selected Essays of Lon L. Fuller.* Holmes's early emphasis on "foreseeability" encompasses the multiplicity of factors involved in these early determinations; as he wrote in 1873, "A more modern example [Holmes had been discussing changes in the liability of innkeepers] is to be found in the rule of the road. After a sufficient amount of *fighting*, a practice is worked out, and a corresponding *expectation* generated. Then this is judicially noticed by the courts, and it is laid down as a rule of law that men are bound to in this instance what by general consent they are *expected* to do" (my italics). *Collected Works* 1: 329.

40. Nancy Cartwright, *Dappled World: A Study of the Boundaries of Science* (Cambridge: Cambridge University Press, 1999), 1; Kellogg, *Holmes and Legal Logic*, 144.

41. Hooker, *Ideal Code, Real World* (Oxford: Oxford University Press, 2000).

42. Kellogg, *Holmes and Legal Logic*.

43. Kellogg, *Holmes and Legal Logic*. Holmes, "Law in Science and Science in Law," *Collected Works* 3: 406.

44. John Rawls, *A Theory of Justice* (Cambridge, MA & London: Harvard University Press, 1971).

45. Michael Ridge, "Climb Every Mountain," *Ratio (new series)* XXII 1:22 (2009).

46. Ridge, "Climb Every Mountain," 59.

47. Ridge, "Climb Every Mountain," 60–61.

48. Ridge, "Climb Every Mountain," 62.

49. Parfit, *On What Matters* 1: 278.

50. Ridge, "Climb Every Mountain," 60.

51. Parfit, *On What Matters* 1: 44.

52. "We need not look further than the many points of contact between Parfit and the philosophers referenced in this very review, the number of which would easily be ten times higher were it not for space restrictions, to come away with this impression. This strongly indicates that, while our discipline lost a philosophical giant when Parfit passed away shortly before the publications of Volume Three and Singer's collection, moral philosophy has a bright future ahead of it. I would count this as a reason why it is rational to be optimistic about the possibility of moral progress." Laskowski, "Review of Parfit's *On What Matters*."

## BIBLIOGRAPHY

Cartwright, Nancy. *The Dappled World: A Study of the Boundaries of Science.* Cambridge: Cambridge University Press, 1999.

Dancy, Jonathan. *Ethics without Principles*. Oxford: Clarendon Press, 2004.

———. *Moral Reasons*. Oxford and Cambridge, MA: Blackwell 1993.

Fuller, Lon. *The Law in Quest of Itself.* Boston: Beacon Press, 1940.

———. *The Principles of Social Order: Selected Essays of Lon L. Fuller.* Edited by Kenneth Winston. Oxford & Portland, OR: Hart Publishing, 2001.

Holmes, Oliver Wendell, Jr. *The Collected Works of Justice Holmes: Complete Public Writings and Selected Opinions of Oliver Wendell Holmes*. Edited by Sheldon M. Novick. Chicago and London: University of Chicago Press, 1995.

———. *The Common Law*. Boston: Little Brown and Co., 1881.

Hooker, Brad. *Ideal Code, Real World.* Oxford: Oxford University Press, 2000.

———. "Rule Consequentialism." *Stanford Encyclopedia of Philosophy*, 2018.

Kellogg, Frederic R. *Oliver Wendell Holmes and Legal Logic.* Chicago: University of Chicago Press, 2018.

———. *Oliver Wendell Holmes, Legal Theory, and Judicial Restraint.* Cambridge: Cambridge University Press, 2009.

———. "The Snake and the Roundabout: Ethical Particularism and the Patterns of Normative Induction." *Duc in Altum Cadernos de Direito* 8, no. 16 (December 2016). See also https://papers.ssrn.com/sol3/papers.cfm?abstract_id=2888196.

Laskowski, Nicholas. "Review of Derek Parfit's *On What Matters*," vol. 3. *Ethics* 128 (2): 496–505 (2018)

Levi, Edward H. *An Introduction to Legal Reasoning.* Chicago and London: University of Chicago Press, 1949.

Lyons, David. *Forms and Limits of Utilitarianism.* Oxford: Clarendon Press, 1965.

Mackie, J. L. *Ethics: Inventing Right and Wrong.* New York: Penguin Books, 1977.

Parfit, Derek. *Reasons and Persons.* Oxford: Clarendon Press, 1984.

———. *On What Matters*. Draft of December 4, 2008, http://www-bcf.usc.edu/~jacobmro/coursedocs/parfit-whatmatters.pdf.

Peirce, Charles S. *Writings of Charles S. Peirce: A Chronological Edition*. 6 vols. Max H. Fisch, Christian J. W. Kloesel, Edward C. Moore, Don D. Roberts, Lynn A. Ziegler, Nathan Houser, Marc Simon, Ursula Niklas, André De Tienne, Cornelis de Waal, Jonathan K. Eller, and Albert Lewis, eds. Bloomington: Indiana University Press, 1982–2000.

Perry, Ralph Barton. *General Theory of Value.* Cambridge, MA: Harvard University Press, 1967.

Rawls, John. "Two Concepts of Rules," in *Theories of Ethics*. Foot, ed. Oxford: Oxford University Press, 1967.

———. *A Theory of Justice.* Cambridge, MA, & London: Harvard University Press, 1971.

———. *Lectures on the History of Moral Philosophy.* Cambridge, MA, & London: Harvard University Press, 2000.

Ridge, Michael. "Climb Every Mountain" *Ratio* (new series) XXII 1:22 (2009).

Sleeper, Ralph. *The Necessity of Pragmatism: John Dewey's Conception of Philosophy.* New Haven: Yale University Press, 1986.

Weber, Eric Thomas. *Rawls, Dewey and Constructivism: On the Epistemology of Justice.* Continuum, 2010.

## *Chapter Four*

# The Social Darwinist

Seth Vannatta and Sarah H. Woolwine

Social Darwinism eludes a simple definition.[1] The term covers a set of particulars bearing a family resemblance including, but not limited to: (1) the extension of evolutionary biology, though not necessarily Darwinian, to social phenomena; (2) a biological explanatory device for the success of certain more biologically "fit" groups, ethnicities, races, or nations over others; (3) an acceptance of the use of force by the "fit" to succeed over the "unfit" in the struggle for existence;[2] (4) a preference for competition in the marketplace and a resulting laissez-faire ideology.[3] (5) Snaking across these particulars, the serpent of Social Darwinism leaves a trail of the eugenics movement in its wake. Further, those charged with being Social Darwinists rarely embrace the term; it is usually a term of opprobrium cast from the prejudices of those in one era upon those of a prior one deemed morally retrograde.

Evidence is found that Holmes's judicial and non-judicial philosophy fits each of these instantiations. (1) He commonly applied the language of evolution and metaphors gleaned from evolutionary biology to social phenomena including law.[4] (2) Holmes's fatalism often moves from the is to the ought, such that a description of given socio-economic states are taken as prescriptions that the status quo, explained in evolutionary terms, ought to be just what it is. And his decisions regarding the civil liberties of racial minorities exhibits a racism at least concomitant with a biological account of racial superiority.[5] (3) Holmes accepted that force was the ultimate arbiter between two conflicting groups with mutually exclusive worldviews bound to enact them.[6] (4) He defended free speech using the metaphor of a competitive marketplace of ideas, and despite his deference to state legislative measures, thought that socialism and redistributive legislation were sentimental hopes that did not work.[7] (5) The trail of eugenics leads his commentators directly to his decision in *Buck v. Bell* and his infamous dictum: "three generations of imbeciles are enough."[8]

Nevertheless, assessing the suitability of the label of Social Darwinist for Holmes demands contextual nuance, semantic analysis, and scholarly humility. The historical and jurisprudential context of Holmes's decisions used to support the claim must be illustrated. The meaning of the words "fit" and "survival," "strong" and "weak" need interrogation. And we must balance our right to judge Holmes morally with a healthy skepticism of the moral progress some claim we have made because, as Holmes reminds us, our ultimates are not likely those of the cosmos. This chapter proceeds by explaining the origins and meanings of Social Darwinism. Next, it examines the evidence supporting the five features of Social Darwinism in Holmes's writings. Then, space is given to an evaluation of the repugnant trail of eugenics in Holmes's *Buck v. Bell* decision. Last, the analysis pivots to concluding reflections on Holmes's contested legacy and on the evidence for labeling him a Social Darwinist. We conclude that while much explanatory work can situate Holmes as a man of his time, some of Holmes's prejudices were morally problematic. Our admiration for Holmes ends where his classism, racism, and ableism, fueled by the spirit of Social Darwinism, begin. We conclude that in addition to his place in intellectual history as the first legal pragmatist, the label of Social Darwinist suits Justice Holmes.

## EARLY EXPRESSIONS AND ORIGINS OF SOCIAL DARWINISM

An early instantiation of the spirit of Social Darwinism came from the mouth of Callicles in his verbal dispute with Socrates in Plato's *Gorgias*. Callicles tells Socrates that, when claiming that it is more disgraceful to do than to suffer injustice, he is engaging in "popular fallacies, looking to what is fine and noble, not by nature, but by convention."[9] Callicles claimed that laws are written and passed for the advantage of the weak, such that convention makes it shameful to seek an advantage over the many. But "nature herself makes it plain that it is right for the better to have the advantage over the worse, the more able over the less."[10] Callicles analogizes the natural law for humans to the ways of nature for both animals and "entire states and races of mankind."[11] Conventional law turns the strongest, "young like lion cubs" into slaves, saying that they should be contented with equality.[12] Callicles embodies the proto-Nietzschean claim that eventually a strong man will rise up, burst through his fetters and reveal himself to be master, showing the true, *natural* concept of justice.[13]

Friedrich Nietzsche channels this sentiment when he contrasts the good as the noble, strong and healthy, clean and pure, truthful and beautiful, with the bad as the weak and sickly, the unclean and soiled, the double-minded and ugly. The nobles, a warrior class, valued their own qualities, those to which they could attribute their own station. The weak, their slaves, suffered in quiet rancor, in whispering, bitter resentment. But by a clever trick, they inverted the value system and elevated a new set of priestly values, meekness, other-centeredness, charity, forgiveness, and love. However, their love stemmed from the greatest hate. The pleasure of heaven was for them watching their enemies burn in hell. The priests thought those who partake in the rape and violence of life's will shall feel bad, bad in their consciences, guilty.[14] Both Callicles and Nietzsche extend the ways of nature to social phenomena, elevate competition as a test for fitness, and give voice to a naturalistic explanatory device for the success of certain more "fit" groups, ethnicities, races, or nations over others. Further, they accept the use of force by the "fit" to succeed over the "unfit."

Of course, neither Callicles nor Nietzsche used the term Social Darwinism to name their version of natural law or the natural will to power, respectively. The term was first used in Joseph Fisher's 1877 article on *The History of Landholding in Ireland* published in the *Transactions of the Royal Historical Society.*[15] The American historian, Richard Hofstadter, popularized the term in 1944.[16] Hofstadter used the term to decry a reactionary ideology that trafficked in competitive strife, racism, and jingoism. Hofstadter recounts that Herbert Spencer coined the term "survival of the fittest" and criticized state interference with the natural working of the market. Public assistance to the poor and regulations on businesses were both forms of conventional law, the product of the weak and unfit, disturbing the law of nature, which favored the fit and strong. Spencer's followers then used Darwinian evolutionary science to legitimize Spencer's social philosophy.[17]

## EVIDENCE OF SOCIAL DARWINISM IN HOLMES'S PHILOSOPHY

### The Extension of Evolutionary Biology to Social Phenomena

The ancient and the nineteenth-century instantiations of the attitude of Social Darwinism loom large in Holmes's career. Holmes certainly extended evolutionary biology to the social phenomenon of law. He saw himself as fulfilling Sir Henry Maine's historical method in *Ancient Law* in a post-Darwinian world. Holmes's *The Common Law* is "first of all an account of legal change, and its object in this respect is to exhibit the workings of Darwinian evolution in law."[18] In light of this fact, Jan Vetter states explicitly that Holmes "is best seen [. . .] as a kind of Social Darwinist."[19] He referred to early conceptions of law as embryonic, and attempted to show that law, responding to externalities, evolves by organic necessity.[20] Holmes's first lecture in *The Common Law*, "Early Forms of Liability," treats the law as an organic, evolving form. Referring to the evolutionary nature of law, he states, "Just as the clavicle in the cat only tells of the existence of some earlier creature to which a collarbone was useful, precedents survive in the law long after the use they once served is at an end and the reason for them has been forgotten."[21] In the first three lectures of *The Common Law*, Holmes shows that the modern concept of liability began from a concept grounded in vengeance and the passion for revenge, where the action for damages was brought against the owner of the *deodand*, or, in even more primitive cases, liability was attached to the offending thing, not the human agent.[22] The long evolution of the concept of liability from primitive to modern was one from vengeance to compensation and one from inanimate objects to living things, to owners of living things, to knowledge of the owner of the living thing, and finally to the point where attention is paid to negligence and culpability.[23]

Holmes's essay, "Law in Science and Science in Law" attempted to overcome the teleological tendency to explain law by showing its fitness for ends. In place of this approach, Holmes wanted to "trace the order and process of its growth and development."[24] Here Holmes claims that the survival of some legal concepts and practices is in part a function of "the struggle for life among competing ideas," aiming at and demonstrating "the ultimate victory and survival of the fittest."[25] He claims that out of the practice of the giving of hostages grew the legal concept of surety, a development independent of the growth toward debt or formal contract.[26] He concludes: "There was a clash between competing ideas, and just as commerce was prevailing over war the children of the sale drove the child of the hostage from the field."[27] Appealing to Spencer's concept of Integration, Holmes illustrates that historical inquiry into the origin of legal rules often shows their somewhat accidental survival.[28]

The practical turn in the essay aims to show that "the justification of a law for us cannot be found in the fact that our fathers always have followed it. It must be found in some help which the law brings toward reaching a social end which the governing power of the community has made up its mind that it wants."[29] In fact, that the jury brings to its decision a host of popular prejudices is an advantage because the jury needs to channel the shifting principle of reasonable conduct in line with social ends the populace supports. In this same essay, however, Holmes manifests a pragmatist legal analysis. His repeated remark, "we must think things not words," means that accepting legal rules and inventing grounds of policy as their base must be met with skepticism.[30] Empty generalizations must be investigated analytically and historically. Further, some consequentialist measure, some social aim, though not one antecedently purported as universal, will be the ultimate arbiter in many legal decisions.

## A Biological Explanatory Device for the Fitness of Certain Groups

A version of determinism, or *amor fati*, permeates Holmes's thought, and a biological interpretation of his fatalism is plausible. For example, consider Holmes's reflections as he thought he was dying after being wounded at Ball's Bluff in the Civil War: "Then came in my Philosophy—I am to take a leap in the dark—but now as ever I believe that whatever shall happen is best—for it is in accordance with a general law—and *good & universal* (or *general law*) are synonymous terms in the universe."[31] He told Harold Laski that he accepted "a rough equation between isness and oughtness."[32] And he wrote to Morris Cohen that he worshipped the inevitable.[33] In another public address, he channeled something similar: "I always say yes—whatever is, is right—but not necessarily will be for thirty seconds longer."[34] Holmes held a view that nature uses tricks to get us to work. We operate under the illusion of self-striving, and effort is the means by which the inevitable comes to pass. That is, we are but functions of a much larger, natural cosmos whose destiny we cannot fathom, but which our efforts help fulfill. One version of his determinism came in a speech at the dinner of the Alpha Delta Phi Club: "We all have cosmic destinies of which we cannot divine the end, if the unknown has ends. Our business is to commit ourselves to life, to accept at once our functions and our ignorance and to offer our heart to fate."[35]

If fitness is the product of biological evolution within a changing environment, whether or not such a result is determined or contingent, perhaps the most concise statement resounding in the spirit of Social Darwinism comes from Holmes's opinion in *The Gas-Stokers' Strike*. I cite it at length here:

> The struggle for life, undoubtedly, is constantly putting the interests of men at variance with those of the lower animals. And the struggle does not stop in the ascending scale with the monkeys, but is equally the law of human existence. Outside of legislation this is undeniable. It is mitigated by sympathy, prudence, and all the social and moral qualities. But in the last resort a man rightly prefers his own interest to that of his neighbors. And this is true in legislation as in any other form of corporate action. All that can be expected from modern improvements is that legislation should easily and quickly, yet not too quickly, modify itself in accordance with the will of the *de facto* supreme power in the community, and that the spread of an educated sympathy should reduce the sacrifice of minorities to a minimum. But whatever body may possess the supreme power for the moment is certain to have interests inconsistent with others which have competed unsuccessfully. The more powerful interests must be more or less reflected in legislation; which like every other device of man or beast, must tend in the long run to aid the survival of the fittest.[36]

The Spencerian language here is strong and rather harsh. Even while Holmes holds out hope for "the spread of an educated sympathy," his remarks resound of Thrasymachus's in Book I of Plato's *Republic*: "Justice is nothing but the advantage of the stronger."[37]

Further, there is an aesthetic dimension to the vitalism in Holmes's thought.[38] In his Speech at the Bar Association of Boston in 1900, Holmes stated: "The end of life is life. Life is action, the use of one's powers. As to use them to their height is our joy and duty, so it is the one end that justifies itself." He continues, "More complex and intense intellectual efforts mean a fuller and richer life. They mean more life. Life is an end in itself, and the only question as to whether it is worth living is whether you have enough of it."[39] The aesthetic dimensions of this vitalism come through in a speech to the class of '61: "Life is a roar of bargain and battle, but in the very heart of it there rises a mystic spiritual tone that gives meaning to the whole. It transmutes the dull details into romance."[40] He compared life to a boat race and a game of solitaire, treating experience as competitive, the constant overcoming of obstacles, but he was skeptical of attributing to life experiences an ultimate *telos*.

Relevant to an inquiry into Holmes's views on biological fitness is his record on cases involving race and the rights of racial minorities. G. Edward White makes the convincing case that Holmes was "no friend of [. . .] the rights of minorities," at least in the first thirteen years on the Supreme Court.[41] He infers this conclusion from an examination of several court cases, two of which make the point plainly. In *Giles v. Harris*, Holmes denied the effort of a black citizen of Alabama to be registered by the state to vote prior to the institution of more restrictive voting qualifications in 1903, which purposely disenfranchised only black voters. Holmes refused to grant equitable relief because traditionally "proceedings in equity have not embraced a remedy for political wrongs."[42] His curious dichotomy between the political wrongs of states' anti-black legislation and legal wrongs is manifest further in his claim that federal courts possess "no constitutional power to control [state] action by any means," indicating that the federal courts could not enforce the Fifteenth Amendment.[43] White claims that Holmes was implying that federal courts should not enter into the area of race relations. While this implication may be true, it also evinces Holmes's thoroughgoing prediction theory of law and the seriousness with which he takes the dogmatic dictum of public taste and public will. In the opinion, Holmes makes the following conditional statement: "Unless we are prepared to supervise the voting in that state by officers of the court, it seems to us that all that the plaintiff could get from equity would be an empty form."[44] The implication here is that the court is not willing to supervise the voting in that state (26 years after the end of Reconstruction). He was likely predicting accurately that the public will would not support it.

In *Bailey v. Alabama*, Holmes wrote a dissent, plainly betraying his habit of anti-formalism in a case involving a black litigant. Bailey had been contracted to work as an agricultural laborer for $12 a month, but received an advance of $15, and was required to repay it by ensuing deductions. Bailey left his employment after a month without repaying. Alabama had passed a statute in 1903 indicating that a breach of contract was "prima facie evidence of the intent to injure or defraud [one's] employer," making a breach of contract a criminal offense. An amicus brief argued that the law was designed to enslave blacks. The majority opinion held that the prima facie evidence of the intent to defraud infringed upon the right of defendants to be presumed innocent and was inconsistent with the Thirteenth Amendment.[45] Holmes dissented, arguing that it was evidence "that a man has a fraudulent intent if he receives an advance upon a contract over night and leaves in the morning."[46] He deferred to the jury to determine if there was a legitimate excuse for breaking the contract by examining external circumstances, as a rule of evidence barred Bailey, charged with fraud, from testifying. Thus, Holmes thought deference to an all-white jury in a case of fraud involving a black sharecropper would be impartial enough to weigh circumstances and determine legitimate from fraudulent breaches of contract. Ignoring the purpose of the law and relying on a formal distinction between conclusive and rebuttable presumptions, Holmes wrote, "the fact that it mainly concerns the blacks does not matter."[47] This is a substantive ruling hiding behind the evening wear of formal logic—the type of disingenuousness of which Holmes was ordinarily so critical.

Two rulings in cases involving African Americans does not a racist make. But when these cases run against the grain of Holmes's habits of argument and judicial decision making and these methodological exceptions are in cases of racial minorities, the case for Holmes's anti-black racism becomes more pronounced, and this is apiece with the spirit of his Social Darwinism evinced elsewhere. The need to write a dissenting opinion in the Bailey case also suggests more than a deference to state legislatures. However, Holmes's deference to the will of the majority, even racial majorities, is consistent. It evokes a conservative methodology that law is not the instrument of change in moral sentiments. The law follows the sentiments that motivate will of the public. He wrote, "It cannot be helped, it is as it should be, that the law is behind the times."[48] Other modes of culture than law work on the sensibilities, and law follows changes therein.

## An Acceptance of the Use of Force by the "Fit" Over the "Unfit"

Holmes accepted without any moral qualms the use of force and the reality of an evolutionary life struggle. He wrote to Harold Laski, "All society has rested on the death of men and must rest on that or on the prevention of the lives of a good many, I naturally shrink from the moral tone."[49] In a Calliclean tone, Holmes writes, "Nature is an aristocrat or at least makes aristocrats, e.g. the cat—and one recognizes certain bloods that generation after generation turn out superior men with here and there a genius."[50] In "The Soldier's Faith," he laments the fashionable "literature of sympathy" that portends that suffering is a wrong, reminding his audience that times of peace are but "a little space of calm in the midst of the tempestuous untamed streaming of the world."[51] To Holmes, a broken neck of a polo player was a price well spent for the breeding of a race fit to rule.[52]

Holmes's commentators have not overlooked his admiration for the life struggle. Grant Gilmore wrote, "Put out of your mind the picture of the tolerant aristocrat, the great liberal, the eloquent defender of our liberties, the Yankee from Olympus. All that was a myth, concocted principally by Harold Laski and Felix Frankfurter, about the time of World War I. The real Holmes was savage, harsh, and cruel, a bitter and lifelong pessimist who saw in the course of human life nothing but a continuing struggle in which the rich and powerful impose their will on the poor and weak."[53]

Similar to Nietzsche, whom Holmes read, Holmes glorified the life struggle. Holmes wrote, "I know of no true measure of men except the total of human energy which they embody—counting everything, with due allowance for quality . . . the final test of this energy is battle in some form."[54] Holmes's amoral realism in this regard is evident when he wrote: "man is at present a predatory animal. I think that the sacredness of human life is a purely municipal ideal of no validity outside the jurisdiction. I believe that force, mitigated so far as may be by good manners, is the *ultimata ratio*, and between two groups that want to make inconsistent kinds of world I see no remedy except force. . . . Every society rests on the death of men."[55] His reflections on World War I only bolstered his dark view: "[WWI] shows us that classes as well as nations that mean to be in the saddle have got to be ready to kill to keep their seat; and that the notion that all that remained for the civilized world was to sit still, converse, and be comfortable was humbug."[56]

His skepticism toward the sentimentalism of Christian ethics also affected his view of William James's pragmatism. He wrote, "As to pragmatism . . . I now see . . . that the aim and end of the whole business is religious."[57] He thought James had succumbed to wishful thinking, making room for a warm God that loves us.[58] Holmes wrote to John Wigmore, "Doesn't this squashy sentimentality of a big minority of our people about human life make you puke?" In the same letter, he referred to the universe itself as predatory.[59] Holmes rebelled at what he called the Neo-Kantian idealism of Del Vecchio's "Formal Bases of Law." In response, Holmes wrote:

> I confess that I rebel at once. If we want conscripts, we march them up to the front with bayonets in their rear to die for a cause in which perhaps they do not believe. The enemy we treat not even as a means but as an obstacle to be

> abolished, if so it may be. I feel no pangs of conscience over either step, and naturally am slow to accept a theory that seems to be contradicted by practices that I approve.[60]

In the same essay, Holmes again criticizes the social reformers of his day, who think they "can get something for nothing by legislation."[61] In response, Holmes claims the best we can do is to "shift disagreeable burdens from the shoulders of the stronger to those of the weaker."[62]

Although he took constructed values seriously, he refused to ascribe to them any transcendent source, often reducing them to functions of taste, as "more or less arbitrary."[63] In "Natural Law," Holmes stated that in his youth he defined truth as the majority opinion of the nation that could "lick all others."[64] However, he took the arbitrariness of aesthetic values so seriously as to state, "When men differ in taste as to the kind of world they want the only thing to do is to go to work killing."[65] Our emotions express our "imperfect social generalizations," and these generalizations are all there is to morality.[66] He wrote to Lewis Einstein, "The world has produced the rattlesnake as well as me; but I kill it if I get a chance, as also mosquitos, cockroaches, murderers and flies. My only judgment is that they are incongruous with the world I want."[67]

To sum up this line of thinking, Holmes not only ascribed biological evolutionary thinking to social phenomena, he often reduced social phenomena, including moral values and abstractions such as rights and duties, to functions of a natural cosmos whose purposes we could not cognize. Since we have no epistemic access to the transcendent, all we have are our more or less arbitrary tastes. But these tastes are dogmatic, and we are willing to fight to defend them. Thus, any sentimentalism about the sanctity of human life is drivel. Every civilization rests on human struggle and loss of life. He stated bluntly, "Nature has but one judgment on wrong conduct—if you can call that a judgment which seemingly has no reference to conduct as such—the judgment of death."[68]

## Preference for Competition in the Marketplace and a Resulting Laissez-Faire Ideology

Holmes disliked Progressive programs of wealth redistribution. In "Ideals and Doubts," he railed against the aspirations of social reformers. The wholesale social regeneration that the reformers expect cannot be achieved by "tinkering with the institution of property, but only by taking in hand life and trying to build a race. That would be my starting point for an ideal of the law."[69] Here, he couples his skepticism of socialism and wealth redistribution with the language of Social Darwinism, "building a race." G. Edward White labeled Holmes "an unreconstructed social Darwinist on economic issues," insofar as he did not fully support the idea that "a beneficent state should become more of a presence as a policymaking force."[70] Holmes's default position was skeptical of redistribution. He stated, "State interference is an evil, where it cannot be shown to be a good."[71] He thought that "objections to unlimited private ownership [were] sentimental or political, not economic."[72] While Holmes did not view profit seeking as a good in itself, he thought that a Rockefeller, "under the illusion of self-seeking or in the conscious pursuit of power," did direct their ability to an "economically desirable end."[73] Further, he referred to men such as Rockefeller in a Calliclean vein as "the ablest men."[74]

Holmes had a "standing war" with his socialist correspondent, Harold Laski, whose affinity for "equality" Holmes thought to be "drool."[75] He thought socialism would only receive serious treatment when it "prevents the continuance of the unfit."[76] Holmes wrote, "[Harold Laski] seems to believe in the fundamental thesis that the rich exploit the poor and the ideal of equality, both of which (with some slight explanation) I believe to be drool. Indeed they provoke me out of intellectual indifference into a fiercely contemptuous wrath"[77] While Holmes is famous for allowing for social experimentation in progressive legislation, and perhaps wrongly lauded as a progressive for doing so, he did so "without enthusiasm" because he thought that "Malthus is right in his general view."[78] In *The Common Law*, Holmes argued that the government's "cumbrous and expensive machinery ought not to be set in motion unless some clear benefit is to be derived from disturbing the status quo. State interference is an evil, where it cannot be shown to be a good."[79] He told Lewis Einstein that most government meddling was "noxious."[80]

Holmes's reputation as a progressive judge after his retirement was largely unearned. The premises supporting the label of progressive were his support for organized labor, his deference toward progressive legislation, and his free speech opinions.[81] However, Holmes himself was not sympathetic to labor unions, as evidenced in his letters to Laski. Rather, he held a detached view that collective labor was free to compete in the same marketplace for a competitive advantage as combinations of capital.[82] In fact, Holmes's detached self-restraint and deference toward state legislative experimentation was not entirely consistent, especially when it came to the cause of racial minorities, as we have seen above.

Holmes was disdainful of social reformers whose aims seemed to be unworthy and beneath Holmes's heroic, risk-taking, and bellicose ideals: "But who of us could endure a world, although cut up into five-acre lots and having no man upon it who was not well fed and well housed, without the divine folly of honor, without the senseless passion for knowledge outreaching the flaming bounds of the possible, without ideals the essence of which is that they never can be achieved?"[83] The social reformers aimed too low.

They, like Nietzsche's last man, aimed only for material comfort and stasis, but these were unworthy aims for Holmes. Thus, tinkering with the institution of property only served to level and to deaden higher human ideals, which were permeated with a romantic bellicosity: "The struggle for life is the order of the world, at which it is vain to repine."[84]

## EUGENICS IN HOLMES'S *BUCK V. BELL* DECISION

Even as Holmes expressed his view that life was an end in itself, he had no qualms about upholding a law meant to hinder its perpetuation. His decision in *Buck v. Bell* to defend a Virginia statute for the sterilization of inmates of state institutions deemed to have heritable insanity or imbecility illustrates how Social Darwinism and eugenics are close cousins. Carrie Buck was detained in a Virginia Colony in 1924 for being allegedly epileptic, feeble-minded, and morally delinquent.[85] Dr. Albert Priddy, the Virginia Colony superintendent, petitioned to have her sterilized. The sterilization order was approved, and was subsequently appealed all the way to the United States Supreme Court.

The plaintiff in error argued that the statute infringed upon the due process and equal protection clauses of the Fourteenth Amendment.[86] Holmes argued that the statute did not violate due process requirements because, although sterilization statutes had been dismissed because of procedural issues, in *Buck*, "the rights of the patient are most carefully considered, and as every step in this case was taken in scrupulous compliance with the statute after months of observation, there is no doubt that in that respect the plaintiff in error has had due process of law."[87] Holmes argued that the appeal was not a matter of procedure, but one of substance. He straightforwardly upheld the grounds of the law. Because Buck is "the probable potential parent of socially inadequate offspring," her sterilization will promote the welfare of society.[88]

The spirit of Social Darwinism provides the measure of the welfare of society. Society calls on "the best citizens" to give their lives in war, and so it would be odd if those that are a drain on society could not be called on to prevent the perpetuation of their kind, the "manifestly unfit."[89] As Phillip Thompson wrote, "Imbeciles threatened to create generations of incompetent people who, at a minimum, would either starve or rely on public or private charity. In a worst-case scenario, generations of 'degenerate offspring' would threaten society with their predatory and criminal activity."[90]

Eugenics was an extension of the logic of Social Darwinism, deploying science to justify its message.[91] Gregor Mendel's work on genetics found renewed interest in the early twentieth century, and scientists inferred that psychological traits, such as imbecility, feeble-mindedness, or criminality, were heritable.[92] Thompson argues that Holmes used Malthusian economics, Social Darwinism, and eugenics for the "theoretical ballast in his scientific jurisprudence, as applied in *Buck v. Bell*."[93] As we have already seen, Holmes respected Herbert Spencer, and he held the view that reform measures to assist the poor were wrong-headed, and one reason for this was that they "increased the population beyond a desirable level."[94] Thompson writes that Social Darwinism "annealed these Malthusian claims."[95]

Susan Haack argues that Holmes's decision in *Buck* exemplifies his moral fallibilism. As we have seen, Holmes was skeptical of any philosopher, judge, or theorist to act as a little god in the presumption that his ultimate ideals somehow matched those of the universe. The law evolves to reflect the moral sensibilities of a culture, but those sensibilities evolve too. The rise and fall of eugenics laws reflect this evolution and, according to Haack, confirms Holmes's commitment to fallibilism, a central tenet of philosophical pragmatism.[96] Haack argues both that the decision represented a failure in moral imagination, given what we now know about the atrocities of Nazi eugenics laws, for instance, and that the decision reflects the ways that "experience," including considerations of social advantage and prejudices judges share with their colleagues, contribute to a judicial decision more so than formal logic.

Allen Mendenhall provides another illuminating spin on *Buck*. Without dismissing the horror of the decision, Mendenhall notes that the equal protection clause of the Fourteenth Amendment had not yet been applied as it was after *Brown v. Board of Education* in 1954.[97] Further, the expansive reading and activist use of the Fourteenth Amendment was, during Holmes's career, a tool of the right wing of the court. It had used the equal protection and due process clauses to strike down state and federal legislation that was progressive: restrictions on working hours (*Lochner v. New York*, 1905), restrictions on child labor (*Hammer v. Dagenhart*, 1918), legislation protecting labor unions (*Duplex Printing Press Co. v. Deering*, 1921), and regulations on the coal industry (*Carter v. Carter Coal Company*, 1936), to name just a few.[98] Mendenhall writes, "Striking down Virginia's eugenics law would have required Holmes to adopt the Fourteenth Amendment jurisprudence of the justices on the right wing of the United States Supreme Court."[99] Rather, Holmes applied the Fourteenth Amendment in a much more limited manner, one in line with the progressives of his time, even though his moral sensibilities were often at odds with the social reformers.[100] Mendenhall's last point is that requirements that judges be impartial and refrain from advocacy mean that Holmes could only address the arguments made by the parties involved in the case. Judges must often rule in favor of parties whose arguments are based on morally appalling laws.[101]

## CONCLUDING REFLECTIONS ON HOLMES'S CONTESTED LEGACY

This volume relies on at least three premises. First, Holmes's legacy is a contested one. Each chapter offers reflections and analyses into a label that Holmes's commentators have applied to him. Yosal Rogat summed up the paradoxes of his reputation: "Remarkably dogmatic, Holmes exemplifies 'humility.' Fatalistic, mistrustful of reason, obsessed with the ubiquity of force, Holmes is nevertheless classified with John Dewey. Generally indifferent to civil liberties interests, Holmes is regarded as their champion. Unconcerned with contemporary realities, Holmes inspired a school of 'realists.' Uninvolved with the life of his society, Holmes affected it profoundly. The apotheosis of Holmes defeats understanding."[102] This volume aims to recover what Rogat claimed was a defeated understanding of Holmes.

The second premise is that Holmes was a pragmatist, sharing significant methodological similarities with other pragmatists of his day including experimentalism, fallibilism, and skepticism of a priori thinking. The final chapter of this volume makes the argument for Holmes's pragmatism despite his disagreements with Peirce, James, and Dewey on a host of philosophical issues including Social Darwinism. The beliefs that disenfranchised groups are evolutionary losers, that the progression of history is unilinear, and that natural selection proceeds toward a fixed end of biological perfection run contrary to the views of the early pragmatists. Peirce, James, and Dewey were highly critical of Herbert Spencer's social philosophy. James and Dewey attacked Spencer's philosophy on ethical grounds. Hofstadter wrote, "Darwin himself offered somewhat confused counsel on the ethical implications of his own discoveries. . . . If there were, in Darwin's writings, texts for rugged individualists and imperialists, those who stood for social solidarity and fraternity could . . . match them text for text with some to spare."[103] Spencer, by contrast, presented a consistent ethical theory grounded in what he took to be a fundamental law of nature—namely, the elimination of the unfit. Those who are fit, he wrote, "do live, and it is well that they should live." Moreover, those who are not die, and it is best that they should die."[104] In accordance with this view, Spencer advocated an ethos of adaptation rather than collective intervention into the problematic affairs of individuals. According to this ethos, "evil" consists in the failure of the individual to adjust to situational givens while "goodness" is attributable to his or her success in acclimating to them.

Spencer's commitment to non-interventionism stemmed from the mechanistic and deterministic elements of his thought. He held that evolution moves inexorably toward its end, driven by a mechanical principle.[105] This end is species perfection as embodied by the "fittest" individuals. Spencer additionally thought of evolution as a universal and unalterable law of nature.

By contrast, Peirce held that natural laws are statements of probability that never rise to the level of absolute certainty. Therefore, one ought to regard evolutionary principles as provisional. Consistent with Peirce's view is the idea that evolution, as a process, is subject to alteration and lacks fixed ends. The ethical applications of this revised concept of evolution lead to an understanding of moral and social progress quite distinct from Spencer's.

James wrote, "Mental interests, hypotheses, postulates, so far as they are bases for human action—action which to a great extent transforms the world—help to *make* the truth which they declare." Thus, "there belongs to mind, from its birth upward, a spontaneity, a vote."[106] The future is open because the universe is unfinished, and because our most established theories about its workings and ourselves remain experimental. Thus, we can alter the course of history, whether for good or for ill. James criticized Spencer for not explaining significant changes within communities from generation to generation. James attributed such changes to innovations by unusual or outstanding individuals. Spencer, by contrast, "attributed social changes to geography, environment, external circumstances—in brief, to everything except human control."[107] This absence of indeterminacy removes any possibility of shifting the course of history for the better, making social progress, and perhaps morality itself, impossible on James's view. "Calling a thing bad means, if it means anything at all, that the thing ought not be, that something else ought to happen in its stead," he wrote.[108] Determinism is consistent with moral pessimism, although Holmes claimed to be neither a pessimist nor an optimist.

The last premise of the volume is that Holmes shared with other men and women of his era significant identifiable prejudices. This last premise is somewhat bifurcated. On the one hand, of course Holmes was prejudiced. To be human is to bring some angle of vision to one's interpretative projects, and that angle of vision is cultured, the product of one's history and social context. These prejudices likely account for his poor record on cases involving minority rights. On the other hand, Holmes, like Edmund Burke before him and Hans-Georg Gadamer after him, made prejudice a concept ripe with normative content.[109] In a manner similar to Charles Sanders Peirce, we should rely on our inherited prejudices and be skeptical of overturning the inductive generalizations of the history of our race because of ratiocination.[110] Not only did Holmes pull off the formalist mask of jurisprudence and wash its pretenses with "cynical acid," he also knew that the public was as prejudiced as the judge was, and the will of the majority could not be contravened easily.[111] Thus, deference to legislation, even legislation that grates on our contemporary moral sensibilities, was the most prudential course of action. Judges had to predict the consequences of their decisions in ways similar to the bad men Holmes claimed defined law by their prophecies. Judges had to ask, implicitly or explicitly, what the consequences of this decision were in terms of policy advantages and costs of enforcement. These predictions included taking the prejudice of the public seriously. Was their public will to enforce the decision? If not, that answer contributed to the decision, even if the decision wore the evening dress of formal logic.

The spirit of Social Darwinism contributed much to Holmes's background beliefs. It was his bog of inquiry, but, ever the skeptic and fallibilist, he knew the bog was not solid ground. Part of his context was the accepted science of the day, and much of this science accepted eugenics, which was an extension of the Social Darwinism in the air during Holmes's career. His unique, personal experiences also contributed to this spirit. His Civil War experience must have shaped his acceptance of the reality and inevitability of struggle, suffering, and death. As David Luban has argued, Holmes overused military metaphors and overemphasized physical enforcement of laws.[112] Holmes was the product of the Darwinian and Spencerian revolutions, whose spirit contributed to his evolutionary view of law, his understanding of social fitness, his acceptance of the use of force in the struggle of competition in the marketplace and on the battlefield. Beyond his enthusiasm for Darwin and his Nietzschean skepticism of Christian morality, he was not ahead of his time. He was the product of it. The ugliness of the Spirit of Social Darwinism, according to our lights, was manifest in his poor record of civil rights for racial minorities and culminated in his decision in *Buck v. Bell.* We conclude that in addition to his place in intellectual history as the first legal pragmatist, the label of Social Darwinist suits Justice Holmes.

## NOTES

1. Portions of this essay were previously published in Vannatta, Seth. "Justice Holmes, the Social Darwinist." *The Pluralist*. Proceedings from the 2018 Meeting of SAAP, Vol. 14, No. 1 (2019), 78–90. They are reprinted here with permission.

2. Mike Hawkins, *Social Darwinism in European and American Thought, 1860–1945* (Cambridge, Cambridge University Press, 1997), 31.

3. I am working with a fairly stereotypical understanding of Social Darwinism, not one that is strictly Spencerian.

4. See Holmes, "Law in Science and Science in Law," *Harvard Law Review*, Vol XII, No. 7, Feb. 25, 1899.

5. See *Giles v. Harris* 189 U.S. 475 (1903); *Bailey v. Alabama* 219 U.S. 219 (1911); *United States v. Reynolds* 235 U.S. 133 (1914); *United States v. Ju Toy* 198 U.S. 253 (1905).

6. To Frederick Pollock, February 1, 1920. *The Essential Holmes*, ed. Richard Posner (Chicago: University of Chicago Press, 1992), 103.

7. Oliver Wendell Holmes, "Ideals and Doubts" [1915], in *Collected Legal Papers* (New York: Harcourt, Brace, and Company, 1921), 305.

8. *Buck v. Bell* 274 U.S. 200 (1927): 15.

9. *Plato: The Collected Dialogues*, ed. Edith Hamilton and Huntington Cairns (Princeton: Princeton University Press, 1989), 482d-e.

10. *Plato*, 483c-d.

11. *Plato*, 483d.

12. *Plato*, 483e.

13. *Plato*, 484a.

14. See Friedrich Nietzsche, *The Birth of Tragedy & The Genealogy of Morals*, trans. Francis Golffing (New York: Doubleday, 1956).
15. See Joseph Fisher, "The History of Landholding in Ireland," *Transactions of the Royal Historical Society* (1877) V: 228–326.
16. Richard Hofstadter, *Social Darwinism in American Thought* (Boston: Beacon Press, 1992).
17. Hofstadter, *Social Darwinism in American Thought*, xiv.
18. Jan Vetter, "The Evolution of Holmes, Holmes and Evolution," 72 *Calif. L. Rev*. 343, (May 1984), 238.
19. Vetter, "The Evolution of Holmes, Holmes and Evolution," 238.
20. Holmes, *American Law Review* 1: 554 (1867), *Collected Works of Justice Holmes*, Vol. 1, ed. Sheldon Novick (Chicago: University of Chicago Press, 1995), 189.
21. Holmes, *The Common Law*, Lecture 1, in *Collected Works of Justice Holmes*, Vol. 3 (Chicago: University of Chicago Press, 1995), 132.
22. Holmes, *Collected Works*, Vol. 3, 6. Deodand is a thing forfeited or given to God, specifically, in law, an object or instrument which becomes forfeit because it has caused a person's death. The English common law of deodands traces back to the eleventh century and was applied, on and off, until Parliament finally abolished it in 1846.
23. Holmes, *Collected Works*, Vol. 3, 10.
24. Holmes, "Law in Science and Science in Law" in *Collected Works of Justice Holmes*, Vol. 3, (Chicago: University of Chicago Press, 1995), 406.
25. Holmes, *Collected Works*, Vol. 3, 410.
26. Holmes, *Collected Works*, Vol. 3, 410.
27. Holmes, *Collected Works*, Vol. 3, 410.
28. Holmes, *Collected Works*, Vol. 3, 411. Spencer argued that structures develop from simple and undifferentiated homogeneity to more complex and differentiated heterogeneity, which was concomitant with a process of greater *integration* of the parts. The progress of ideas in the law, such as replacing primitive notions, as put forth in Holmes's legal history in *The Common Law* qualify as social evolution under Spencer's general theory of social progress only if the changes in the common law benefit or improve society. However, our definition of Social Darwinism is not specifically Spencerian, so we are silent on whether or not these evolutionary changes in the law do in fact benefit society.
29. Holmes, *Collected Works*, Vol. 3, 412.
30. Holmes, "Law in Science and Science in Law," in *Collected Works*, Vol. 3, 412, 418.
31. *Oliver Wendell Holmes: Touched with Fire*, ed. Mark D. Howe (1946), 28.
32. Letter from Oliver Wendell Holmes to Harold J. Laski, June 1, 1927, in *Holmes-Laski Letters*, ed. Mark DeWolfe Howe (Cambridge: Harvard University Press, 1953), 948.
33. Letter from Oliver Wendell Holmes to Morris Cohen, Jan. 20, 1921, in *The Essential Holmes*, ed. Richard Posner (Chicago: University of Chicago Press, 1992), 33–34.
34. Holmes, Address to the Class of 61 at the Fiftieth Anniversary of Graduation, June 28, 1911, in *The Essential Holmes*, 7.
35. Holmes, "Reflections on Past and Future," in *The Essential Holmes*, 6.
36. Holmes, *The Gas Stokers' Strike*, 44 *Harvard Law Review*, 795–96 (1931), reprinted from 7 *American Law Review*, 583 (1873).
37. Plato, *Republic* (New Dehli: General Press, 2016), 338c.
38. See David Luban, "Justice Holmes and the Metaphysics of Judicial Restraint," *Duke Law Journal*, Vol. 44, No. 3 (Dec. 1944), 479.
39. Holmes, *Collected Legal Papers*, 247–48.
40. Holmes, June 28, 1911, *The Essential Holmes*, ed. Richard Posner (Chicago: University of Chicago Press, 1992), 219.
41. G. Edward White, *Justice Oliver Wendell Holmes: Law and the Inner Self* (Oxford: Oxford University Press, 1993), 348.
42. *Giles v. Harris* 189 U. S. 486.
43. *Giles v. Harris* 189 U. S. 488.
44. *Giles v. Harris* 189 U. S. 488.
45. *Bailey v. Alabama* 219 U. S. 234.

46. *Bailey v. Alabama* 219 U. S. 248.
47. *Bailey v. Alabama* 219 U. S. 246.
48. Holmes, "Law and the Court," in *Collected Works*, Vol. 3, 506.
49. Holmes to Laski, December 9, 1921, in *The Essential Holmes*, 115.
50. Holmes to Alice Stopford Green, Nov. 9, 1913, *The Essential Holmes*, 22.
51. Holmes, "The Soldier's Faith," in *Collected Works*, Vol. 3, 489.
52. Holmes, "The Soldier's Faith," in *Collected Works*, Vol. 3, 489.
53. Grant Gilmore, *The Ages of American Law* (New Haven: Yale University Press, 1977), 48–49.
54. Holmes to George Otis Shattuck (1897), in *The Essential Holmes*, 97.
55. Holmes to Pollock, February 1, 1920, in *The Essential Holmes*, 103.
56. Holmes to Lewis Einstein, October 12, 1914, in *The Essential Holmes*, 101.
57. *Holmes-Pollock Letters*, ed. M. Howe (June 17, 1908), 140.
58. *Holmes-Pollock Letters*, ed. M. Howe (September 1, 1910), 167.
59. Letter from Oliver Wendell Holmes to John Wigmore, November 1915, quoted in Sheldon M. Novick, *Honorable Justice: The Life of Oliver Wendell Holmes* (1989), 469, n.11.
60. Holmes, "Ideals and Doubts" in *Collected Works of Justice Holmes*, Vol. 3 (Chicago: University of Chicago Press, 1995), 443.
61. Holmes, "Ideals and Doubts," in *Collected Works of Justice Holmes*, Vol. 3, 443.
62. Holmes, "Ideals and Doubts," in *Collected Works of Justice Holmes*, Vol. 3, 443.
63. Letter from Oliver Wendell Holmes to Lady Pollock, September 6, 1902, in *Holmes-Pollock Letters: The Correspondence of Mr. Justice Holmes and Sir Frederick Pollock 1872–1932*, ed. Mark D. Howe (1941), 104–5.
64. Holmes, "Natural Law," *Collected Legal Papers*, 310.
65. Letter from Holmes to Laski (December 3, 1917) in *Holmes-Laski Letters*, ed. Mark DeWolfe Howe (Cambridge: Harvard University Press, 1953), 116.
66. *Holmes-Einstein Letters*, ed. James Bishop Peabody (New York: St. Martin's Press, 1964), 92–93.
67. *Holmes-Einstein Letters*, 92–93.
68. Holmes, "Address at the Dedication of the Northwestern University Law School Building," October 20, 1902, in *The Essential Holmes*, 98.
69. Oliver Wendell Holmes, *Collected Legal Papers* (New York: Harcourt, Brace, and Company, 1921), 306.
70. G. Edward White, *Justice Oliver Wendell Holmes: Law and the Inner Self* (Oxford: Oxford University Press, 1993), 360.
71. Vetter, "The Evolution of Holmes, Holmes and Evolution," 236. Vetter cited Holmes, *The Common Law*, ed. M. Howe (1963), 77.
72. Holmes, "Economic Elements," *Collected Legal Papers*, 280.
73. Holmes, "Economic Elements," *Collected Legal Papers*, 279–80.
74. Holmes, "Economic Elements," *Collected Legal Papers*, 280.
75. *Justice Oliver Wendell Holmes: His Book Notices and Uncollected Letters and Papers*, ed. H. Shriver (Boston: De Capo Press, 1973), 181.
76. *Justice Oliver Wendell Holmes: His Book Notices and Uncollected Letters and Papers*, 197.
77. *The Essential Holmes*, ed. Richard Posner (Chicago: University of Chicago Press, 1992), 72.
78. Letter from Holmes to Louis D. Brandeis, April 20, 1919, in Phillippa Strum, *Louis D. Brandeis: Justice for the People* (1984), 310.
79. Holmes, "Trespass and Negligence," in *Collected Works*, Vol. 3, 164.
80. *Holmes-Einstein Letters*, 33–34.
81. White, *Justice Oliver Wendell Holmes*, 333.
82. White, *Justice Oliver Wendell Holmes*, 333.
83. Holmes, "The Soldier's Faith," in *Collected Works*, Vol. 3, 487.
84. Holmes, "The Soldier's Faith," in *Collected Works*, Vol. 3, 487.
85. Terms such as imbecility and "feeble-minded" were at least somewhat technical in the psychology of the day.

86. *Buck v. Bell*, 274 U.S. 200 (1927).
87. *Buck v. Bell*, 274 U.S. 207 (1927).
88. *Buck v. Bell*, 274 U.S. 207 (1927).
89. *Buck v. Bell*, 274 U.S. 207 (1927).
90. Phillip Thompson, "Silent Protest: A Catholic Justice Dissents in *Buck v. Bell*," *Cath. Law*. 43 (2004): 129.
91. Hofstadter, *Social Darwinism in American Thought*, 38–40.
92. Thompson, "Silent Protest," 130, and Susan Haack, "Law, Pragmatism, and Morality: The Lessons of *Buck v. Bell*," *European Journal of Pragmatism and American Philosophy* (2011), III, 2, 76.
93. Thompson, "Silent Protest," 129.
94. Letter from Holmes to Harold Laski, August 24, 1924, *The Essential Holmes*, 51, and Thompson, "Silent Protest," 129.
95. Thompson, "Silent Protest," 129–30.
96. Haack, "Law, Pragmatism, and Morality," 86.
97. Allen Mendenhall, *Oliver Wendell Holmes, Jr., Pragmatism, and the Jurisprudence of Agon: Aesthetic Dissent and the Common Law* (Lewisburg: Bucknell University Press, 2017), 132.
98. Mendenhall, *Oliver Wendell Holmes, Jr., Pragmatism, and the Jurisprudence of Agon*, 132.
99. Mendenhall, *Oliver Wendell Holmes, Jr., Pragmatism, and the Jurisprudence of Agon*, 132.
100. Mendenhall, *Oliver Wendell Holmes, Jr., Pragmatism, and the Jurisprudence of Agon*, 132.
101. Mendenhall, *Oliver Wendell Holmes, Jr., Pragmatism, and the Jurisprudence of Agon*, 133.
102. Yosal Rogat, "The Judge as Spectator," 31 U. *Chicago Law Review* 213 (1964), 256.
103. Richard Hofstadter, *Social Darwinism in America*, revised edition (United States: American Historical Association 1955), 90–91. Special thanks to Sarah Woolwine for her commentary on and contributions to this portion of the chapter. Society for the Advancement of American Philosophy, March 9, 2018.
104. Herbert Spencer, *Social Statics, Abridged and Revised, together with The Man Versus the State* (New York: D. Appleton & Company 1897), 206.
105. Chauncey Wright criticized Spencer's theory of evolution by arguing that Spencer's theory was a teleological evolution, not derived by induction, imposed on the data, by a mind driven by the idea of universal progress. Chauncey Wright, "The Philosophy of Herbert Spencer," 100 *North American Review* 423 (1865), 454.
106. William James, *Collected Essays and Reviews* (New York: Longmans, Green & Company 1920), 67.
107. Hofstadter, *Social Darwinism in American Thought*, 132.
108. William James, *The Will to Believe* (New York: Longmans, Green & Company 1897). 161.
109. See Ryan Holston, "Two Concepts of Prejudice," *History of Political Thought*, Vol. 35, No. 1 (2014), 174–203, and Seth Vannatta, *Conservatism and Pragmatism in Law, Politics, and Ethics* (London: Palgrave Macmillan, 2014).
110. Charles Sanders Peirce, *Reasoning and the Logic of Things*, ed. Kenneth Laine Ketner (Cambridge: Harvard University Press, 1992), 111.
111. Holmes, "The Path of the Law," in *Collected Works*, Vol. 3, 394.
112. David Luban, "Justice Holmes and the Metaphysics of Judicial Restraint," *Duke Law Journal*, Vol. 44, No. 3 (December 1944), 514.

## BIBLIOGRAPHY

*Bailey v. Alabama* 219 U.S. 219 (1911).
*Buck v. Bell* 274 U.S. 200 (1927).

Fisher, Joseph. "The History of Landholding in Ireland." *Transactions of the Royal Historical Society* (1877) V: 228–326.
*Giles v. Harris* 189 U.S. 475 (1903).
Gilmore, Grant. *The Ages of American Law*. New Haven: Yale University Press, 1979.
Haack, Susan. "Law, Pragmatism, and Morality: The Lessons of *Buck v. Bell*." *European Journal of Pragmatism and American Philosophy*. (2011) III, 2.
*Plato: The Collected Dialogues*. Ed. Edith Hamilton and Huntington Cairns. Princeton: Princeton University Press, 1989.
Hofstadter, Richard. *Social Darwinism in American Thought*. Boston: Beacon Press, 1992.
Holmes, Jr. Oliver Wendell. "Science in Law and Law in Science." *Harvard Law Review*. Vol. XII. No. 7 (Feb. 25, 1899).
Holmes, Jr. Oliver Wendell. *Collected Legal Papers*. New York: Harcourt, Brace, and Company, 1921.
Holmes, Jr. Oliver Wendell. *American Law Review* 1: 554 (1867).
*Holmes-Pollock Letters: The Correspondence of Mr. Justice Holmes and Sir Frederick Pollock 1872–1932*. Ed. Mark D. Howe. Cambridge: Belknap Press, 1941.
*Holmes-Laski Letters*. Ed. Mark D. Howe. Cambridge: Harvard University Press, 1953.
*Collected Works of Justice Holmes*. Vol. 1. Ed. Sheldon Novick. Chicago: University of Chicago Press, 1995.
*Collected Works of Justice Holmes*. Vol. 3. Ed. Sheldon Novick. Chicago: University of Chicago Press, 1995.
*The Essential Holmes*. Ed. Richard Posner. Chicago: University of Chicago Press, 1992.
Hawkins, Mike. *Social Darwinism in European and American Thought, 1860–1945*. Cambridge: Cambridge University Press, 1997.
Hofstadter, Richard. *Social Darwinism in America*, revised edition. United States: American Historical Association, 1955.
Holston, Ryan. "Two Concepts of Prejudice," *History of Political Thought*. Vol. 35. No. 1 (2014), 174–203.
James, William. *Collected Essays and Reviews*. New York: Longmans, Green & Company 1920.
———. *The Will to Believe*. New York: Longmans, Green & Company, 1897.
Luban, David. "Justice Holmes and the Metaphysics of Judicial Restraint." *Duke Law Journal*. Vol. 44. No. 3 (Dec. 1944), 449–523.
Mendenhall, Allen. *Oliver Wendell Holmes, Jr., Pragmatism, and the Jurisprudence of Agon: Aesthetic Dissent and the Common Law*. Lewisburg: Bucknell University Press, 2017.
Nietzsche, Friedrich. *The Birth of Tragedy & the Genealogy of Morals*. Trans. Francis Golffing. New York: Doubleday, 1956.
Novick, Sheldon M. *Honorable Justice: The Life of Oliver Wendell Holmes*. New York: Little, Brown, 1989.
Peirce, Charles Sanders. *Reasoning and the Logic of Things*. Ed. Kenneth Laine Ketner. Cambridge: Harvard University Press, 1992.
Rogat, Yosal. "The Judge as Spectator," 31 U. *Chicago Law Review* 213 (1964), 213–256.
*Justice Oliver Wendell Holmes: His Book Notices and Uncollected Letters and Papers*. Ed. H. Shriver. Boston: De Capo Press, 1973.
Spencer, Herbert. *Social Statics Abridged and Revised, together with The Man Versus the State*. New York: D. Appleton & Company, 1897.
Strum, Phillippa. *Louis D. Brandeis: Justice for the People*. Cambridge: Harvard University Press, 1984.
Thompson, Phillip. "Silent Protest: A Catholic Justice Dissents in *Buck v. Bell*." *Cath. Law*. 43, 125–148.
*United States v. Ju Toy* 198 U.S. 253 (1905).
*United States v. Reynolds* 235 U.S. 133 (1914).
Vannatta, Seth. *Conservatism and Pragmatism in Law, Politics, and Ethics*. London: Palgrave Macmillan, 2014.
Vetter, Jan. "The Evolution of Holmes, Holmes and Evolution." 72 *Calif. L. Rev* 343 (May 1984), 343–268.

White, G. Edward. *Justice Oliver Wendell Holmes: Law and the Inner Self.* Oxford: Oxford University Press, 1993.

Wright, Chauncey. "The Philosophy of Herbert Spencer." 100 *North American Review* 423 (1865), 423–476.

## *Chapter Five*

# The Natural Law Theorist

Allen Mendenhall

Michael Hoffheimer has argued that the prevailing scholarly assumption that Holmes did not believe in natural law in any form was misguided. He claims that Ralph Waldo Emerson's transcendentalism encompassed a kind of natural law that influenced Holmes, and that Holmes rejected only specific strands—rather than the entire field—of natural-law theory. "Notwithstanding his forceful criticism of natural law," Hoffheimer submits, "Holmes retained an interest throughout his life in the champion of transcendentalism,"[1] namely Emerson, whose exhilarating philosophy and lyrical prose anticipate elements of Holmes's writing.

This chapter investigates Holmes's skepticism of natural law and explores the kind of natural law that he represents: a curious form of Emersonian transcendentalism. Although there is no name for this type of natural law,[2] which, because of its inherent flux and fluidity, defies classification, it might be described as pragmatic in the sense in which that term refers to seminal features of an American literary tradition that includes Emerson, William and Henry James, George Santayana, Wallace Stevens, Gertrude Stein, and Robert Frost.[3] Its transcendentalist premises involve radical subjectivity and individuality as necessary conditions for the spontaneous order that emerges through the superintending forces of nature.

Figures as diverse as Harold Bloom, Richard Poirier, Louis Menand, Joan Richardson, and Jonathan Levin have examined this American literary tradition for its pragmatic qualities and effects.[4] Situating Holmes's transcendentalist rhetoric and affinities within this literary tradition illuminates the Emersonian characteristics of his oft-unnoticed natural-law tendencies. Standing against the derivative "over-influence"[5] of scholarly consensus, this chapter heeds Emerson's rousing imperative "never imitate"[6] by striving for originality in the marriage of literary and legal scholarship to explore Holmes's overlooked but subtle support for a certain paradigm of natural law. It also corrects growing misconceptions about the purportedly absolute divide between natural law and positive law that are the result of tendentious twentieth-century theorizing.[7] Studying Holmes's relationship to Emersonian transcendentalism reveals the embeddedness of normative principles and natural-law reasoning in the textual deposit of cases and customs.

## HOFFHEIMER'S DISRUPTION OF THE SETTLED CONSENSUS ON HOLMES AND NATURAL LAW

Little has changed since Hoffheimer wrote, in 1992, that "Holmes remains considered almost universally as a utilitarian, positivist, pragmatist, or realist in his basic theory."[8] Researchers continue to agree that Holmes "was not a proponent of natural law in any form" and to "assume that continental rationalist and idealist strains of thought—and American proponents like Emerson—had no important influence on [his] mature theory."[9] Related conjecture accepts as given that Holmes's "intellectual development was achieved by a radical break with the transcendentalist views that he held in his early adulthood."[10]

Holmes may have broken from the transcendentalism of his youth,[11] but its influence remained. He acknowledged as much by claiming to have been enamored of Emerson throughout his life. He once wrote that the "only firebrand of my youth that burns as brightly as ever is Emerson."[12] In a different letter with a similar tone, he stated:

> You put it much too strongly when you say that I had no sympathy with Emerson. When he was breaking and I was still young, I saw him on the other side of the street and ran over and said to him: "If I ever do anything, I shall owe a great deal of it to you," which was true. He was one of these who set one on fire—to impart a [thought] was the gift of his genius.[13]

These lines declare and represent Emerson's sway. The figurative use of "fire" recalls Emerson's reference in "The American Scholar" to those "concentrated fires" that "set the hearts of their youth on flame."[14] Genius, of course, was a superlative concept central to Emerson's thought, and in calling Emerson a genius Holmes conceivably tied him as well to such notions as "absolute truth"[15] that are connected to the moral and normative claims of natural-law theory. At the time of his death, Holmes's book collection contained 24 volumes of Emerson's work, a fact that demonstrates at a minimum his ongoing fondness for the Sage of Concord and, in light of his early writing to and about Emerson, a probable familiarity with Emerson's numerous essays and teachings.[16]

Stylistic similarities between Emerson and Holmes have long been recognized, and the influence of Emerson on Holmes has been discussed and debated at length. Mark DeWolfe Howe, the first expert on Holmes, noticed many decades ago that Emerson had affected Holmes.[17] Francis J. Mellen Jr., a practicing attorney, in the late 1970s, contributed a most insightful piece about Holmes and Emerson, arguing that "a fundamental change in American aesthetic thought in the late 18th and early 19th centuries heralded a corresponding change in other intellectual disciplines, including law, in the late 19th and early 20th centuries; and that . . . Holmes[,] whose aesthetic beliefs had been strongly influenced by . . . Emerson, was a leader in the change in legal doctrine because he, sooner than most of his contemporaries, understood and accepted the change."[18] What has not been sufficiently examined, despite Hoffheimer's groundbreaking work, is the link between Emerson and Holmes in terms of natural law and transcendentalism.

Hoffheimer has determined that Holmes's early writings were less hostile to natural law, or at least to doctrines representative of natural law, than were his later writings.[19] He found that Holmes retained the transcendentalism of his youth in his non-legal writings but avoided it in his professional or legal writings such as case opinions.[20] Moreover, he observed that, as Holmes matured as a jurist he grew increasingly impatient with substantive propositions rooted in natural law, which he associated with a version of horizontal federalism whereby federal courts justified their intervention into state matters through appeals to philosophical abstraction involving rights claims.[21]

Holmes could nevertheless practice what he purported to repudiate. His earliest arguments against natural law were limited in scope and lacked the strong language that characterized his essay "Natural Law."[22] Mindful, perhaps, that "[a] foolish consistency is the hobgoblin of little minds,"[23] he "shared important doctrines and ideas with the legal philosophy"—i.e., natural law—"that he sought to destroy."[24] He once employed natural-law reasoning to challenge natural-law premises, going so far as to invoke philosophical absolutes as markers of legal authority.[25] In this, Holmes established an improbable rapprochement between positivist and natural-law paradigms, one that recalls transcendentalism in its ability to synthesize ostensibly incompatible methods and principles.

Holmes scrupulously accomplished an unlikely Emersonian synthesis between airy intuitive romanticism and proto-positivist instrumentalism in his early essays such as "Plato."[26] Only through the ever-open, all-receptive forces of vigorous transcendentalism could his seemingly irreconcilable modes of thought come together in an operative fusion. Holmes's apparent contradictions may represent, not confusion or ignorance, but transcendentalist synthesis. One recalls Walt Whitman's suggestive quip: "Do I contradict myself? / Very well then . . . I contradict myself; / I am large . . . I contain multitudes."[27]

Hoffheimer does not definitively establish or adequately describe what elements of Holmes's jurisprudence signal transcendentalism. I take his conclusion to be that Holmes did not renounce natural law per se so much as he disavowed ways of knowing and discovering natural law.[28] On this view, Holmes's chief concern was epistemological, not ontological or metaphysical.

Unlike classical natural-law theory, which generally holds that moral norms articulated as legal principles are discernable by, and conformable to, right reason, Holmes's jurisprudence was skeptical of the ability of the fallible human mind, with its limited knowledge and selective memory, to ascertain and exercise right reason.[29] He believed that knowledge about the law was necessarily social and embedded in evolving historical conditions and standards with concrete manifestations in cases, statutes, and other legal documents.[30] This premise does not exclude right reason and moral absolutes as indicia of truth that correspond with the natural or normative order of society; rather, it considers reason and morality to be intelligible only through mediated networks of language and discourse and learned through collective contestation, not individual revelation. One may proclaim a truth, but only after several qualified minds evaluate and verify the truth-claim will it gain currency. A truth must establish itself as such for societies to profess it.

Regrettably, Hoffheimer's treatment of the transcendentalist properties of Holmes's jurisprudence is thin on details and substance. There is thus a felt need in the academic literature to pick up where Hoffheimer left off and fill in what he left out.

## DETACHED SKEPTICISM OF NATURAL LAW IN "NATURAL LAW"

A brief and preliminary overview of the conceptions of natural law attributed to Holmes will help to satisfy this felt need. Because an exhaustive or comprehensive synopsis of the numerous studies of Holmes and natural law is not feasible here, I will focus on the essay "Natural Law" from which most commentators derive their understanding of Holmes's relationship to natural-law theory.

"Natural Law" opens with the suggestion that an innate human drive for the superlative probably accounts for "the jurist's search for criteria of universal validity which he collects under the head of natural law."[31] A critique of "universal validity" as a touchstone of natural law appears odd if it is predicated on an assertion of universal validity, to wit, the notion that "[t]here is in *all* men a demand for the superlative."[32] Holmes seems to be articulating a natural law in these first lines of an essay generally agreed to be antithetical to natural-law theory. Could it be that his essay is more complex and nuanced than commentators have allowed?

Recalling the value pluralism of William James as exemplified in "The Varieties of Religious Experience," as well as James's theories of truth in "Pragmatism" and "The Meaning of Truth," Holmes states that "our test of truth is a reference to either a present or an imagined future majority in favor of our view."[33] He expresses with these words a consensus-based mode of knowing and understanding: If a proposition is true, it must satisfy not only the individual thinking or uttering it (after all, "[c]ertitude is not the test of certainty")[34] but also a broad community—a majority—of critical thinkers. A lack of consensus calls into question the validity of the truth claim. It would hardly seem reasonable to call something natural that nobody else believed in or about which there was much controversy and disagreement. Could there be a natural law that no one followed or acknowledged, that existed independently of any human mind? If so, it could not be apprehended, there being no brain equipped or willing to recognize it.

Holmes advocates intellectual modesty and tolerance in light of his conviction that preferences are necessarily experiential.[35] One who has immersed himself in a field of discourse to the exclusion of another field of discourse will naturally favor the former over the later. One who has grown up in a culture with discernable normative codes may find foreign normative codes to be strange, and thus must overcome his ingrained predilections to respect or understand the foreign way. Attachments to childhood and youthful associations—for Holmes, these would be his "earliest joys" such as "granite rocks and barberry bushes"—form entrenched biases upon which one constructs an identity and worldview.[36] To a certain extent, one cannot help but value those ideas he has studied to a far greater degree than he values unfamiliar concepts. "It is true," Holmes says to this end, "that beliefs and wishes have a transcendental basis in the sense that their foundation is arbitrary. You can not help entertaining and feeling them, and there is an end of it."[37] This grasp of the experiential basis of preference-making accounts, in Holmes's view, for the universalizing motivations of natural-law theorists. "The jurists who believe in natural law," he says, "seem to me to be in that naïve state of mind that accepts what has been familiar and accepted by them and their neighbors as something that must be accepted by all men everywhere."[38]

Just because Holmes considers conceptions of "rights and duties" and other such categories of natural-law theory to be socially conditioned and discursively formed[39] does not mean he believes the objects of those categories (i.e., the things that constitute a right or a duty) to be nonexistent or unreal. Holmes is not concerned with the ontological or metaphysical properties of rights, duties, or law but with epistemology, or the modes and methods by which we apprehend laws or their subsidiaries such as rights and duties.

The distinction is important: maybe natural laws exist as real phenomena in the material world, but in any case our knowledge of them is not a priori.

Holmes never says rights are not real or do not exist. He says, rather, that not just for *any* purposes, but specifically "for *legal* purposes a right is only the hypostasis of a prophecy—the imagination of a substance supporting the fact that the public force will be brought to bear upon those who do things said to contravene it—just as we talk of the force of gravitation accounting for the conduct of bodies in space."[40] Holmes is careful not to enter into philosophical debate here regarding the existence or essence of universal natural laws. He limits his discussion to the legal context, perhaps because judges are not philosophers: they lack the equipment and training to undertake complex philosophical reasoning or to derive conclusions in the manner of scientists. His most categorical and unqualified assertion—one that provokes the ire of his opponents—is that the "most fundamental of the supposed preexisting rights—the right to life—is sacrificed without a scruple not only in war, but whenever the interest of society, that is, of the predominant power in the community, is thought to demand it."[41] Even this bold statement, I think, is meant to apply to the legal community only and not to humanity writ large because Holmes follows it by mentioning a "very tenderhearted judge" who would choose to allow a fire to kill a man (i.e., who would abstain from acting to extinguish the flames) if doing so would save precious cargo from burning.[42] Accordingly, Holmes expresses skepticism regarding the ability of a jurist to divine absolute natural law and points to philosophical disparities as a reason for the need to tolerate antagonistic views.

Holmes is thus arguing for viewpoint toleration; he cannot simultaneously advocate intolerance towards conceptions of natural law. His message, then, is cautionary and directed at judges whose operative rulings bind the populace within the subject jurisdiction, and perhaps at jurisprudents or others who champion hermeneutical modes of judging. When you inhabit an official position with the authority to control the lives and actions of others, his warning runs, you must not confuse your personal wants with a body of controlling rules backed by the coercive powers of the state. "Men to a great extent believe what they want to," he remarks, "although I see in that no basis for a philosophy that tells us what we should want to want."[43] This statement impliedly cautions against conflating extant rules with absolute, universal, and inevitable norms.

Then Holmes turns to the celestial. "Now when we come to our attitude toward the universe," he muses, "I do not see any rational ground for demanding the superlative—for being dissatisfied unless we are assured that our truth is cosmic truth, if there is such a thing—that the ultimates of a little creature on this little earth are the last word of the unimaginable whole."[44] Before the religious scholar of natural law takes these lines about intellectual humility as antithetical to natural-law theory, he might recall these words of the prophet Isaiah: "For as the heavens are higher than the earth, so are my ways higher than your ways and my thoughts than your thoughts."[45] Holmes, in the passage I have just quoted, is no more a "positivist" than Isaiah. The conditional phrase "if there is such a thing" reveals his openness to the possibility of cosmic truth, a concept that surely comprises natural law.

Although modesty was not a distinguishing feature of his personality, it was a defining attribute of his philosophy and jurisprudence. Elsewhere I have attributed this modesty to his feeling that the Civil War—and the death and carnage it produced—represented the tragic consequence of an uncompromising spirit of certainty possessed by adversarial ideological camps that were totally convinced not only of the absolute rightness of their cause but also of the necessity for violence in the face of opposition.[46]

Also noticeable here is Holmes's echo of Emerson's essay "Nature," in particular section III in which Emerson refers to beauty as "an ultimate end."[47] Just as a human for Holmes is merely a little creature on a little earth, so beauty for Emerson "is not ultimate" but "must stand as a part, and not as yet the last or highest expression of the final cause of Nature."[48] Holmes's troping of Emerson in these lines seems to go beyond the borrowing of diction; it signals, to me, the idea, central to Emerson, that the constituent elements of an abstract and universal "whole" are meaningful only insofar as they communicate with, and participate in, that "wholeness."[49] Holmes's personal book collection, it should be noted, contained two volumes of Emerson's "Nature," one published in 1836 (probably a first edition) and the other in 1849;[50] thus, it is plausible he was reiterating Emersonian points and themes from "Nature" either consciously or subliminally.

Holmes does not loudly and proudly celebrate skepticism or cynicism. In light of his troping of "Nature," where Emerson is concerned about the unattainability of representational perfection,[51] Holmes seems cautious and reticent about his own values. He does not dismiss values out of hand. He criticizes French skeptics "for getting upon a pedestal and professing to look with haughty scorn upon a world in ruins."[52] He is thus not a delighted nihilist bent on the destruction of thought systems or inherited and longstanding ideas. Actually, his reading habits and reverence for the common law suggest that, in fact, he was a keen observer and longsuffering student of centuries of law, literature, philosophy, and political theory. He was not interested in the total annihilation or demolition of cherished principles. He claimed that people may, for unknown reasons, believe "that significance, consciousness and ideals are more than marks of the finite."[53] Such unreasoned convictions make people humble and modest in the acceptance of their intellectual limitations and experience. "The real conclusion," Holmes says, "is that the part can not swallow the whole—that our categories are not, or may not be, adequate to formulate what we can not know."[54] Here again he calls for humility and discreetly cautions against assuming that, because one favors something and categorizes it according to his own preferences, it must be universally true and good for everyone else as well. This call channels Section III in "Nature" where Emerson states that the human soul seeks beauty for unknown reasons.[55] For Emerson, nature is a "final cause" and beauty is "one expression for the universe,"[56] but what constitutes nature and beauty defies complete comprehension and can be only incompletely understood. An inability to fully comprehend nature or beauty, however, does not mean that nature and beauty are nonexistent or unreal, just as the inability to totally ascertain natural laws through right reason does not mean natural laws are merely empty words and fictions.

Holmes is talking about more than the law at this point. His vision is cosmic in scope, hence his axiom that, "[i]f we believe that we come out of the universe, not it out of us, we must admit that we do not know what we are talking about when we speak of brute matter."[57] He does not recommend ideational capitulation or angst: Although "the universe has in it more than we understand," humans as acting agents need not be paralyzed, disempowered, or meaningless in our life pursuits.[58] Rather, most humans embrace life, pursue the ideas they prize and enjoy, and defend causes for which they are passionate. "We still shall fight," Holmes says, "all of us because we want to live, some, at least, because we want to realize our spontaneity and prove our powers, for the joy of it, and we may leave to the unknown the supposed final valuation of that which in any event has value to us."[59] The suggestion Holmes has been building is that humans are unqualified and unsuited to evaluate the ultimate merits of their hierarchy of values in their own moment and space. Assessment of our ideas and actions is best left to the test of time as carried out by subsequent generations of probing minds seeking constructive consensus about right conduct and belief.

The unnamed targets of Holmes's critique of natural law apparently place themselves before the universe, as though their passions and motivations were the vital and inevitable drivers of the universal natural order of all life and existence. Holmes may have derived this critique from Emerson, who said, "Man is conscious of a universal soul within or behind his individual life, wherein, as in a firmament, the natures of Justice, Truth, Love, Freedom, arise and shine."[60] Emerson is not criticizing but acknowledging what he considers to be a fact about modest human involvement within the manifold circuits of life in the measureless cosmos. He reverses the priority of man and nature, stating that the latter owns or possesses the former: "This universal soul he calls Reason: it is not mine, or thine, or his, but we are its; we are its property and men."[61] Holmes articulates a similar position in "Natural Law": "It is enough for us that the universe has produced us and has within it, as less than it, all that we believe and love."[62]

This similarity involves submission to natural forces that are greater than those possessed by conditioned human minds; to know and understand, a human must not seek to impose his or her socially acquired values on the universe but must remain open and receptive to the facts and data the universe makes manifest. Emerson and Holmes treat humans as one slight piece of the "multitude of uses that enter as parts into [the final cause of the world]."[63] "If we think of our existence not as that of a little god outside, but as that of a ganglion within," Holmes says, "we have the infinite behind us. It gives us our only but our adequate significance."[64] Emerson likewise calls "man" an "analogist" who "studies relations in all objects."[65] Man, he claims, "is placed in the centre of beings, and a ray of relation passes from every other being to him."[66] So conceived, human ideational significance depends upon its ties and connections to other things, not in isolated, disconnected, or closed modes of thought, even if man is spatially central in and to the known universe. Only in this transcendental context does Holmes's mention of "the vision of ourselves as parts inseverable from the rest" begin to make sense.[67] Emerson himself said that "[w]e live in succession, in division, in parts, [and] in particles" while "within man is the soul of the whole."[68] For both Holmes and Emerson, then, the sum of one person's knowledge is the whole of that person, yet the whole of that person is not the whole of The Whole, although it contributes to and thus remains indispensable to the composition of The Whole.

## EMERSON AND TRANSCENDENTAL NATURAL LAW

In light of the foregoing, transcendentalist associations between Holmes and Emerson should be apparent. Yet how does Emerson's transcendentalism pertain to the law? What themes or other elements of his work involve natural law, and what does natural law look like in the transcendentalist paradigm? This section sheds light on these questions and exposits the seminal elements of a school of jurisprudence that might be denominated as transcendentalist, although the impetus of transcendentalism is to resist rigid labels and accept flux and flow as, paradoxically, the spontaneous order that organizes known experience.

Two elements of transcendentalism, as I conceive it, act upon natural-law legal theory or jurisprudence: the concept of a universal order or ultimate unity and the idea of history as a guiding force behind the distinctly human capacity for creativity and originality. That the new springs from the old is another sign of transcendentalism. It recalls the axiom that nothing exists in a vacuum or that something cannot come from nothing. The rules and principles in the common-law system that Holmes adored are likewise rooted in custom and, the theory goes, traced to time out of mind or time immemorial,[69] making their transmission over the generations similar to that which marks ideas and creativity according to Emersonian transcendentalism.

## Natural Law, Classification, and Unified or Universal Order

To be "natural" means to be caused or existent in nature, the tangible and physical phenomenon that is the starting point of Emerson's philosophy of law. In fact, the natural world and moral laws mirror one another in Emerson's thinking: "The laws of moral nature answer to those of matter as face to face in a glass."[70] Emerson elsewhere names "these two facts, namely, that the mind is One, and that nature is its correlative," thereby suggesting that laws inhere in the union of mind and nature.[71] To this point, moreover, he adds that "[t]he axioms of physics translate the laws of ethics,"[72] and that "a law of one organization . . . holds true throughout nature."[73] To the extent that the laws of moral nature and ethics amount to natural law, Emerson suggests that nature and the natural world display and comprise laws, or a system of rules and principles. "Nature," he posits, "is an endless combination and repetition of a very few laws."[74]

Discussing Emerson's views of natural law is difficult, however, because he considered the properties and meaning of nature to be incommunicable, its material forms external to, and hence mediated by, fallible human sensations and faculties. "We know more from nature than we can at will communicate," he writes. "Its light flows into the mind evermore, and we forget its presence."[75] Here he implies that knowledge of nature comes as a spark of recognition that may quickly vanish. Elsewhere he says that "the mind opens and reveals the laws which traverse the universe and make things what they are, then shrinks the great world at once into a mere illustration and fable of this mind."[76] The point of these statements, I think, is to highlight "our imperfect apprehension" of the "outrunning laws" that "traverse the universe."[77] On this view, flashes of brilliance or genius may spontaneously impress themselves upon open minds, revealing the universal and moral laws, or traces and shadows of those laws, yet any full understanding eludes us because of the innate limitations of the human mind. Therefore, although he believes that universal and moral laws are real and present, he does not name or describe them with precision.

Emerson's discourse on nature can seem vague, there being a "mystery"[78] to his subject that is "full of a sublime family likeness throughout her works."[79] One must exercise faculties to transform the vague into the familiar, and in reading Emerson we witness the processes of his mind as he does just that, working through ambiguities and training them into familiar ideas or concepts. We follow along as he seeks to show the manner in which the faculties take in sensible objects and then settle into opinion or beliefs about their apparent truths. The incommunicable characteristics of nature that comprise law involve sensory impressions or spontaneous feelings: things which require sustained contemplation before they can be classified or arranged in such a manner as to reveal underlying patterns of likeness that suggest continuity or universality.

Classification is key to understanding the laws of nature, Emerson suggests in the "Discipline" section of "Nature." In "The American Scholar," he includes "law" in his definition of classification, which is, he says, "the perceiving that these objects [i.e., the phenomena in nature] are not chaotic, and are not foreign, but have a law which is also the law of the human mind."[80] The process of training the mind through classificatory methodology aims at discerning the natural law, or that part of nature which corresponds with human thought. Disciplined and pensive individuals labor to account for the laws that are intrinsic to external data. "The ambitious soul," Emerson says of these individuals, "sits down before each refractory fact; one after another reduces all strange constitutions, all new powers, to their class and their law, and goes on forever to animate the last fibre of organization, the outskirts of nature, by insight."[81]

One struggles to disambiguate Emerson's statement that "[t]he law of nature is, Do the thing, and you shall have the power."[82] What is *the* thing? And what is *the* power? It may have something to do with Emerson's emphasis on the working powers of the human mind, which, in his paradigm, should remain ever active and animated lest it fall into a disabling state of stasis. "It seems as if the law of the intellect," he maintains, referring to the human mind, "resembled that law of nature by which we now aspire, now expire breath; by which the heart now draws in, then hurls out the blood—the law of undulation."[83] Here the law of undulation might refer to mobility or energy: features of a dynamic mind that generates, originates, and creates. Still his meaning is vague. He is clearer in his assertion that the "relation between the mind and matter"[84] match or correspond such that "the universe becomes transparent, and the light of higher laws than its own shines through it."[85] Conforming the mind to nature is, accordingly, the key to understanding the law; understanding the law is not immediate, however. It is a gradual process of growing and becoming that begins with spontaneous impressions of nature that later refine and perfect themselves through the purposeful development of rigorous thought.

Holmes said that "[a]ll law is directed to conditions of things manifest to the senses,"[86] a proposition that squares with Emerson's notion of moral law, which "lies at the centre of nature[,] radiates to the circumference"[87] and "traverse[s] the universe and make[s] things what they are."[88] This moral law begins with the immediate opening of the human mind[89] to external data and only later systematizes into categories and taxonomies. Belief in the "absolute existence of nature" is "instinctive,"[90] in this view, and materializes whenever the faculties achieve harmony with the forms, outlines, and rules of nature. Yet prudence, a cultivated or learned trait, moves matter "after the laws of matter,"[91] i.e., exercises mental powers to create new material from existing material and conform events to one's will.[92] Though the law as manifest in nature can be knowable without hesitancy and though our untaught understanding of it may precede conscious deliberation, the effort to classify disciplines the mind to apprehend truths.[93] Apprehending truths of nature thus involves an influx of revelation, spontaneous and intuitive, but it also involves the cataloging and grouping of sensory impressions, a sign of intellectual maturity.

"To the young man," Emerson remarks of this process of classification, which furnishes the mind with gradual discernment, "every thing is individual, stands by itself. By and by, it finds how to join two things and see in them one nature; then three, then three thousand; and so, tyrannized over by its own unifying instinct, it goes on tying things together, diminishing anomalies, discovering roots running under ground whereby contrary and remote things cohere and flower out from one stem."[94] One might imagine putting an eye to the dirt to examine an ant up close, then standing up and surveying the ant in its broader environment, then moving upward and outward, further and further, until the ultimate significance of the particular ant—its minor yet vital role on the planet—becomes increasingly perceptible while at the same time increasingly subsumed into the general workings of the vast physical order.

Classification thus aids perspicuity of thought by sloughing off and weeding out irrelevant or useless data, allowing one to observe the beautiful harmony—or the universal law—that inheres in nature. And it places any remaining or residual data into constructive context, allowing one to distinguish the important and significant from the unimportant and insignificant. This process of contextualization and classification according to Emerson runs like this: Initial sensory impressions about external data, as well as the inchoate testimonies of excited feelings, generate introspection, which leads in turn to the integrating tendencies of rigorous examination and the concomitant categorization of organized facts. "Every property of matter is a school for the understanding," Emerson submits as his starting point;[95] then sustained investigation of the properties of matter empowers inductive faculties from which derive insights into general and universal forms; at length, ideas about matter and matter itself achieve a state of accord.[96] Through this complex process, extant phenomena increasingly become more harmonized or integrated as they prove themselves to be agreeable to reason.[97]

Substituting Holmes's notion of undeveloped society or "primitive time"[98] for "young man" in Emerson's statement about classification ("To the young man . . .") reveals how closely Holmes's understanding of maturing rules or formulas in a common-law system track Emerson's musings regarding a developing perspective about ultimate unities. "The customs, beliefs, or needs of a primitive time establish a rule or a formula," says Holmes.[99] "In the course of centuries," he continues, "the custom, belief, or necessity disappears, but the rule remains. The reason which gave rise to the rule has been forgotten, and ingenious minds"—here I must mention that Emerson, too, thought genius involved the kind of classification that enables understanding of generals out of particulars[100]—"set themselves to inquire how it is to be accounted for."[101]

Holmes, like Emerson, believed that knowledge of the past contextualizes the particulars and facilitates insight into the general. "As a first step towards a generalization," he explains, "it will be necessary to consider what is to be found in ancient and independent systems of law."[102] The chief difference between Holmes and Emerson on this score is that the latter saw in expository generalities workings of divine knowledge.[103] But both men saw law first as something to be observed and only later to be classified and arranged; law is natural, in this regard, because it is pre-political, prior to any person's reflection on it. Reflection provides taxonomies and vocabularies for that which is immanent in nature or the given state of the world. The past supplies important context for understanding how those taxonomies and vocabularies came into existence and achieved wide acceptance. Knowledge of the past shows, in Holmes's conception, that rules occupying a certain time and space consist in a more general orderliness; it may be difficult in the instant to apprehend the successive order in which the rules live. But taking the long view affords us the opportunity to analyze the career of laws, attentive to their patterns and precedents over time. A closer look at how historical awareness features in both Holmes and Emerson reveals additional commonalities regarding their views pertaining to natural law.

## The Common Law, Creative Destruction, and the Transmission of Influence over Generations

Holmes portrayed the common law as an evolutionary system engrained in custom that develops in stages over time.[104] It involved, he said, "the struggle for life among competing ideas,"[105] "the ultimate victory and survival of the strongest," and "the struggle for existence between competing ideas and forms."[106] He claimed the history of the law of torts revealed "another evolutionary process which Mr. Herbert Spencer has made familiar to us by the name of integration."[107] Maintaining that "the law is always approaching, and never reaching, consistency,"[108] he looked back, as a legal historian as well as a jurist, over the long, stadial course of rules and principles in the Anglo-American legal tradition, which, he said, "is forever adopting new principles from life at one end" while always "retain[ing] old ones from history at the other, which have not yet been absorbed or sloughed off."[109] This organic, filtering tradition will, he determined, "become entirely consistent only when it ceases to grow."[110] One gets the distinct impression, though, that he believed the common-law system would never cease to grow, or if it would, the resulting stasis would come at considerable expense, removing from the common law the plasticity and malleability that are its essential features.

If the common law evolves by slow degrees, then knowledge of its past is key to understanding its present state and conditions, Holmes believed.[111] "The history of what the law has been is necessary," he claimed, "to the knowledge of what the law is."[112] Sustained study of legal history therefore reveals through-lines and continuities.

In a short piece in the *American Law Review*—incidentally, the forum in which he first employed the famous phrase about the life of the law being logic, not experience—Holmes wrote that "[t]he form of continuity [in the law] has been kept up by reasonings purporting to reduce everything to a logical sequence; but that form is nothing but the evening dress which the new-comer puts on to make itself presentable according to conventional requirements."[113] This line about current law representing the repackaging or rearticulating of extant principles—a recurring theme in Holmes—recalls similar declarations by Emerson, who in various ways propounded the evolutionary notion that the new always springs from the old, or that the old must give way to make room for the new.

"What are called new views here in New England," Emerson wrote in an essay that was delivered as a lecture in 1842, "are not new, but the very oldest of thoughts cast into the mould of these new times."[114] "We are stung by the desire for new thought," he mused, "but when we receive a new thought it is only the old thought with a new face."[115] Speaking of the history of religious institutions and religious expression, he said, "[L]et the breath of new life be breathed by you through the forms already existing. For if once you are alive, you shall find they shall become plastic and new."[116] "The introduction of these elements," he wrote of technology and innovation, "gives new resources to existing proprietors."[117] Of art, he stated: "[T]he artist must employ the symbols in use in his day and nation to convey his enlarged sense to his fellow-men. Thus the new in art is always formed out of the old."[118] "The new position of the advancing man," he remarked in another essay, "has all the powers of the old, yet has them all new. It carries in its bosom all the energies of the past, yet is itself an exhilaration of the morning."[119]

"New arts destroy the old,"[120] still another essay proclaims. Such destruction is both the source of and the condition for *construction*. This Emersonian model of growth through demolition anticipates the capitalist economic theory of creative destruction, coined by Joseph Schumpeter,[121] which holds, in short, that the "process of industrial mutation . . . incessantly revolutionizes the economic structure *from within*, incessantly destroying the old one, incessantly creating a new one."[122] Creative destruction is a driving force behind the spontaneous order described by F. A. Hayek, who proposed that, "[i]f old truths are to retain their hold on men's minds, they must be restated in the language and concepts of successive generations. What at one time are their most effective expressions gradually become so worn with use that they cease to carry a definite meaning."[123] Holmes had his own pronouncements regarding creative destruction, namely in the context of what he called the "doctrine of survival."[124]

The connection between Emerson, Holmes, and Hayek is pregnant with possibility and requires more treatment than this short piece can provide. Suffice it to say that in their evolutionary paradigm the processes of creative destruction generate order out of replacement, subdual, and obliteration. If, as Emerson believed, human knowledge and its successive transmission reflected the processes of nature, then evidence of creative destruction in nature—i.e., evidence of *natural* law—might include the fact that fire can stimulate the seeding and germination of forests, or that snakes shed their old skin to strengthen and renew their new skin.

In fact, Emerson turns to natural metaphors to explain how creative destruction operates. I quote at length because this passage demonstrates so well the parallels Emerson envisions between the rejuvenating operations of both nature and the human mind, the latter presented in the ideal of the poet:

> Nature, through all her kingdoms, insures herself. Nobody cares for planting the poor fungus; so she shakes down from the gills of one agaric countless spores, any one of which, being preserved, transmits new billions of spores to-morrow or next day. The new agaric of this hour has a chance which the old one had not. This atom of seed is thrown into a new place, not subject to the accidents which destroyed its parent two rods off. She makes a man; and having brought him to ripe age, she will no longer run the risk of losing this wonder at a blow, but she detaches from him a new self, that the kind may be safe from accidents to which the individual is exposed. So when the soul of the poet has come to ripeness of thought, she detaches and sends away from it its poems or songs—a fearless, sleepless, deathless progeny, which is not exposed to the accidents of the weary kingdom of time; a fearless, vivacious offspring, clad with wings (such was the virtue of the soul out of which they came) which carry them fast and far, and infix them irrevocably into the hearts of men. These wings are the beauty of the poet's soul. The songs, thus flying immortal from their mortal parent, are pursued by clamorous flights of censures, which swarm in far greater numbers and threaten to devour them; but these last are not winged. At the end of a very short leap they fall plump down and rot, having received from the souls out of which they came no beautiful wings. But the melodies of the poet ascend and leap and pierce into the deeps of infinite time.[125]

Notice how nature, so conceived, is self-regulatory, seemingly with an agency of its own as it selectively eliminates that which holds it back, confines its powers, and suppresses its potential. Notice, too, that nature is an analogue of the human mind, which creates language and lyrics that rise above the fray of criticism and separate themselves from their less fit, less durable challengers.

Might Holmes have had such lines in mind when he wrote of obsolete principles being "sloughed off,"[126] suggested that "old implements" can be "adjusted to new uses,"[127] or emphasized that "[t]he doctrine of contract has been so thoroughly remodeled to meet the needs of modern times"?[128] If not Emerson's precise language, Holmes at least may have recalled the concepts that language articulated. Was it not Holmes, after all, who, borrowing the nature metaphor, stated, "The development of our law has gone on for nearly a thousand years, like the development of a plant, each generation taking the inevitable next step, mind, like matter, simply obeying a law of spontaneous growth. It is perfectly right and natural that it should have been so."[129] He drove this point home in his essay "Law in Science and Science in Law," where he repeatedly asserted that the legal community circulated lexica and doctrines (e.g., the "uninstructive and indolent use of phrases to save the trouble of thinking closely"[130]) absent any knowledge or awareness of the principles from which they arose.[131]

Jonathan Levin, a scholar of Emerson, has described the hard-to-identify moment when the creator repurposes the old for the new as transitional.[132] This is also the moment when the poet overcomes the anxiety of influence, Harold Bloom's seminal concept, to break into new aesthetic territory. Bringing together Bloom's and Emerson's views on influence and inspiration, Levin refers to the "poetics of transition" to describe the move from a settled state or stasis to one of mobility and energy. Levin attributes this theory to Emerson, but its manifestation in the common law, where it appears less in the form of aesthetics than in the form of creative modification or application of extant rules and precedents, is astonishing.

"No truth is so sublime but it may be trivial to-morrow in the light of new thoughts. People wish to be settled; only as far as they are unsettled is there any hope for them,"[133] Emerson said. Imagine this statement in terms of the common law, in which settled case precedents embody the right rule—the truth—that new circumstances and technologies disrupt, thereby forcing creative judges to articulate the rule in novel ways, which is to say, to unsettle what was settled to supply hope for future rulings. The judge who in these circumstances imaginatively repurposes extant principles in light of changed conditions realizes the poetics of transition, at least the judicial equivalent to it. "Heaven forbid that I should find fault with an expression because it is new," Holmes remarked of legal vocabularies he found inadequate.[134] He went on to say that "[j]udges commonly are elderly men, and are more likely to hate at sight any analysis to which they are not accustomed, and which disturbs repose of mind, than to fall in love with novelties."[135] Holmes concludes this line of thought with an Emersonian axiom: "Every living sentence which shows a mind at work for itself should be welcomed."[136] These lines suggest that Holmes contemplated the poetics of transition in some form in the common-law system.

Of course, Emerson's poetics of transition are more assertively and extravagantly exclaimed than is appropriate for, or germane to, judicial modes and practices. For example, a judge may not strictly speaking "cast away in this new moment all [his or her] once hoarded knowledge, as vacant and vain."[137] A judge, rather, must operate within statutory and constitutional frameworks and, in a common-law system, from established and recognized case precedents. Nevertheless, the spirit or essence of Emerson's message—that the creator must break free from the restraints of the past to realize the right rule or principle for the current moment—can animate and enthuse the common-law judge. In fact, the past supplies the conditions and precedents that inspire and necessitate its own displacement, the new past; thus, the settling of past paradigms is, paradoxically, requisite to the cultivation of new forms. A judge may use prior cases to forge a new direction in the pattern of precedents, giving the law an interior logic and heritability to accompany his or her originality and innovation.

Evolution by successive transition is *natural*, an organic and ongoing process that unfolds in inevitable phases. "In nature," Emerson submits, "every moment is new; the past is always swallowed and forgotten; the coming only is sacred. Nothing is secure but life, transition, the energizing spirit."[138] In "Circles," his exposition of creative destruction is couched in metaphorical language about nature, suggesting that the most important law of nature is the very fluidity of the laws of nature.[139]

Holmes directly links the evolution of the law to the organic, transitional processes of nature.[140] Putting his own mark on the *natural* law of inevitable, animating transition, he attributes an organic process to the common-law system, which reflects bottom-up orderings derived from custom and reworked or adapted for present exigencies and technologies: "Some ground of policy is thought of, which seems to explain [the reason that gave rise to the rule] and to reconcile it with the present state of things; and then the rule adapts itself to the new reasons which have been found for it, and enters on a new career. The old form receives a new content, and in time even the form modifies itself to fit the meaning which it has received."[141] Accordingly, natural law in the Emersonian and Holmesian transcendentalist paradigm is not teleological or immutable; still it could be universal in light of the coherence that emerges, paradoxically, out of the incoherence of the natural order; the transcendentalist sees in dynamic evolution the ultimate unity and interrelatedness of all knowable phenomena.

Holmes like Emerson possessed a strong sense of history. This historical knowledge, again paradoxically, was indispensable to their resistance of historical forces that wed us to customs that are demonstrably unfit or disadvantageous. "The past gives us our vocabulary and fixes the limits of our imagination; we cannot get away from it," Holmes explained of the role history must play in our present calculations.[142] "There is, too," he continues, "a peculiar logical pleasure in making manifest the continuity between what we are doing and what has been done before," a fact he knew well, having mapped continuities within the Anglo-American legal tradition in *The Common Law* and having edited James Kent's *Commentaries on American Law*, which traced legal history.[143] "But," he concludes, "the present has a right to govern itself so far as it can; and it ought always to be remembered that historical continuity with the past is not a duty, it is only a necessity."[144] Fidelity to history, on this view, requires the repurposing and revision of history. To be faithful to history requires reworking it for the present.

Natural law, too, is plugged into historical networks and channels, transmitted through discursive formalities, and mediated by human minds attuned to their own time and place. It may be knowable by the exercise of reason, but the basis and form of that reason are circumscribed by historical forces and factors. A proper understanding of natural law, in Holmes's paradigm, must therefore be pragmatic, which is to say, tested by experience in light of practical effects and proven successes in concrete circumstances.

## HOLMES'S EMERSONIAN PRAGMATIC NATURAL LAW

Emerson and Holmes were indisposed to assert exactly what they believed natural laws to be or consist of. They were content merely to describe the methodical and ideational processes by which natural laws are divined or apprehended. Holmes even ridiculed those who moved beyond these processes and assumed as operative and vital their own cherished assumptions about natural law that others did not share. Given Emerson's and Holmes's deliberate vagueness, or their focus on mental methods and processes rather than the final attainment of definite rules, it is not possible to reduce their belief in natural law to fixed, unassailable doctrines, formulas, or decrees. Much can be made, however, of the probable effects that Emerson's personalized, individual, and interior sense of natural law had on Holmes.

The strangeness of Emersonian natural law involves its claims of radical individuality as a basis of universal "oneness." Nowhere is this curiosity more apparent than in his essay "Self-Reliance." Here he celebrates "the law in his person"[145] and "a law of his own,"[146] i.e., the qualia and sentience that guide human attitudes and actions and remain antecedent to corrupting social influences. "No law can be sacred to me but that of my nature," he says, adding that "[g]ood and bad are but names very readily transferable to that or this: the only right is what is after my constitution; the only wrong what is against it."[147] A few years later he expanded on this theme in "Politics," stating, "For any laws but those which men make for themselves are laughable. If I put myself in the place of my child, and we stand in one thought and see that things are thus or thus, that perception is law for him and me."[148]

If the laws of nature inhabit individual minds working in isolation, then an individual following his conscience does not transgress against those inner laws. In Emerson's words, "no man can violate his nature. All the sallies of his will are rounded in by the law of his being."[149] This law of absolute subjectivity is *natural*, even constitutive of nature: "a true man belongs to no other time or place, but is the centre of things. Where he is, there is nature."[150] But if the natural law is interior to the individual, and utterly subjective, then how can it become systematized as a governing scheme? Does it represent some variety of Nietzschean perspectivalism?[151] How can the sprawling government, which consists of and controls numerous people within its wide jurisdiction, embody natural-law principles that are essentially and necessarily personal?

The answer to these questions encapsulates the transcendentalist position on natural law. It consists of four discernable steps. First, law exists in nature; second, the human mind apprehends the laws of nature in moments of inspired revelation; third, the human mind—the reflective one, anyway—organizes and classifies those laws according to known and lived experience; fourth, as humans interact, sharing their apprehension of those laws as organized and classified, their views become aggregated into a wider system of organization and classification. Each step in this process emanates from personal revelation or truth.[152]

Notice that these steps do not involve the precise naming or describing of the content of natural law. What is natural, for Emerson as for Holmes, is the organic *process* of law, which adapts to changing features of human experience. Although certain general concepts tend to be fixed—the prohibition of murder, for instance—the details within those concepts always change: killing may be broken down into differing degrees of homicide according to altering notions of safety or culpability.[153] A better example may be found in private-property rights, which Emerson believed to be protected by a "higher law" as humans invariably return to it even after experimentation with different property arrangements.[154] This example shows, as well, Emerson's recognition that positive law may not always comport with higher law, but that higher law would always inevitably win out in the end.[155]

Such focus on the process-oriented, evolutionary features of law enables Emerson to claim universalism out of mutable particulars.[156] The constituent parts of the general whole are never the same, but together they always add up to concepts that represent something permanent and perennial in the human condition. Although numerous people, prejudiced by their unique experiences, possess disparate understandings of the laws of nature that are mediated through their fallible human minds, their discursive transmission of competing ideas and their clashing views organize themselves into systems of behavior and principles. A natural order of rules thus emerges from ostensible chaos and incoherence through regular processes of transition and creative destruction. Individual activity within systems of behavior and principles (i.e., within governing structures) is directed at increasingly higher forms of order that prove themselves, over time, to be self-organizing and self-replicating—to be infinite or universal.

The process just described clarifies Emerson's claim that thoughts about the "infinite relations" that make up "outrunning laws . . . have been the entertainment of the human spirit in all ages."[157] It illuminates Holmes's remark about ideals, which, he says, "furnish us our perspectives and open glimpses of the infinite."[158] The rare person who sees in the common particulars indispensable elements of the infinite whole grasps "the higher law,"[159] which Emerson equated with the moral nature of man.[160]

Nature, in short, is governed by its own laws; it is evolutionary. A feature of the laws of nature is the adaptability of living organisms and the heritability of their given traits. So it is with laws that regulate humans, as recorded, for example, by the bottom-up, organic ordering of the common law that has been passed down over centuries. The law of supply and demand is, according to Emerson, one such natural law of political economy that tends towards equilibrium if it is left to its own devices rather than tinkered with through legislative interference.[161] "The basis of political economy," Emerson states, "is non-interference."[162] Hence, his imperative: "Do not legislate."[163]

The common law is pre-political and prior to legislation.[164] It reflects deep-rooted customs and possesses an internal filtering mechanism that resembles teleonomy. Purposive human behavior does, of course, impact the content of the common law, but that content embodies aggregated human purposes within the jurisdiction, not merely the purposes of a single acting agent. Rules and principles in the common-law system are transmitted through forces like those of natural selection.[165] And the system itself is malleable within permanent paradigms and parameters such as, for example, rules against theft or assault.

## CONCLUSION

Hoffheimer determined that "there is room to doubt how thoroughly and consistently Holmes truly rejected the central tenets of natural law."[166] This chapter, which considers the scientific elements of transcendentalism, in particular as they pertain to the laws of nature or natural law, ought to leave wider room for doubt. It may even inspire confidence that, in fact, Holmes gravitated towards one type of natural law while dismissing the dominant attitudes and ideals of his contemporary proponents of natural-law theory. His judicial restraint signals a type of "hands-off" attitude that was comfortable with, even confident in, the ability of local political communities such as states to organize themselves apart from the controls of centralized or nationalized government structures.

I have not defended the transcendentalist account of natural law, which, I think, raises more questions than it answers. I have, rather, illustrated certain features of it to propound its probable manifestation in Holmes's legal writings. Emerson and Holmes were content to adumbrate the controlling processes of their theories of history and law without depicting the particulars that were being processed. Holmes, for instance, was satisfied that his duties as a justice were fulfilled by allowing the political processes of election and legislative enactment on local levels to run their course without intervention by the federal judiciary. The vagueness of transcendentalist natural-law theory reflects their conception of rules and principles as primarily private and individualized and only secondarily as systematized, from the bottom up, into an integrated body that governs groups of people and institutions. Both men were thrilled by the powers of human faculties but skeptical of large-scale attempts to translate collective consensus into binding mandates to be imposed from the top down. Both men were curious, complicated thinkers whose transcendentalist views of the law warrant more attention.

## NOTES

1. Michael H. Hoffheimer, *Justice Holmes and the Natural Law* (New York: Garland Publishing, 1992), 15.

2. R. H. Helmholz articulates the traditional understanding of natural law: "Natural law theory . . . began . . . with an assumption of congruence between law and basic features of man's nature as they are thought to have existed from the beginning of time. God himself was natural law's source. In creating the world, He had instilled in all of his creatures a knowledge of certain principles. Most of them were known by instinct." R. H. Helmholz, *Natural Law in Court* (Cambridge, Massachusetts and London England: Harvard University Press, 2015), 2. Helmholz then summarizes a different account of natural law: "Natural law also meant, in what was sometimes called its secondary sense, congruence with natural reason, with which God had also imbued his creatures. Men and women knew right from wrong without any special training. . . . Right reason had led to its recognition in every age of human history. The Bible and the great texts of Western law provided additional proof of this principle's hold on human thought and action. So stated, it did not change over time, although it might vary in the details of its application to human life, as the conditions of society themselves required. The underlying principle, it was assumed, would always matter in practice, particularly in doubtful cases. Its observance would promote the rule of justice in human life." Helmholz, *Natural Law in Court*, 2–3. The transcendentalism known to Holmes would not have foreclosed these views of natural law, but it might have downplayed the emphasis on creation or design and focused on the impersonal, spontaneous ordering of the material world by natural forces working to preserve general principles through evolutionary processes. F. A. Hayek describes such a form of natural law, distinguishing it from positive law as follows: "One of the chief sources of confusion . . . is

that all theories which oppose legal positivism are alike labelled and lumped together under the misleading name of 'natural law,' though some of them have nothing in common with each other except their opposition to legal positivism. This false dichotomy is now insisted upon mainly by the positivists, because their constructivist approach allows only that the law should be either the product of the design of a human or the product of the design of a super-human intelligence. But . . . the term 'natural' was used earlier to assert that law was the product not of any rational design but of a process of evolution and natural selection, an unintended product whose function we can learn to understand, but whose present significance may be wholly different from the intention of its creators." F. A. Hayek, *Law, Legislation and Liberty*, Vol. 2 (Chicago and London: University of Chicago Press, 1976), 59. The natural law to which Holmes was open might run along these lines: individual judges responding to concrete cases each exercise reason to resolve disputes, and in that sense they are "doing" natural law, but without total knowledge of the aggregate effects of the resolution of that particular case on the sum of the law, i.e., on the actual content of the natural law. The sum of the laws expressed in cases may reflect a transcendental universalism that cannot be directly or wholly known to any one person or group of people; it exists independently of a judge's opinion about what the natural law is, and the several opinions of numerous judges together represent merely evidence of the transcendental principles that make up the natural law.

3. See Allen Mendenhall, *Oliver Wendell Holmes Jr., Pragmatism, and the Jurisprudence of Agon* (Lewisburg, PA: Bucknell University Press, 2017), xvi, xx, 45.

4. Mendenhall, *Oliver Wendell Holmes Jr., Pragmatism, and the Jurisprudence of Agon*, xvi, 45–54.

5. Ralph Waldo Emerson, "The American Scholar," in *The Essential Writings of Ralph Waldo Emerson*, ed. Brooks Atkinson (New York: Modern Library, 2000), 47.

6. Ralph Waldo Emerson, "Self-Reliance," in *The Essential Writings of Ralph Waldo Emerson*, ed. Brooks Atkinson (New York: Modern Library, 2000), 150.

7. "In my view, the stark jurisprudential dichotomy between natural law and positive law is itself a twentieth century positivist creation that has kept us from seeing the way in which all legal structures inevitably embody normative positions." Morton J. Horwitz, "History and Theory," *Yale Law Journal* 96 (1987): 1834.

8. Hoffheimer, *Justice Holmes and the Natural Law*, 5.

9. Hoffheimer, *Justice Holmes and the Natural Law*, 7. Holmes's classmate at Harvard, William A. Holbrook, accused Holmes of airing "a dreamy, transcendental, artistic religion" in Holmes's essay "Notes to Albert Dürer." See Mark DeWolfe Howe, *Justice Oliver Wendell Holmes: The Shaping Years, 1841–1870* (Cambridge, MA: Belknap Press, 1957), 59.

10. Hoffheimer, *Justice Holmes and the Natural Law*, 7.

11. Mendenhall, *Oliver Wendell Holmes Jr., Pragmatism, and the Jurisprudence of Agon*, 115; see also Hoffheimer, *Justice Holmes and the Natural Law*, 29. Regarding transcendentalism's influence on the young Holmes, see Hoffheimer, *Justice Holmes and the Natural Law*, 31–43.

12. Quoted in Mendenhall, *Oliver Wendell Holmes Jr., Pragmatism, and the Jurisprudence of Agon*, 14.

13. Quoted in Mendenhall, *Oliver Wendell Holmes Jr., Pragmatism, and the Jurisprudence of Agon*, 14.

14. Ralph Waldo Emerson, "The American Scholar," 49.

15. Ralph Waldo Emerson, "The American Scholar," 47 ("The one thing in the world, of course, is the active soul. This every man is entitled to; this every man contains within him. . . . The soul sees absolute truth and utters truth, or creates. In this action it is genius").

16. Oliver Wendell Holmes Jr., John G. Palfrey (1875–1945) Collection of Oliver Wendell Holmes Jr. Papers, 1715–1938, Family and Personal Material, Personal: Box 61, Folder 5, List of OWH's books, 1935, seq. 11, http://nrs.harvard.edu/urn-3:HLS.Libr:8268117?n=11; Oliver Wendell Holmes Jr., John G. Palfrey (1875–1945) Collection of Oliver Wendell Holmes Jr. Papers, 1715–1938, Family and Personal Material, Personal: Box 61, Folder 5, List of OWH's Books, 1935, seq. 13, http://nrs.harvard.edu/urn-3:HLS.Libr:8268117?n=13. Note: seq. 12 consists of a blank page.

17. Mark DeWolfe Howe, *Justice Oliver Wendell Holmes: The Shaping Years*, 44, 54–55, 58–59, 203–4.

18. Francis J. Mellen Jr., "Ralph Waldo Emerson, Mr. Justice Holmes and the Idea of Organic Form in American Law," *New England Law Review* 14 (1978–1979), 148.

19. Hoffheimer, *Justice Holmes and the Natural Law*, 18.

20. Hoffheimer, *Justice Holmes and the Natural Law*, 17.

21. Hoffheimer, *Justice Holmes and the Natural Law*, 18; see also 19 ("Natural law judging did not offend him because of its results but rather because of its philosophical postulates") and 21 (referring to Holmes's "hostility to the creation of legal rights from claims of moral obligations").

22. Hoffheimer, *Justice Holmes and the Natural Law*, 8.

23. Ralph Waldo Emerson, "Self-Reliance," 138. "With consistency," Emerson added, "a great soul has simply nothing to do."

24. Hoffheimer, *Justice Holmes and the Natural Law*, 25.

25. Hoffheimer, *Justice Holmes and the Natural Law*, 25.

26. Hoffheimer, *Justice Holmes and the Natural Law*, 40 (Holmes "sought to harmonize aspects of idealism and empiricism by associating each with different intellectual activities").

27. Section 51 of Walt Whitman, "Song of Myself," in *The Portable Walt Whitman*, ed. Mark Van Doren (New York: Penguin Books, 1973), 96.

28. Hoffheimer, *Justice Holmes and the Natural Law*, 90–91.

29. Hoffheimer, *Justice Holmes and the Natural Law*, 90–91.

30. Hoffheimer, *Justice Holmes and the Natural Law*, 91. Consider these famous lines from *The Common Law*: "The felt necessities of the time, the prevalent moral and political theories, intuitions of public policy, avowed or unconscious, even the prejudices which judges share with their fellow men, have had a good deal more to do than the syllogism in determining the rules by which men should be governed. The law embodies the story of a nation's development. . . . In order to know what it is, we must know what it has been, and what it tends to become. We must alternatively consult history and existing theories of legislation. But the most difficult labor will be to understand the combination of the two into new products at every age." Oliver Wendell Holmes Jr., *The Common Law* (Chicago: ABA Publishing, [1881] 2009), 1.

31. Oliver Wendell Holmes Jr., "Natural Law," *Harvard Law Review* 32 (1918–1919), 40.

32. Holmes, "Natural Law," 40 (italics added).

33. Holmes, "Natural Law," 40.

34. Holmes, "Natural Law," 40.

35. Holmes, "Natural Law," 41.

36. Holmes, "Natural Law," 41.

37. Holmes, "Natural Law," 41.

38. Holmes, "Natural Law," 41.

39. "I see no *a priori* duty to live with others and in that way, but simply a statement of what I must do if I wish to remain alive. If I do live with others they tell me that I must do and abstain from doing various things or they will put the screws on to me. I believe that they will, and being of the same mind as to their conduct I not only accept the rules but come in time to accept them with sympathy and emotional affirmation and begin to talk about duties and rights." Holmes, "Natural Law," 42.

40. Holmes, "Natural Law," 42, italics added.

41. Holmes, "Natural Law," 42.

42. Holmes, "Natural Law," 42.

43. Holmes, "Natural Law," 43.

44. Holmes, "Natural Law," 43.

45. Isaiah 55:9.

46. Mendenhall, *Oliver Wendell Holmes Jr., Pragmatism, and the Jurisprudence of Agon*, xxi, 83–84, 98–99, 111, 113–16, 126.

47. Ralph Waldo Emerson, "Nature," in *The Essential Writings of Ralph Waldo Emerson*, ed. Brooks Atkinson (New York: Modern Library, 2000), 13. Holmes echoed Emerson before. His essay "Books" represents a copy of Emerson's essay by the same title. See Allen Menden-

hall, "Oliver Wendell Holmes Jr. Is the Use of Calling Emerson a Pragmatist: A Brief and Belated Response to Stanley Cavell," *Faulkner Law Review* 6 (2014), 224–26.

48. Ralph Waldo Emerson, "Nature," 13.

49. Ralph Waldo Emerson, "Nature," 13 ("Nothing is quite beautiful alone; nothing but is beautiful in the whole. A single object is only so far beautiful as it suggests this universal grace").

50. Oliver Wendell Holmes Jr., John G. Palfrey (1875–1945) Collection of Oliver Wendell Holmes Jr. Papers, 1715–1938, Family and Personal Material, Personal: Box 61, Folder 5, List of OWH's Books, 1935, seq. 13, http://nrs.harvard.edu/urn-3:HLS.Libr:8268117?n=13.

51. See Emerson's discussion of language as signs of natural facts in Ralph Waldo Emerson, "Nature," 13–19.

52. Holmes, "Natural Law," 43.

53. Holmes, "Natural Law," 43.

54. Holmes, "Natural Law," 43.

55. Ralph Waldo Emerson, "Nature," 13 ("No reason can be asked or given why the soul seeks beauty").

56. Ralph Waldo Emerson, "Nature," 13.

57. Holmes, "Natural Law," 43.

58. Holmes, "Natural Law," 43.

59. Holmes, "Natural Law," 43.

60. Ralph Waldo Emerson, "Nature," 14.

61. Ralph Waldo Emerson, "Nature," 14.

62. Holmes, "Natural Law," 43–44.

63. Ralph Waldo Emerson, "Nature," 7.

64. Holmes, "Natural Law," 44.

65. Ralph Waldo Emerson, "Nature," 14.

66. Ralph Waldo Emerson, "Nature," 14–15.

67. Holmes, "Natural Law," 44.

68. Ralph Waldo Emerson, "The Over-Soul," *The Essential Writings of Ralph Waldo Emerson*, ed. Brooks Atkinson (New York: Modern Library, 2000), 237.

69. Most scholars date the common law back to Henry II's rule in the twelfth century.

70. Ralph Waldo Emerson, "Nature," 17.

71. Ralph Waldo Emerson, "History," *The Essential Writings of Ralph Waldo Emerson*, ed. Brooks Atkinson (New York: Modern Library, 2000), 130.

72. Ralph Waldo Emerson, "Nature," 17.

73. Ralph Waldo Emerson, "Nature," 23.

74. Ralph Waldo Emerson, "History," 119.

75. Ralph Waldo Emerson, "Nature," 16.

76. Ralph Waldo Emerson, "An Address," *The Essential Writings of Ralph Waldo Emerson*, ed. Brooks Atkinson (New York: Modern Library, 2000), 63.

77. Ralph Waldo Emerson, "An Address," 63.

78. Ralph Waldo Emerson, "An Address," 63.

79. Emerson, "History," 119.

80. Ralph Waldo Emerson, "The American Scholar," 45.

81. Ralph Waldo Emerson, "The American Scholar," 45.

82. Ralph Waldo Emerson, "Compensation," *The Essential Writings of Ralph Waldo Emerson*, ed. Brooks Atkinson (New York: Modern Library, 2000), 165.

83. Ralph Waldo Emerson, "Intellectual," *The Essential Writings of Ralph Waldo Emerson*, ed. Brooks Atkinson (New York: Modern Library, 2000), 266.

84. Ralph Waldo Emerson, "Nature," 17.

85. Ralph Waldo Emerson, "Nature," 18.

86. Holmes, *The Common Law*, 33.

87. Ralph Waldo Emerson, "Nature," 21–22.

88. Ralph Waldo Emerson, "An Address," *The Essential Writings of Ralph Waldo Emerson*, ed. Brooks Atkinson (New York: Modern Library, 2000), 63.

89. Emerson, "An Address," 63.

90. Ralph Waldo Emerson, "Nature," 25.

91. Ralph Waldo Emerson, "Prudence," *The Essential Writings of Ralph Waldo Emerson*, ed. Brooks Atkinson (New York: Modern Library, 2000), 215.

92. Emerson insists that humans may learn this creative skill at a young age: "From the child's successive possession of his several senses up to the hour when he saith, 'Thy will be done!' he is learning the secret that he can reduce under his will not only particular events but great classes, nay, the whole series of events, and so conform all facts to his character." Emerson, "Nature," 21.

93. Emerson says, "Nature is a discipline of the understanding in intellectual truths. Our dealing in sensible objects is a constant exercise in the necessary lessons of difference, of likeness, of order, of being and seeming, of progressive attainment; of ascent from particular to general; of combination to one end of manifold forces." Emerson, "Nature," 19. Here the purposeful development of truth attained through classificatory methodology is evident.

94. Ralph Waldo Emerson, "The American Scholar," 45.

95. Ralph Waldo Emerson, "Nature," 19.

96. "The understanding [of the solidity or resistance, inertia, extension, figure, and divisibility of matter] adds, divides, combines, measures, and finds nutriment and room for its activity in this worthy scene. Meantime, Reason transfers all these lessons into its own world of thought, by perceiving the analogy that marries Matter and Mind." Ralph Waldo Emerson, "Nature," 19.

97. Hoffheimer was aware of this penchant for classification as an element of his transcendentalism as it pertains to the law. "There is," he says, "the problem of the vision behind *Natural Law*—expressed, perhaps, in its style, too—that meaning derived from connection to a greater whole that was known to be, even if known to be unknowable in its details." Hoffheimer, *Justice Holmes and the Natural Law*, 13.

98. Holmes, *The Common Law*, 3.

99. Holmes, *The Common Law*, 3–4.

100. Ralph Waldo Emerson, "History," 118 ("Genius studies the casual thought, and far back in the womb of things sees the rays parting from one orb, that diverge, ere they fall, by infinite diameters. Genius watches the monad through all his masks as he performs the metempsychosis of nature. Genius detects through the fly, through the caterpillar, through the grub, through the egg, the constant individual; through countless individuals the fixed species; through many species the genus; through all genera the steadfast type; through all the kingdoms of organized life the eternal unity").

101. Holmes, *The Common Law*, 4.

102. Holmes, *The Common Law*, 5.

103. "Generalization is always a new influx of the divinity into the mind." Emerson, "Circles," 256.

104. See generally Allen Mendenhall, "Oliver Wendell Holmes Jr. and the Darwinian Common Law Paradigm," *European Journal of Pragmatism and American Philosophy*," 7, no. 2 (2015). See also Oliver Wendell Holmes Jr., "Law in Science and Science in Law," *Harvard Law Review* 12 (1899), 447 ("We have evolution in this sphere of conscious thought and action no less than in lower organic stages, but an evolution which must be studied in its own field").

105. Oliver Wendell Holmes Jr., "Law in Science and Science in Law," 449.

106. Oliver Wendell Holmes Jr., "Law in Science and Science in Law," 450.

107. Oliver Wendell Holmes Jr., "Law in Science and Science in Law," 450.

108. Holmes, *The Common Law*, 25.

109. Holmes, *The Common Law*, 25.

110. Holmes, *The Common Law*, 25.

111. "History sets us free and enables us to make up our minds dispassionately whether the survival [of rules or traditions] which we [judges] are enforcing answers any new purpose when it has ceased to answer the old." Oliver Wendell Holmes Jr., "Law in Science and Science in Law," 452.

112. Holmes, *The Common Law*, 25. He also claimed that, "to understand their [the seemingly self-sufficient propositions of law] scope fully, to know how they will be dealt with by

judges trained in the past which the law embodies, we must ourselves know something of that past." Holmes, *The Common Law*, 25.

113. Mark DeWolfe Howe, Research Materials Relating to Life of Oliver Wendell Holmes Jr., 1858–1968, MDH Research Materials, Holmes—Uncollected Essays, Vol. IV, January 1873–January 1880: Box 32, Folder 31, [Book Notice] A Selection of Cases on the Law of Contracts, with a Summary of the Topics Covered by the Cases, *American Law Review* 14 (March 1880), 233, seq. 2–3, http://nrs.harvard.edu/urn-3:HLS.Libr:8527870.

114. Ralph Waldo Emerson, "The Transcendentalist," in *The Essential Writings of Ralph Waldo Emerson*, ed. Brooks Atkinson (New York: Modern Library, 2000), 81.

115. Ralph Waldo Emerson, "Intellect," in *The Essential Writings of Ralph Waldo Emerson*, ed. Brooks Atkinson (New York: Modern Library, 2000), 270.

116. Emerson, "An Address," 78.

117. Ralph Waldo Emerson, "English Traits," in *The Essential Writings of Ralph Waldo Emerson*, ed. Brooks Atkinson (New York: Modern Library, 2000), 545.

118. Ralph Waldo Emerson, "Art," in *The Essential Writings of Ralph Waldo Emerson*, ed. Brooks Atkinson (New York: Modern Library, 2000), 275.

119. Ralph Waldo Emerson, "Circles," in *The Essential Writings of Ralph Waldo Emerson*, ed. Brooks Atkinson (New York: Modern Library, 2000), 261.

120. Emerson, "Circles," 253.

121. See Allen Mendenhall, "Oliver Wendell Holmes Jr. Is the Use of Calling Emerson a Pragmatist: A Brief and Belated Response to Stanley Cavell," *Faulkner Law Review* 6 (2014), 215–16.

122. Joseph Schumpeter, *Capitalism, Socialism and Democracy* (London: Routledge, [1943] 1994), 83.

123. F. A. Hayek, *The Constitution of Liberty*, ed. Ronald Hamowy (Chicago: University of Chicago Press, [1960] 2011), 47.

124. Oliver Wendell Holmes Jr., "Law in Science and Science in Law," 454. He says, e.g.: "At that time there were few rules of evidence. Later our laws of evidence were systematized and developed. But the authority of Lord Hale has caused his dictum to survive as law in the particular case, while the principle upon which it would have to be justified has been destroyed. The exception in other words is pure survival, having nothing or very little to back it except that the practice is established." Oliver Wendell Holmes Jr., "Law in Science and Science in Law," 453. Interestingly, Hoffheimer talks about transcendentalism in Holmes's thought as if it were itself subject to the doctrine of survival, i.e., as if it were a holdover or survival from Holmes's early years. Hoffheimer, *Justice Holmes and the Natural Law*, 17.

125. Ralph Waldo Emerson, "The Poet," in *The Essential Writings of Ralph Waldo Emerson*, ed. Brooks Atkinson (New York: Modern Library, 2000), 297.

126. Holmes, *The Common Law*, 25.

127. Holmes, *The Common Law*, 25.

128. Holmes, *The Common Law*, 167.

129. Oliver Wendell Holmes Jr., "The Path of the Law," 10 (1896–97), 468.

130. Oliver Wendell Holmes Jr., "Law in Science and Science in Law," 461.

131. See also his concern about phrasing taking the place of real reasons. Oliver Wendell Holmes Jr., "Law in Science and Science in Law," 459.

132. Jonathan Levin, *The Poetics of Transition: Emerson, Pragmatism & American Literary Modernism* (Duke University Press, 1999), ix.

133. Emerson, "Circles," 261.

134. Oliver Wendell Holmes Jr., "Law in Science and Science in Law," *Harvard Law Review* 12 (1899), 455.

135. Oliver Wendell Holmes Jr., "Law in Science and Science in Law," *Harvard Law Review* 12 (1899), 455.

136. Oliver Wendell Holmes Jr., "Law in Science and Science in Law," *Harvard Law Review* 12 (1899), 455.

137. Emerson, "Circles," 261.

138. Emerson, "Circles," 261.

139. Emerson, "Circles," 252–63: "There are no fixtures in nature. The universe is fluid and volatile. Permanence is but a word of degrees. Our globe seen by God is a transparent law, not a mass of facts. The law dissolves the fact and holds it fluid. Our culture is the predominance of an idea which draws after it this train of cities and institutions. Let us rise into another idea; they will disappear. The Greek sculpture is all melted away, as if it had been statues of ice; here and there a solitary figure or fragment remaining, as we see flecks and scraps of snow left in cold dells and mountain clefts in June and July. For the genius that created it creates now somewhat else. The Greek letters last a little longer, but are already passing under the same sentence and tumbling into the inevitable pit which the creation of new thought opens for all that is old. The new continents are built out of the ruins of an old planet; the new races fed out of the decomposition of the foregoing."

140. "I confess that such a development as that fills me with interest, not only for itself, but as an illustration of what you see all through the law—the paucity of original ideas in man, and the slow, coasting way in which he works along from rudimentary beginnings to the complex and artificial conceptions of civilized life. It is like the niggardly uninventiveness *of nature in its other manifestations*, with its few smells or colors or types, its short list of elements, working along in the same slow way from compound to compound until the dramatic impressiveness of the most intricate compositions, which we call *organic life*, makes them seem different in kind from the elements out of which they are made, when set opposite to them in direct contrast." Oliver Wendell Holmes Jr., "Law in Science and Science in Law," 446–47.

141. Holmes, *The Common Law*, 4.

142. Oliver Wendell Holmes Jr., "Learning and Science," *North Carolina Law Review* 24 (1946), 103 (reprint of an 1895 address Holmes delivered for the Harvard Law School Association).

143. Oliver Wendell Holmes Jr., "Learning and Science," 103.

144. Oliver Wendell Holmes Jr., "Learning and Science," 103.

145. Emerson, "Self-Reliance," 141.

146. Emerson, "Self-Reliance," 141.

147. Ralph Waldo Emerson, "Self-Reliance," 135.

148. Ralph Waldo Emerson, "Politics," in *The Essential Writings of Ralph Waldo Emerson*, ed. Brooks Atkinson (New York: Modern Library, 2000), 386.

149. Emerson, "Self-Reliance," 138.

150. Emerson, "Self-Reliance," 140.

151. For a treatment of the Nietzschean elements of Holmes's jurisprudence, see Seth Vannatta and Allen Mendenhall, "The American Nietzsche? Fate and Power in the Pragmatism of Justice Holmes," *UMKC Law Review* 85 (2016). It is notable that Emerson is the one thinker who had a demonstrative influence on both Holmes and Nietzsche.

152. A person's "fidelity to new revelations of the incessant soul" and "faithfulness to his truth" make up the law that "writes the laws of cities and nations"—i.e., the law which "it is in vain to build or plot or combine against." Ralph Waldo Emerson, "Compensation," 157–58. See also Ralph Waldo Emerson, "Prudence," 218 ("Let a man keep the law—any law—and his way will be strown with satisfactions. . . . If you think the senses final, obey their law. If you believe in the soul, do not clutch at sensual sweetness before it is ripe on the slow tree of cause and effect").

153. See Emerson, "Compensation," 159 ("Crime and punishment grow out of one stem. Punishment is a fruit that unsuspected ripens within the flower of the pleasure which concealed it. Cause and effect, means and ends, seed and fruit, cannot be severed; for the effect already blooms in the cause, the end preëxists in the means, the fruit in the seed").

154. See, e.g., Ralph Waldo Emerson, "Politics," 381–82 ("The law may do what it will with the owner of property; its just power will still attach to the cent. The law may in a mad freak say that all shall have power except the owners of property; they shall have no vote. Nevertheless, by a higher law, the property will, year after year, write every statute that respects property. The non-proprietor will be the scribe of the proprietor. What the owners wish to do, the whole power of the property will do, either through the law or else in defiance of it").

155. Ibid.

156. See, e.g., Ralph Waldo Emerson, "The Over-Soul," 237.

157. Emerson, "An Address," 63.

158. Oliver Wendell Holmes Jr., "Law in Science and Science in Law," 462–63. This remark comes on the heels of Holmes's brief aside about knowledge of generals depending upon understanding of the particulars of which they consist. See Oliver Wendell Holmes Jr., "Law in Science and Science in Law," 461 (discussing "the danger of reasoning from generalizations unless you have the particulars which they embrace in mind"). Here Holmes states that a "generalization is empty so far as it is general. Its value depends on the number of particulars which it calls up to the speaker and the hearer."

159. Emerson, "Nature," 38 ("The invariable mark of wisdom is to see the miraculous in the common. What is a day? What is a year? What is summer? What is woman? What is a child? What is sleep? To our blindness, these things seem unaffecting. We make fables to hide the baldness of the fact and conform it, as we say, to the higher law of the mind. But when the fact is seen under the light of an idea, the gaudy fable fades and shrivels. We behold a higher law. To the wise, therefore, a fact is true poetry, and the most beautiful of fables").

160. Emerson, "An Address," 73–74.

161. Ralph Waldo Emerson, "Conduct of Life," in *The Essential Writings of Ralph Waldo Emerson*, ed. Brooks Atkinson (New York: Modern Library, 2000), 631–32.

162. Ralph Waldo Emerson, "Conduct of Life," 631.

163. Ralph Waldo Emerson, "Conduct of Life," 631.

164. See, e.g., F. A. Hayek, *The Constitution of Liberty*, 310–15 (on the rule of law working as a limitation on legislation).

165. For the most profound expression, in my view, of the evolutionary nature and characteristics of the common-law system, see Allan C. Hutchinson, *Evolution and the Common Law* (Cambridge: Cambridge University Press, 2005).

166. Hoffheimer, *Justice Holmes and the Natural Law*, 13.

## BIBLIOGRAPHY

Emerson, Ralph Waldo. *The Essential Writings of Ralph Waldo Emerson*. Ed. Brooks Atkinson. New York: Modern Library, 2000.

Hayek, F. A. *The Constitution of Liberty*. Ed. Ronald Hamowy. Chicago: University of Chicago Press, [1960] 2011.

———. *Law, Legislation and Liberty, Vol. 2*. Chicago and London: University of Chicago Press, 1976.

Helmholz, R. H. *Natural Law in Court*. Cambridge, MA: Harvard University Press, 2015.

Hoffheimer, Michael H. *Justice Holmes and the Natural Law*. New York: Garland Publishing, 1992.

Holmes Jr., Oliver Wendell. John G. Palfrey (1875–1945) Collection of Oliver Wendell Holmes Jr. Papers, 1715–1938, Family and Personal Material, Personal: Box 61, Folder 5, List of OWH's books, 1935, seq. 11, http://nrs.harvard.edu/urn-3:HLS.Libr:8268117?n=11; Oliver Wendell Holmes Jr., John G. Palfrey (1875–1945) Collection of Oliver Wendell Holmes Jr. Papers, 1715–1938, Family and Personal Material, Personal: Box 61, Folder 5, List of OWH's Books, 1935, seq. 13, http://nrs.harvard.edu/urn-3:HLS.Libr:8268117?n=13. Note: seq. 12 consists of a blank page.

———. John G. Palfrey (1875–1945) Collection of Oliver Wendell Holmes Jr. Papers, 1715–1938, Family and Personal Material, Personal: Box 61, Folder 5, List of OWH's Books, 1935, seq. 13, http://nrs.harvard.edu/urn-3:HLS.Libr:8268117?n=13.

———. *The Common Law*. Chicago: ABA Publishing, [1881] 2009.

———. "Natural Law." *Harvard Law Review* 32 (1918–19).

———. "Law in Science and Science in Law." *Harvard Law Review* 12 (1899).

———. "Learning and Science." *North Carolina Law Review* 24 (1946).

Horwitz, Morton J. "History and Theory." *Yale Law Journal* 96 (1987).

Howe, Mark DeWolfe. *Justice Oliver Wendell Holmes: The Shaping Years, 1841–1870*. Cambridge, MA: Belknap Press, 1957.

———. Research Materials Relating to Life of Oliver Wendell Holmes Jr., 1858–1968, MDH Research Materials, Holmes—Uncollected Essays, Vol. IV, January 1873 – January 1880: Box 32, Folder 31, [Book Notice] A Selection of Cases on the Law of Contracts, with a Summary of the Topics Covered by the Cases, *American Law Review* 14 (March 1880), 233, seq. 2–3, http://nrs.harvard.edu/urn-3:HLS.Libr:8527870.

Hutchinson, Allan C. *Evolution and the Common Law.* Cambridge: Cambridge University Press, 2005.

Levin, Jonathan. *The Poetics of Transition: Emerson, Pragmatism & American Literary Modernism.* Durham, NC: Duke University Press, 1999.

Mellen Jr., Francis J. "Ralph Waldo Emerson, Mr. Justice Holmes and the Idea of Organic Form in American Law." *New England Law Review* 14 (1978–79).

Mendenhall, Allen. *Oliver Wendell Holmes Jr., Pragmatism, and the Jurisprudence of Agon.* Lewisburg, PA: Bucknell University Press, 2017.

———. "Oliver Wendell Holmes Jr. Is the Use of Calling Emerson a Pragmatist: A Brief and Belated Response to Stanley Cavell." *Faulkner Law Review* 6 (2014).

———. "Oliver Wendell Holmes Jr. and the Darwinian Common Law Paradigm." *European Journal of Pragmatism and American Philosophy*. Vol. 7, no. 2 (2015).

Schumpeter, Joseph. *Capitalism, Socialism and Democracy.* London: Routledge, [1943] 1994.

Vannatta, Seth and Allen Mendenhall. "The American Nietzsche? Fate and Power in the Pragmatism of Justice Holmes." *UMKC Law Review* 85 (2016)

Whitman, Walt. "Song of Myself." *The Portable Walt Whitman.* Ed. Mark Van Doren. New York: Penguin Books, 1973.

*Chapter Six*

# The Positivist

Catharine Wells

Holmes wrote about law in the same way that a poet might write about a bouquet of flowers. We listen and say: "How remarkable! How clearly he has captured the essence of that sunflower." Then we take some time to reflect. We think about what he really meant and whether it is true. But, by the time we turn to ask, he is on to the peony.

While this way of writing has made Holmes a subject of continuing interest, it has also created considerable confusion about the substance of his views. No expert on American law has been subject to as many differing interpretations as he. And no area of his writing is more controversial than what he has said about the relationship between law and morality. Central to the debate is the charge that Holmes advocates a theory known as legal positivism. Exhibit A for this allegation is the following quote from "The Path of the Law":

> I think it desirable at once to point out and dispel confusion between morality and law. . . . You can see very plainly that a bad man has as much reason as a good one for wishing to avoid an encounter with the public force, and therefore you can see the practical importance of the distinction between morality and law. A man who cares nothing for an ethical rule which is believed and practiced by his neighbors is likely nevertheless to care a good deal to avoid being made to pay money, and will want to keep out of jail if he can.[1]

In writing this, Holmes makes a fundamental distinction between law and morality. Morality, he says, states the requirements for being a good person; while law merely tells us how to avoid being jailed.

To the uninitiated, this distinction may seem logical and practical. However, it runs against two distinct themes of American democracy. The first is the idea of freedom subject to law. In a country founded upon notions of individual liberty, law represents a concession to the necessities of public order and welfare. This means that law cannot be arbitrary; its coercive power can only be justified by reference to legitimate public need; and this, in turn, requires reference to a governing normative theory. The second is the rule of law. It is a hallmark of the American system that we are ruled by laws rather than by individuals. As a result, everyone has a moral obligation to obey the law even in the absence of enforcement. For example, we expect a motorist to obey traffic signals even if there is no one around to dispense a ticket; and, for the same reason, we expected President Nixon to turn over his tapes even though the Justice Department was unlikely to storm the White House. Thus, when Holmes separates law and morality, some legal writers become uneasy. They are worried that obedience to law will be seen as morally optional with each citizen doing whatever they wish so long as they can evade the consequences or are willing to bear them. They are also fearful that lawyers will see their job as facilitating evasion. These are real concerns. Indeed, we find ourselves in a legal world that increasingly slants in that direction. Nevertheless, we must ask ourselves: what does legal positivism have to do with this problem? And more specifically: In what way did Holmes contribute to the trend?

To shed light on this debate, I will do three things in this chapter. First, I will briefly recap the criticism of Holmes's positivism. Second, I will examine legal positivism and its limitations as an analysis of law. Third, I will set out what I take to be Holmes's position with respect to law and morality. Readers will then be able to decide for themselves whether Holmes had a troubling influence on American law.

## HOLMES AND HIS CRITICS

In the last part of his life, Holmes had become the beloved icon of American law. His record of heroism in the Civil War together with fifty years on the bench and a lifetime of quotable speeches were sufficient to cement his first-rate reputation. Then came the rise of fascism and the Second World War, and these two events effectively changed the way that American legal scholars thought about law. Before the war, the emphasis had been on law's instrumental possibilities. There was little need for abstract morality as progressive lawyers sought to lay the groundwork for a rapidly developing nation. This left plenty of room for moral skepticism; and, for this reason, Holmes's doubts about moral theorizing had not sounded like abject cynicism. To the contrary, his contemporaries saw a certain humility and an admirable willingness to listen to the other side. After the war, however, the emphasis was on idealism. Americans had come to value the kind of moral certitude that makes it possible to stand up to a bully. They believed that it was high ideals that had defeated fascism and that would soon, they hoped, insure a victory in the Cold War. Thus, legal theorists did not like to be reminded that law was a form of coercion. Instead they saw it as a mechanism for facilitating a self-perfecting democratic state. And, in this vein, they saw law as central to the movement for Civil Rights. Thus, when Holmes described rights as mere prophecies of what the courts will do in fact,[2] he seemed to be missing an important point: namely, that civil rights should be understood as moral claims.

In this context, the first attacks on Holmes were shrill. Critics opposed him both for his legal and political views. For example, in an article entitled *Holmes, Hobbes and Hitler*, Robert Palmer concluded:

> (H)is basic principles lead straight to the abasement of man before the absolutist state and the enthronement of a legal autocrat—whether individual, minority or majority—a legal autocrat who may perhaps be as genial as Holmes, benevolently paternalistic, perhaps grim and brutal as any Nazi or Japanese totalitarian, but none the less an autocrat in lineal succession from Caesar Augustus and Nero through Hobbes and Austin and Mr. Justice Holmes.[3]

A second group of attacks took a more moderate tone. Lon Fuller, for example, criticized Holmes by arguing that he had paid insufficient attention to the moral aspirations of the legal profession.[4] This led to an ongoing debate in the pages of the *Harvard Law Review*.[5] Like the earlier attacks, these articles did not focus upon the theoretical questions posed by legal positivism. Nor were they scholarly attempts at interpreting Holmes's thought. Instead, the participants expressed their concerns about Holmes's influence on American law. Mark DeWolfe Howe, a Harvard Law School professor, a Holmes law clerk, and Holmes's official biographer, summed it up nicely. He wrote that many legal theorists were troubled that

> Holmes' philosophy of law was inconsistent with the highest traditions and aspirations of western thought and that his scale of moral and political values was badly suited to measure the needs of a progressive and civilized society."[6]

More recently, there has been a strand of Holmes's scholarship that has focused on debunking the myth of Justice Holmes as the great figure of American law. This has taken the form of showing: (1) that his legal opinions were never as progressive as they seemed; (2) that his experience in the Civil War made him detached, ambitious, self-centered, and mean-spirited; (3) that he held despicable views on eugenics; and (4) that he had a poor record on civil rights. But the idea that Holmes was despicable or even mean-spirited seems to contradict what we know of his life. Holmes was well liked and generally understood to be affable and kind. But his critics charge that behind the charming exterior lurked a worldview that was cynical and demoralizing.

And, with a little cherry picking, it was easy for them to make the case. Here are some of Holmes's words chosen by one of his latest critics:

- I think that the sacredness of human life is a purely municipal ideal of no validity outside the jurisdiction. I believe that force, mitigated so far as may be by good manners is the ultimo ratio . . . [E]very society rests on the death of men.[7]
- Doesn't this squashy sentimentality of a big minority of our people about human life make you puke? (That minority includes) people who believe there is an onward and upward—who talk of uplift—who think that something in particular has happened and that the universe is no longer predatory. Oh bring in a basin.[8]
- I don't think you can do much by tinkering with property without taking in hand life. I meant what I suppose what he would think horrible—restricting propagation by the undesirables and putting to death infants that didn't pass the examination, etc., etc.[9]

We should note that all three of these quotations come from private correspondence where overstatement often serves as a mark of emphasis and feeling. Nevertheless, each of them sounds a distinctly Holmesian theme. The first involves the denial of a universal system of morality; the second expresses skepticism about the perfectibility of human nature; and the third is more complicated. It seems to attack the idea that all human life is sacred; but, if you read it carefully and, in its context, he is in fact ridiculing the socialists and their idea that we can radically change society by "tinkering" with property. At worst, these statements reinforce the view that Holmes, as a man of his time, held views on property rights, racial differences, and even eugenics that would not be acceptable today. Added to this is the fact that he disliked do-gooders and ridiculed the progressive notion that things must always get better. Like Emerson, he disdained the kind of mindless charity that people use to inflate their sense of self-worth. He was opposed to abstract moral systems and quick to see hypocrisy in inflated proclamations of moral ideals.

While none of these attitudes are particularly troubling, the same cannot be said for the lack of compassion that sometimes appears in his public pronouncements. His opinion in *Buck v. Bell*[10] provides a notable example. Holmes, writing for the majority, upholds a Virginia statute providing for the sterilization of "feeble-minded" women. For him it seemed an easy case:

> We have seen more than once that the public welfare may call upon the best citizens for their lives. It would be strange if it could not call upon those who already sap the strength of the State for these lesser sacrifices, in order to prevent our being swamped with incompetence. It is better for all the world if,

> instead of waiting to execute degenerate offspring for crime or to let them starve for their imbecility, society can prevent those who are manifestly unfit from continuing their kind.[11]

And, as if he had not already said enough, he finished with a flourish: "Three generations of imbeciles are enough."[12]

The opinion, and this passage in particular, demonstrate the clear limits of Holmes's moral vision. Note how casually he makes the distinction between "the best citizens" and "those who already sap the strength of the State." Note how quickly he gives up any hope that "degenerate offspring" can avoid crime and live dignified, meaningful lives. But, it is important to remember that, like many of his era, his views on eugenics were tied to considerations of human welfare. Misguided though they were, the men who had brought Carrie Buck to court believed that they were acting in her best interest. Of course, they were not.[13] Nor was Justice Holmes. Looking back, one feels that he has made a big moral mistake, but a mistake is not the same thing as abject cynicism. Further, as we shall see in the third section, it is a mistake unrelated to his so-called positivism.

## LEGAL POSITIVISM AND THE SEPARATION THESIS

Legal positivism is related to a broader philosophical movement that began with Auguste Comte and reached its peak with logical positivists of the mid-twentieth century. The logical positivists were empiricists who believed that sense data defined the limits of meaningful discourse.[14] This meant that what could not be observed or verified could not form the basis of an objective theory. Consequently, positivism created an unbridgeable gap between facts and values. One could use an objective method to determine factual questions, but value questions, the positivists said, were irretrievably subjective. Thus, positivism left the law in a precarious position. The positivist must either admit that law, like morality, is entirely subjective or he or she must elevate its claims to the level of fact. The legal positivists chose the latter course. For example, John Austin, an important early expositor of legal positivism, argued that law represented a series of social facts.[15] Its fundamental constituent was the power of the Sovereign to issue commands and a corresponding habit among the citizens of obeying these commands. For those who did not obey, the sovereign had the power to punish disobedience. Thus, the study of law was a kind of anthropological and sociological discipline. Knowing the law of a given jurisdiction was to know who the sovereign was, how he expressed his commands, and the mechanisms by which they obtained obedience among his subjects. This view had the benefit of placing law squarely on the fact side of the fact/value dichotomy.

But Austin's positivism had a number of disadvantages. For one thing, it lacked a theory of legislation. A rule became law whenever the sovereign made it so. So long as the sovereign retained his power, there was no limit on his authority. His laws could be arbitrary, unfair and even cruel, but there would be no ground for criticism. Under positivism, one could speak of "good laws" and "bad laws," but all such talk would be understood as expressions of preference. The statement—"I like laws that are fair"—would have the same moral weight as "I like vanilla ice cream." As a result, the only way to counter tyranny was by revolution—a revolution aimed not at reform but at installing a new and more agreeable Sovereign.

Besides this problem, legal positivism seemed ill suited to describing the far-flung pockets of power that exist in a modern democracy. To accommodate this, modern positivists such as H. L. A. Hart have traded talk of a sovereign for talk about the origins of law and the "pedigree" of individual laws. In *The Concept of Law*, Hart argued that the legal system utilizes two distinct types of rules. He wrote:

> Under rules of . . . the basic or primary type, human beings are required to do or abstain from certain actions, whether they wish to or not. Rules of the other type are in a sense parasitic upon or secondary to the first; for they provide that human beings may by doing or saying certain things introduce new rules of the primary type, extinguish or modify old ones, or in various ways determine their incidence or control their operations. Rules of the first type impose duties; rules of the second type confer powers, public or private.[16]

This distinction has the beneficial effect of separating law from the actions of a single sovereign. A society may make any number of arrangements by which proposed rules become binding law. These arrangements are codified by the secondary rules. And it is the secondary rules that provide a framework for defining the primary or substantive rules of law. Thus, to determine whether or not a given primary rule is binding within a specific society, one must determine whether or not its pedigree conforms to the requirements of the secondary rules. Thus, Hart's modification dispenses with a unitary sovereign but still results in a factual description of law.

In 1958, Hart entered the controversy over Holmes's positivism.[17] Since he was about to publish his own version of legal positivism, he was anxious to clarify the doctrine and to contest the idea that it was morally suspect. He began the essay by noting a certain confusion over what counts as a positivist theory. He therefore separated three distinct claims:

1. The claim that law must be kept separate from morality
2. The claim that law utilizes a distinctive vocabulary that should not be confused with the homonyms used to describe morality
3. The claim that every law can be understood as a command

This clarification helps us to see that it is only the first of these claims—the so-called Separation Thesis[18]—that is truly controversial. The second seems to be no more than helpful advice to those who wish to study law, while the third clearly misstates the nature of modern law.[19] Since Holmes's critics saw law and morality as the intertwined pillars of a free society, it was the Separation Thesis that drew their ire. Their attacks, however, were misplaced. To understand why, it is necessary to think about the process of adjudication.

Any act of interpretation—whether it is by a judge or a public official—presupposes a normative theory of interpretation. Interpretive decisions are not supposed to be arbitrary. If not arbitrary, then they must be rule-bound; that is, each act of interpretation must be governed by a set of standards that govern the interpretive process. Thus, in order to speak of the correctness of an interpretive decision, we must refer to a normative meta-theory. Indeed, the literature about Constitutional decision making is filled with disputes over the choice of such a theory. For example, all of the following principles have their defenders:

- Decide in accordance with the intent of the framers (original intent)
- Decide consistently with the plain meaning of the terms used
- Decide in such a way that efficiency is maximized
- Decide in terms of contemporary notions of fairness

This puts positivism in a difficult position. To maintain the factual nature of their account, proponents would have to insist that learning the meta-rules is a matter of empirical inquiry; that a student of law could simply observe that one or another of them was operating at any given point. The problem with this is that it leaves the theory toothless. It describes past instances of law making; but it cannot shed any light on the central questions of jurisprudence: What should a judge do in deciding cases? What makes a good judge?

To answer these questions, it is important to recognize that making a decision is an activity and not a static state that is amenable to factual description. This insight was central to pragmatists like Holmes. It is a point persuasively made by Lewis Carroll in the classic essay, "What the Tortoise said to Achilles."[20] The point of his essay is to clarify the difference between descriptive propositions and rules of inference. Propositions describe states of affairs such as: "All persons are mortal." Rules of inference, on the other hand, permit a movement from one belief, or set of beliefs, to another. Thus, for example, we have a rule that licenses the following inference.

If one believes that all persons are mortal and that Tom is a person then one can, or should, also believe that Tom is mortal.

This is, in fact, an instance of a familiar logical rule:

Modus ponens: If ((if A then B) and A) then B.

As I have just written it, the principle of modus ponens looks like a proposition. But, as Carroll makes clear, if we treat it as one, it will lose its essential ability to license real world inferences. He illustrates this with a pointed story about Achilles and the Tortoise.

The story begins with a challenge to Achilles. The Tortoise sets out three propositions from Euclid:

> (A) Things that are equal to the same are equal to each other.
> (B) The two sides of this Triangle are things that are equal to the same.
> (Z) The two sides of this Triangle are equal to each other.

and claims to believe that A and B are true but that Z is not. He then challenges Achilles to "force (him), logically, to accept Z as true." Achilles replies that, obviously, the problem is that the Tortoise does not accept the hypothetical: "If A and B are true, then Z must be true."

When the Tortoise acknowledges this, Achilles writes down the hypothetical as:

(C) If A and B, then Z

and asks the tortoise to accept it as a premise. So then there are three premises—A, B, and C—and when Achilles once again asks the Tortoise to acknowledge the truth of Z, the Tortoise replies that he will do so only if Achilles will add yet another premise to those he has written on his tablet. The premise is:

> (D) If A and B and C, then Z.
> Achilles adds the premise and the conversation continues:
> "And at last we've got to the end of this ideal race-course! Now that you accept A and B and C and D, of course you accept Z."
> "Do I?" said the Tortoise innocently. "Let's make that quite clear. I accept A and B and C and D. Suppose I still refuse to accept Z?"
> "Then logic would take you by the throat and force you to do it!" Achilles triumphantly replied. "Logic would tell you 'You can't help yourself. Now that you've accepted A and B and C and D, you must accept Z!' So you've no choice, you see."
> "Whatever Logic is good enough to tell me is worth writing down," said the Tortoise. "So enter it in your book, please. We will call it—
> (E) If A and B and C and D are true, Z must be true.
> Until I've granted that, of course, I needn't grant Z. So it's quite a necessary step, you see?"
> "I see," said Achilles; and there was a touch of sadness in his tone.[21]

Obviously, this line of argument will postpone the inference indefinitely. The Tortoise will not make the inference unless the rule is included among the premises and, once it is included among the premises, it loses its power to license the inference.

Carroll's parable illustrates an important point about formal logic: One cannot reach a conclusion solely on the basis of premises, one must also have a rule to license the inference. At the same time, there are puzzling difficulties associated with the seemingly simple phenomenon of following a rule. Wittgenstein put it in his own typically perplexing way: "this was our paradox: no course of action could be determined by a rule, because every course of action can be made to accord with the rule."[22] Keeping Carroll's point in mind, it is not hard to see what Wittgenstein meant. Rules are not, as Carroll makes so clear, propositions that can be written down in Achilles's book. Instead, each rule represents a routinized way of responding to like cases. Rules are amorphous. They may be announced or articulated. They can be evidenced by a course of conduct that is understood as being rule governed. Or they can simply consist of unstated and vague expectations about the nature of future conduct. Suppose, for example, that I wake you up each morning at seven o'clock. I am consistent in this respect for one week; but, on the eighth day, I wake you at eight. Have I changed my rule or was I operating under the rule that I would wake you at seven for the first week and thereafter wake you at eight?[23] There is no clear answer because I am free at any moment to recognize a particular set of circumstances as triggering a particular response under my rule or to decide that the rule does not apply. The rule, unfortunately, can only tell me what happens if it applies, but it cannot go further and tell me whether it applies to the case at hand. Like the Tortoise, I am confronted with an *ad hoc* decision about the application of the rule and, as logical and inevitable as these decisions sometimes feel, they are guided solely by my sense of what the rule means in this specific situation—a sense that is derived from one's personal agency rather than from any particular law of logic.[24]

This means, among other things, that there is a certain ambiguity about statements of the following form:

If the plaintiff is late to court, his case will be dismissed.

On the one hand, this statement could be an empirically derived generalization. It could, for example, be the finding of an anthropologist who had observed the legal system for many years. If he subsequently observes a case in which the plaintiff is late, but nevertheless wins his case, he must regard his prior statement as false. On the other hand, what would we say about a judge who fails to dismiss a case when the plaintiff was late? Has he or she violated the rule? The answer is: not necessarily. While the rule states the consequences for being late, it does so only if the rule applies and if it does not have some relevant but unstated exception. In short, it is binding in this case only if it genuinely requires the judge to decide against the plaintiff. But, whether the judge is so required is the very question that the judge must decide. Remember that rules do not "take you by the throat and force you to do it." From a rule follower's perspective, what is written down is only the starting point. The writing does not tell us what must happen in ambiguous cases. Nor does it specify what might count as an exception. Indeed, to apply a rule, I must understand it well enough to know a number of things:

- Where the rule comes from
- What activity it regulates
- The purpose of that activity
- The purpose of the rule within the context of that activity
- How has it been interpreted in the past
- What exceptions have been recognized
- Who are the decision-makers that are empowered to decide on interpretations and exceptions
- What are the rules governing their activity
- To whom are they accountable

It is only by knowing these things that a judge will be in a position to decide what the rule—now taken in its full sense rather than as its written representation—requires in this case.

Thus, the separation thesis has its limits. It explains one aspect of learning the law. A law student may, for a time, become an amateur anthropologist and study the law from an external perspective. This helps students to avoid confusion when they read cases or study legal treatises. Legal scholars can also undertake an external study of law. They do this when they take the law at face value or when they formulate doctrinal theories and parse the logical relationships between the enunciated rules and substantive decisions. Even practitioners will find it useful to study the law from an external view because it will facilitate predictions about what courts will do. A positivistic theory of law will support all of these research activities. What it does not do—and cannot do—is provide the basis for a theory of judicial decision making. Judges do not predict their own decisions. They are not anthropologists; they are actors in an activity that is bound by the rules. Their perspective is inherently internal. They may, in fact, have very sophisticated doctrinal theories. On the basis of these theories, they may be able to predict what some other judge might do. They might even decide that the predicted result is the right result. But, even with all this, they still have to make a decision; it is not made for them. Nothing can save them from the need to decide for themselves what the law requires in this particular instance.

Inherent in positivism is the distinction between an external view that sees law as consisting of descriptive generalizations and an internal viewpoint that sees it as providing permissions or prohibitions. Hart, of course, embraces such a distinction; and, thirty years ago, I argued that Holmes did as well.[25] Positivism can only describe law from an external perspective. Indeed, once we take the role of a participant, the law becomes inherently normative and something that cannot be described with declarative sentences. From this point of view, the law consists of activities—activities like legislating, interpreting, and obeying—that cannot be understood without reference to an internal perspective in which normative concepts, like intentionality and judgment, are an inevitable part of the discourse.

## HOLMES AND "THE BAD MAN" THEORY OF JURISPRUDENCE

In the last section we examined the strengths and weaknesses of legal positivism. It is now time to consider Holmes's particular views about the relationship between law and morality. The first thing to note is that Holmes is unequivocal in his embrace of the Separation Thesis:

> Manifestly, therefore, nothing but confusion of thought can result from assuming that the rights of man in a moral sense are equally rights in the sense of the Constitution and the law.[26]

But, of course, this does not mean that law and morality are entirely separate. As we saw above, Holmes, like Hart, recognized a distinction between an internal and an external point of view. In the external view, the Separation Thesis facilitates what might be called a science of law—summarizing what courts have done in the past with a view towards predicting what they will do in the future. But prediction is not practice; and it is unlikely that Holmes, as a pragmatist, would miss this point. In fact, he was explicit in endorsing the Separation Thesis only temporarily and for a very specific purpose:

> When I emphasize the difference between law and morals I do so with reference to a single end, that of learning and understanding the law. For that purpose you must definitely master its specific marks, and it is for that that I ask you for the moment to imagine yourselves indifferent to other and greater things.[27]

Thus, for Holmes, legal positivism was a didactic maneuver that facilitated legal study. This left him free to admit that normativity was an essential characteristic of law when seen from the internal view.

In this respect, we should note that as soon as Holmes mentioned the Separation Thesis, he followed it up with a disclaimer:

> I take it for granted that no hearer of mine will misinterpret what I have to say as the language of cynicism. The law is the witness and external deposit of our moral life. Its history is the history of the moral development of the race. The practice of it, in spite of popular jests, tends to make good citizens and good men.[28]

As this passage makes clear, Homes saw that law develops in a particular moral context; and that understanding this context is an important part of understanding the law. This being true, his critics would seem to be wrong in suggesting that he viewed law and morality as entirely distinct.

On the other hand, it is doubtful that Holmes's critics were simply overreacting to his embrace of the separation thesis. As I suggested above, some of his statements suggest an attitude that seems cynical and disinterested in moral questions. If these are not traceable to his positivism, what do they suggest about his underlying views on morality? To answer this, we must consider a question that has been implicit in this chapter from the very beginning. We cannot understand Holmes's views about the relationship between law and morality unless we clarify Holmes's conception of morality itself. This is a subject that Holmes never addresses full on, but when we put his intellectual background together with his occasional utterances, a picture begins to emerge.

With respect to morality, Holmes's chief influence was an especially brilliant member of the Cambridge community named Chauncey Wright. Scholars have largely overlooked Wright's influence for several reasons. One reason was that Holmes's post-war critics tended to view him as a contemporary, without recognizing the fact that Holmes had formed his views in a different historical context. Second, even when we consider Holmes in this context, it is easy to overlook Wright's importance. Wright was a classic underachiever. He was brilliant and relentless in pursuing whatever attracted his interest, but also indolent and indifferent when it came to everything else. He was a man of contradiction. He had many friends but was deeply lonely and prone to long—but not very frequent—bouts of alcoholic intoxication. When sober, however, he had an extremely fast and agile mind. He supported himself as a "calculator," making long and complicated calculations for the American Ephemeris and Nautical Almanac in Cambridge. He was, in fact, so adroit at this that he was able to do a year's work in six months. This left him plenty of time to hang out at Harvard College and chat with whomever would listen. Among his listeners were Holmes and his friends, William James and Charles Peirce. Together with Wright, these men formed a Metaphysical Club that met biweekly to discuss philosophical questions. It was this group that played such a significant role in the formulation of pragmatism.[29] Wright was generally influential among these men; but Holmes, in particular, was specially drawn to Wright's views on moral theory.[30]

Both Wright and Holmes described their views as a form of positivism, but we have already seen that this term engenders confusion. First, there is the potential identification of it with the doctrine of legal positivism discussed above. Second, it suggests a similarity to logical positivism from which it is quite distinct. For Wright, positivism chiefly meant one thing: that one could not use the scientific method to settle moral disputes. Latter positivists would decree that this limitation meant that morality had no cognitive meaning. But this was not Wright's view. His positivism was limited to asserting the impossibility of empirical moral systems.

In his time, Wright was best known for an essay in which he dissected the works of Herbert Spencer. Spencer had coined the phrase "survival of the fittest," and, on the basis of this concept, he had articulated a normative vision for human society. Spencer labeled himself an empiricist, and yet his works were studded with moral "observations." Wright was skeptical; he approached Spencer with a magnifying glass and tweezers, dissecting his arguments and exposing the normative assumptions that Spencer had brought into his work. Describing Spencer, Wright wrote:

> Constrained by his entire sympathy with modern movements in thought and scientific culture, he is perforce a scientific empiricist though his peculiar genius would have found a more congenial employment in scholastic philosophy. Mr. Spencer believes in developments. All his writings are developments and most of them are about developments. He delights in "evolutions from the homogeneous to the heterogeneous"—in "changes from an indefinite incoherent homogeneity to a definite coherent heterogeneity, through continuous differentiations and integrations." He not only discovers them in all the objects of scientific research, but he rings these changes in all his discourses on them. Analysis is his *forte*, and developments are his foibles.[31]

It was Spencer's fascination with "developments" that led him to carelessly bolster his moral pronouncements with an untrustworthy form of moral argument. He would move from the observation that things were evolving towards X, to the conclusion that X was a higher form of the good; and it was this sort of *non sequitur* that Wright's "positivism" had so firmly targeted. To argue for the value of something based on "developments" in that direction, Wright thought, was to make teleology a universal moral premise.

This line of reasoning left Wright unenthusiastic with respect to certain aspects of pragmatism—especially its views on metaphysics, ethics, and religion. In these areas, pragmatism, itself, was prone to Spencerian *non sequiturs*. Nowhere was this more evident than in the pragmatic concept of truth. The pragmatists were idealists who believed that experience was a series of ideas in the mind. This distinguished them from the British empiricists who believed that experience was tethered to an external reality. Because of this difference, the pragmatists did not think of truth in terms of correspondence with reality, but rather in terms of efficacy and coherence among ideas. For example, Peirce defined truth as the object of final opinion in a community that had indefinitely practiced the scientific method.[32] His argument has a similar structure to those deployed by Spencer:

- Over time scientific opinion moves in a certain direction.
- This is progress. Each development of opinion brings us closer to the truth.
- Therefore, the ultimate opinion is truth.

But there is no particular reason why the ultimate opinion could not be just that—an opinion which, for no reason or for reasons unknown, is apparently stable. But if we insist on calling this opinion "true" in a metaphysical sense, it can only be because we assume that our ideas at the end of inquiry are better than those we held at the outset. Peirce himself was an able logician; and, seeing the problem, recognized that his conclusion rested upon a "cheerful hope:"

> [A]ll the followers of science are animated by a cheerful hope that the processes of investigation, if only pushed far enough, will give one certain solution to each question to which they apply it. . . . Different minds may set out with the most antagonistic views, but the progress of investigation carries them by a force outside of themselves to one and the same conclusion. . . . This great hope is embodied in the conception of truth and reality. The opinion which is *fated* (emphasis in original) to be ultimately agreed to by all who investigate, is what we mean by the truth, and the object represented in this opinion is the real.[33]

With respect to moral reasoning, the pragmatists had a similar problem. Again we turn to Peirce who began by affirming that "[e]very man has certain ideals of the general description of conduct that befits a rational animal in his particular station in life, what most accords with his total nature and relations." He continued:

> These ideals have in the main been imbibed in childhood. Still they have been shaped to his personal nature and to the ideas of his circle of society rather by a continuous process of growth than by any distinct acts of thought. Reflecting on these ideals, he is led to intend to make his own conduct conform . . . to them. Next, he usually formulates, however vaguely, certain rules of conduct. . . . Reflection upon these rules, as well as upon the general ideals behind them has a certain effect on his disposition, so that what he naturally inclines to do becomes modified.[34]

Once these rules are internalized, they become active in determining conduct. "Such being his condition," Peirce continued,

> He often foresees that a special occasion is going to arise; thereupon a certain gathering of his forces will begin to work and this working of his being will cause him to consider how he will act, and in accordance with his disposition, such as it now is, he is led to form a resolution as to how he will act upon that occasion. . . . [N]ow he sits down and goes through a process similar to that of

> impressing a lesson upon his memory, the result of which is that the resolution is converted into a . . . really efficient agency.[35]

For Peirce, the ideals of conduct are not static. They must be revised in the light of personal experience. We review our conduct, asking first whether it conformed to our resolution, second whether it conformed to our rules, and third whether it was in accord with our ideal. At each stage, an affirmative answer is marked by a pleasurable feeling of satisfaction. When we are dissatisfied, it is necessary not only to review the relationships among conduct, resolution, rule and ideal; but also, the suitability of our original ideals. Peirce summed it up this way:

> The experience of life is continually contributing instances more or less illuminative. These are digested first, not in the man's consciousness, but in the depths of his reasonable being. The results come to consciousness later. But mediation seems to agitate a mass of tendencies and allow them more quickly to settle down so as to be really more conformed to what is fit for man.[36]

And once again we can see the "cheerful hope" at work. Peirce seems to assume that the course of experience will bring us closer to the truth even when we are considering moral questions. It brings us "examples more or less illuminating" that with proper processing leads us to know "what is fit for man." And this kind of forward looking reasoning fueled not only Pragmatists but much of the Progressive Era. For example, in 1906 Roscoe Pound, Dean of the Harvard Law School, trumpeted exactly these feelings when he argued that society was moving ever upward and that it was up to lawyers to become "conscious factors" who would promote "the course of legal development" and provide the moral leadership for a progressive society.[37]

It is clear, however, that neither Wright nor Holmes could join this parade. Wright described social change as being like the weather—it was not a case of "onward and upward" but that of a dynamic system that moved in accordance with its own unknown imperatives. Holmes agreed; but, even so, their skepticism had limits. They may not have believed in universal moral truths, but they did believe in the importance of morality. Every human society, they recognized, had a set of norms deeply embedded in its culture. To be a member of a community meant that a person had absorbed these norms so thoroughly that they often were invisible. Silently, they shaped one's perceptions, inclinations, and habits. This meant that adherence to these norms was often not a conscious choice—one helped a neighbor because refusing was unthinkable. Thus, even without a priori or teleological arguments, they understood that people could not be disconnected from the values that were so deeply entrenched in their perception of the world.

For a modern reader this view of morality may seem both over-bearing and naïve. It is over-bearing because it allows others to dictate moral conduct and thereby contradicts some basic notions of individuality, rationality, and autonomy. It is naïve because it seems to assume that all societies are homogeneous and generate a monolithic group of shared values. This cannot be true. We note, for example, that there are moral disagreements among families and other groups intimately bound up in the same social circle. But basic norms exist even if they do not settle every argument. We experience conflict; we rebel; we think we can do better. But the point is that there is a standard for judgment that transcends the individual and provides a shared framework within which the community will hold its members accountable.

It is important to recognize that Holmes lived in a time and place different from our own. For two hundred years his ancestors had lived in a tightly regulated New England society. Through that time, there had been controversies and even changes. The stern Puritan values that had been so well adapted to life in the wilderness had given way to a more relaxed regime. Boston had become educated, worldly, and prosperous. To accommodate this, Calvinism had given way to Unitarianism and, for some, Transcendentalism. Nevertheless, their basic worldview persisted. The result was an established moral and religious order that formed the core of Holmes's community. Thus, while we often associate moral positivism with skepticism and amorality, Holmes thought of it in terms of a community that had conditioned them to fulfill the highest aspirations and the most strenuous duties.

The notions of high aspirations and strenuous duties may not seem to fit with the callous tone that Holmes struck in the *Bell* opinion and in his letters. Sometimes it is a long way from one's personal morality to a theory of jurisprudence. But, by examining a few cases, we can see how Holmes combined law with his conception of community values in order to arrive at a decision. We will look at two particular problems. The first is central to common law decision making and was a frequent issue during his tenure at the Massachusetts Supreme Judicial Court. The second concerns the limits of acceptable legislation and this question was common fare as he sat on the United States Supreme Court.

The first issue arises from the fact that the boundaries of a community are not necessarily the same as geographical boundaries. There were many different communities that resided in Boston. As a judge, however, Holmes had to act on behalf of geographical jurisdiction. Thus, as a justice on the Massachusetts Supreme Judicial Court, he acted for everyone within the state, not just for his own particular community. Holmes surely recognized this fact and knew that his values represented only a small sub-group of Boston residents. This being the case, should Holmes simply apply his own values? If not, what values should he apply? In general, how could any judge appeal to community values when the geographical community was value diverse?

Holmes's solution to this problem is evident in a case that he decided while on the Massachusetts Supreme Judicial Court.[38] It was a common law torts case. The plaintiff, Lamson, worked in a factory where he painted the handles of axes. When he finished an axe, he had to hang it on an overhead rack to dry. One day, he noticed that the pegs on the rack were loose and called the dangerous condition to the attention of his supervisor. The supervisor did nothing. Somewhat later, the peg gave way, allowing the axe to fall on Lamson's head. Holmes wrote the opinion, applying the doctrine of assumption of risk. This doctrine had two requirements: the first was that the plaintiff must know of the risk in question; the second was that he must voluntarily act in such a way as to incur the risk. If both requirements were met, then Lamson could not recover. Obviously, the issue in this case was the second requirement: Did the plaintiff voluntarily assume the risk? In Holmes's world of Brahmin Boston, it was clear that he had. Individuals were autonomous. Workers made their own decisions about what working conditions they would accept. In this world, if Lamson had continued working even after he knew of the dangers, it would follow that he did so because he thought that his wages adequately compensated him for the risk. On the other hand, a majority of the community would not have seen it this way. This group did not experience the employment relation as one of autonomy. Workers knew that bad and dangerous working conditions were so prevalent that they had no choice but to accept them. What the employer called autonomy, the worker understood to be coercion. In the context of this narrative, the plaintiff did not voluntarily accept the risk, and the doctrine did not apply. But as willing as Holmes might have been to accept the fact that different parts of the community would take different positions with respect to the case, he firmly pushed forward with the employer's position, stating: "[The plaintiff] stayed and took the risk. He did so none the less that the fear of losing his place was one of his motives."[39] And then he cited six cases and a legal treatise. In doing so, he referred to the common law and not to his own view of the situation. But, of course, the common law was not written by heavenly decree. Rather, by appealing to history and tradition, it reverted to an earlier time when the community was more homogenous—whether that homogeneity had been achieved by true consensus or by enforced silence.

The second problem involves the constitutional limits on legislation. Holmes's attitude toward this problem is explicit. In *Lochner v. New York*,[40] the majority held that a state attempt to limit the working hours of bakers violated the Due Process Clause of the Constitution. Holmes dissented, chiding the majority for turning the Due Process Clause into a set of substantive requirements that were heavily influenced by the social theories of Herbert Spencer. Like Wright, he rejected these theories as pure speculation, and, rejecting them, he interpreted the Constitution as allowing a wide latitude to states to enact such forms of social regulation as they saw fit. He concluded that the court should have refrained from imposing its social views on the State of New York. Communities, he argued, may have differing conceptions of the public interest; but, under the Constitution, that is their privilege. Thus, in constitutional cases, community values became the dominant consideration. In these cases, there was no need to worry about dissenting voices within the community since the assumption was that the legislative process had allowed the community to speak in one voice. The goal in these cases was to uphold the voice of the community against the claims of a Spenserian moral system. Lawyers and scholars have generally praised this way of framing the issues and, by the time Holmes left the court, his view had become the majority view.

The opinion in *Buck* displays this same structure. The state of Virginia had passed a law providing for the involuntary sterilization of the mentally "unfit." The procedure for utilizing this law included evidentiary hearings and independent judgments about whether sterilization would be in the best interest of the patient and society. The record established that all of these safeguards had been followed. Later investigation, however, indicated that the proceedings in the lower court were somewhat of a sham and that Carrie Buck herself had never been properly informed that the case was pending.[41] Not knowing this, Holmes therefore found it an easy case[42]—just as the Constitution allowed the state of New York to make its own decisions about the maximum hours for bakers, it permitted the state of Virginia to curtail the ability of Carrie Buck to have children.

One obvious feature of this decision is Holmes's total lack of empathy for Carrie Buck. A modern reader is struck by the fact that Holmes could not see the significant issues of personal autonomy that were present in the case. Could he really not see the difference between restricting procreation, on the one hand, and limiting working hours on the other? Was the right of a woman to have children really no more important than the right of a capitalist to employ people for sixty hours per week? These questions are important, and it is tempting to answer them with considerations of temperament (Holmes was an intellectual and a New Englander to boot), experience (Holmes himself was childless), intellectual context (he lived in a time when many considered this kind of social experiment as enlightened) and social context (it was also a time when few regarded the rights of women—and in particular the right to sexual autonomy—as being very important). These considerations are all true and are certainly relevant to assessing Holmes's limitations. However, I do not think that they get to the heart of the problem.

*Buck* is a good example of how morality and law operated in Holmes's constitutional jurisprudence. The problem is not that he sees no role for morality. Presumably, there were some legislative enactments that Holmes could not have upheld. What would he have done, for example, if the legislature of Virginia had decided to kill the feeble-minded? Rather the problem is with the particular kind of morality that he brings to bear. The New England moral tradition was inward facing rather than outward facing. The Puritans did not come to the New World as missionaries seeking to benefit others. Their purpose was to seek a deeper relationship with their God. This is how they understood goodness. They did not credit good works for their own sake, but only as an external sign of the virtue within. Service meant service to the family, to one's neighbors, and to the wider religious community. Empathizing with strangers was not part of the moral equation.

This outlook was deeply engraved in Holmes's character. Holmes admired Emerson, and like Emerson, he sought to live a spiritual life. Indeed, he understood this intention as the highest form of virtue. We can understand what this means when we consider these words from Emerson's *Self-Reliance*:

> Trust thyself: every heart vibrates to that iron string. Accept the place the divine providence has found for you, the society of your contemporaries, the connection of events. Great men have always done so, and confided themselves childlike to the genius of their age, betraying their perception that the absolutely trustworthy was seated at their heart, working through their hands, predominating in all their being. And we are now men, and must accept in the highest mind the same transcendent destiny; and not minors and invalids in a protected corner, not cowards fleeing before a revolution, but guides, redeemers, and benefactors, obeying the Almighty effort, and advancing on Chaos and the Dark.[43]

Holmes did not isolate himself from other people, other times, and other places. He read voraciously but the experience of others always became moral lessons that could be applied to his own path through life. For example, when he read a book by Fridtjof Nansen, the Norwegian explorer who had undertaken a nearly fatal trip to the Arctic, he was interested in the adventure. But what he found in the book was an inward lesson—a new metaphor for his own life. He saw his study of law as embodying the same stages that Nansen identified in describing in his trip to the Pole. Given the introverted nature of his outlook, it is not surprising that he had so little empathy or compassion for Carrie Buck or Henry Lamson.

This does not mean that Holmes was a bad judge. Indeed, there were very few judges in 1927 that would have ruled in favor of Carrie Buck. There was only one dissent in the case and that was from a devout Catholic whose religion prohibited any form of birth control. And there was nothing controversial about the court's decision in Lamson. It not only followed established doctrine but it was totally in line with a series of doctrines that made it impossible for employees like Henry Lamson to recover for their injuries. Thus, there is no need for a special explanation of the outcome of these cases. What needs explanation is the enthusiasm which Holmes brought to the task of ruling against these plaintiffs. "Three generations of imbeciles is enough" is not the cry of a man who is compassionate and respectful of others.

Compassion is an important virtue and one that I treasure in my friends. But I am not certain what role it should play in the deliberations of an appellate judge. Traditional jurisprudence assumes that the judge will occupy a distant and impartial space—one that is unmoved by feelings and sympathy. Despite this, I believe that judgments made in such a space are not entirely satisfactory. On the one hand, I recognize that we need a certain distance in order to see the bigger picture and to recognize competing interests. But I also suspect that a closer, more intimate look would help us to understand nuance and what is at stake for each of the parties.[44] Is it possible that judges could cultivate both kinds of sensitivity? I don't know. What I do know is that I would not like to be a party to a lawsuit where the legal system fails to notice that I am entirely absent and unaware of the proceedings. Carrie Buck certainly deserved better.

## CONCLUSION

The discussion of Holmes's positivism has a long and confusing history. Positivism became the convenient label for discussing Holmes's faults as a judge, but it did not shed much light on the subject. From a modern perspective, Holmes's deference to state legislatures made him too slow to recognize the fundamental rights of individual citizens. I have argued that this results from the substance of his moral views rather from a denial of the relevance of morality. Those who find him inadequate in this regard face a daunting task. They must define a moral view, provide normative justification for it, and show that it works well in its application to American Constitutional Law. Lacking this, the Supreme Court has become increasingly political as each side attempts to vindicate their own moral commitments. This, perhaps, is just as Holmes may have feared.

## NOTES

1. Oliver Wendell Holmes, Jr. "The Path of the Law," *Boston Law School Magazine*, 1, no. 4 (February, 1897): 2.

2. Holmes, Jr. "The Path of the Law," 2.

3. Ben Palmer, "Holmes, Hobbes, and Hitler," *American Bar Association Journal* 31, no. 11 (November 1945): 573.

4. Lon L. Fuller, *The Law in Quest of Itself* (Boston: Beacon Press, 1966).

5. See Mark DeWolfe Howe, *The Positivism of Mr. Justice Holmes*, 64 Harv. L. Rev. 529 (1951); Mark DeWolfe Howe, *Holmes' Positivism—A Brief Rejoinder*, 64 Harv. L. Rev. 937 (1951); Lon L. Fuller, *Positivism and Fidelity to Law—A Reply to Professor Hart*, 71 Harv. L. Rev. 630 (1958); but see H. L. A. Hart, *Holmes' Positivism—An Addendum*, 64 Harv. L. Rev. 929 (1951); H. L. A. Hart, *Positivism and the Separation of Law and Morals*, 71 Harv. L. Rev. 593 (1958).

6. Howe, *The Positivism of Mr. Justice Holmes*, 531.
7. Albert W. Alschuler, *Law without Values: The Life, Work and Legacy of Justice Holmes* (Chicago: University of Chicago Press 2000), 24 (citing Holmes to Pollock, Feb. 1920, in 2 *Holmes-Pollock Letters* at 36).
8. Alschuler, *Law without Values*, 27 (citing Holmes to J. H. Wigmore Nov. 1915, quoted in Novick, *Honorable Justice*, 469).
9. Alschuler, *Law without Values,* 28 (citing Holmes to Frankfurter Sept. 1921 in *Holmes and Frankfurter, Their Correspondence*, 124–25,
10. *Buck v. Bell* 274 U.S. 200 (1927).
11. *Buck v. Bell* 274 U.S. 207
12. *Buck v. Bell* 274 U.S.
13. For a factual description of the ins and outs of the Buck case, see Adam Cohen, *Imbeciles: The Supreme Court, American Eugenics, and the Sterilization of Carrie Buck* (New York: Penguin Press, 2016).
14. The logical positivist credited only two sorts of statements with cognitive meaning. The first were statements that were logically deducible from sense data and the second were analytic statements. See generally the arguments in Alfred J. Ayer, *Language, Truth, and Logic* (Mineola, NY: Dover Books, 1952).
15. John Austin, *The Province of Jurisprudence Determined* (London: John Murray, 1861).
16. H. L. A. Hart, *The Concept of Law* (Oxford: Oxford University Press, 1961), 78–79.
17. H. L. A. Hart, *Positivism and the Separation of Law and Morals*, 71, no. 4 (February 1958): 601.
18. The thesis provides that law and morality were separate in the following way: it could not follow from the mere fact that a rule violated standards of morality that it was not a rule of law; and, conversely, it could not follow from the mere fact that a rule was morally desirable that it was a rule of law. Hart, *Positivism and the Separation of Law and Morals*, 599.
19. Hart argues: Some laws require men to act in certain ways or to abstain from acting whether they wish to or not. The criminal law consists largely of rules of this sort: like commands they are simply "obeyed" or "disobeyed." But other legal rules are presented to society in quite different ways and have quite different functions. They provide facilities more or less elaborate for individuals to create structures of rights and duties for the conduct of life within the coercive framework of the law. Such are the rules enabling individuals to make contracts, wills, and trusts, and generally to mould their legal relations with others. Such rules, unlike the criminal law, are not factors designed to obstruct wishes and choices of an antisocial sort. On the contrary, these rules provide facilities for the realization of wishes and choices. They do not say (like commands) "do this whether you wish it or not," but rather "if you wish to do this, here is the way to do it." Under these rules we exercise powers, make claims, and assert rights. Hart, *Positivism and the Separation of Law and Morals*, 604.
20. Lewis Carroll, "What the Tortoise said to Achilles," in *Readings on Logic*, Irving M. Copi and James A. Gould, eds. (New York: Macmillan, 1972), 117.
21. Carroll, "What the Tortoise said to Achilles," 118–19 and 119–20.
22. Ludwig Wittgenstein, *Philosophical Investigations*, section 201. The translation is by Kripke. See Saul Kripke, *Wittgenstein: On Rules and Private Language* (1982).
23. There are a number of ways of interpreting or explaining the Wittgensteinian point. The example I give was inspired by Kripke's interpretation. See note 22.
24. Michal Dummet, the philosopher and logician, makes the exact same point with respect to formal logic:

> A proof proceeds according to certain logical principles or rules of inference. We are inclined to suppose that once we have accepted the axioms from which the proof starts, we have, as it were, no further active part to play; when the proof is shown us, we are mere passive spectators. But in order to follow the proof, we have to recognize various transitions as applications of the general rules of inference. Now even if these rules had been explicitly formulated at the start, and we had given our assent to them, our doing so would not in itself constitute recognition of each transition as a correct application of the rules. . . . Hence at each step we are

free to choose to accept or reject the proof; there is nothing in our formulation of the axioms and of the rules of inference, and nothing in our minds when we accepted these before the proof was given, which of itself shows whether we shall accept the proof or not; and hence there is nothing which forces us to accept the proof. If we accept the proof, we confer necessity of the theorem proved; we "put it in the archives" and will count nothing as telling against it. In doing this we are making a new decision, and not merely making explicit a decision we had already made implicitly. Michael Dummett, "Wittgenstein's Philosophy of Mathematics," in *Readings in the Philosophy of Mathematics: Selected Readings*, Paul Benacerraf and Hilary Putnam, eds. (Upper Saddle River, NJ: Prentice-Hall, 1964), 491.

25. See Hantzis, "Innovation within the Wider Intellectual Tradition, Oliver Wendell Holmes and the Pragmatic Theory of Law," *Northwestern Law Review* 82, no. 3 (Spring, 1988): 541–95.

26. Holmes, "The Path of the Law," 3.

27. Holmes, "The Path of the Law," 2–3.

28. Holmes, "The Path of the Law," 2–3.

29. See Louis Menand, *The Metaphysical Club: A Story of Ideas in America* (New York: Farrar, Strauss and Giroux, 2001).

30. For a discussion of Wright's influence, see Frederic Kellogg, *Oliver Wendell Holmes Jr., Legal Theory and Judicial Restraint* (Cambridge, Cambridge University Press, 2007), 41–42, and sources there cited.

31. Chaucey Wright, "The Philosophy of Herbert Spencer," in *Philosophical Discussions* (New York: Henry Holt and Co. 1878), 57–58.

32. Charles Sanders Peirce, *Collected Papers*, Vol. 5, Charles Hartshorne and Paul Weiss, eds. (Cambridge: Belknap Press, 1934), 384.

33. *CP* 5.407.

34. *CP* 1.592.

35. *CP* 1.592.

36. *CP* 1.599.

37. Pound, Roscoe, "The Need of a Sociological Jurisprudence." *Green Bag*, 19, no. 10 (October, 1907): 615.

A Bench and Bar trained in individualist theories and firm in the persuasion that the so-called legal justice is an absolute and a necessary standard, from which there may be no departure without the destruction of the legal order, may retard but cannot prevent progress to the newer standard recognized by the sociologist. In this progress lawyers should be conscious factors, not unconscious followers of popular thought, not conscious obstructers of the course of legal development.

See also Brandeis, Louis and Warren, Samuel, *The Right to Privacy*, 4 Harvard L. Rev. 193 (1890) where the authors argued for recognition of an expanded right to privacy based upon an analysis of an historical tendency in that direction.

38. *Lamson v. American Axe Tool Co*, 177 Mass. 144 (Mass. 1900).

39. *Lamson v. American Axe Tool Co*, 177 Mass. 144 (Mass. 1900).

40. 198 U.S. 45 (1905).

41. The administrator of the asylum arranged for a lawyer to represent Ms. Buck. It does not appear however that he or the lawyer ever informed her of the proceedings. Indeed she never really understood what had happened to her until much later. For the full story, see Adam Cohen, *Imbeciles: The Supreme Court, American Eugenics, and the Sterilization of Carrie Buck.*

42. It is apparent that respect for the patient's due process rights was essential to the validity of the statute. In reaching his decision Holmes was careful to state: "There can be no doubt that, so far as procedure is concerned, the rights of the patient are most carefully considered, and, as every step in this case was taken in scrupulous compliance with the statute and after months of

observation, there is no doubt that, in that respect, the plaintiff in error has had due process of law." 198 U.S. 200, 201.

43. Ralph Waldo Emerson, "Self-Reliance," in *Essays, First Series*, 49–100 (Philadelphia: David McKay, 1891), 53–54.

44. I develop these views about judging in Catharine Wells, "Situated Decision-Making," *University of Southern California Law Review*, 63, no. 6 (September, 1990): 1727–47.

## BIBLIOGRAPHY


Alschuler, Albert W. *Law without Values: The Life, Work and Legacy of Justice Holmes*. Chicago: University of Chicago Press 2000.

Austin, John. *The Province of Jurisprudence Determined.* London: John Murray, 1861.

Ayer, Alfred J. *Language, Truth, and Logic.* Mineola, NY: Dover Books, 1952.

Brandeis, Louis and Warren, Samuel. "The Right to Privacy." *Harvard Law Review* 4, no. 5 (December, 1890): 193–220.

Carroll, Lewis. "What the Tortoise said to Achilles." In *Readings on Logic*, edited by Irving M. Copi and James A. Gould, 117. New York: Macmillan, 1972.

Cohen, Adam. *Imbeciles: The Supreme Court, American Eugenics, and the Sterilization of Carrie Buck.* New York: Penguin Press, 2016.

Dummett, Michael. *Wittgenstein's Philosophy of Mathematics.* In *Readings in the Philosophy of Mathematics: Selected Readings*, edited by Paul Benacerraf and Hilary Putnam, 491. Upper Saddle River, NJ: Prentice-Hall, 1964.

Emerson, Ralph Waldo. "Self-Reliance." In *Essays, First Series*, 49–100. Philadelphia: David McKay, 1891.

Fuller, Lon. *The Law in Quest of Itself.* Boston: Beacon Press, 1966.

Hantzis, Catharine Wells, "Innovation within the Wider Intellectual Tradition, Oliver Wendell Holmes and the Pragmatic Theory of Law." *Northwestern Law Review* 82, no. 3 (Spring, 1988): 541–95.

Hart, H. L. A. *The Concept of Law.* Oxford: Oxford University Press, 1961.

———. "Positivism and the Separation of Law and Morals." *Harvard Law Review* 71, no. 4 (February 1958): 593–629.

Holmes, Oliver Wendell, Jr. "Brown University Commencement" [1897]. In *Collected Legal Papers*, 164–66. New York: Peter Smith, 1952.

———. "The Path of the Law," *Boston Law School Magazine* 1, no. 4 (February, 1897): 1–18.

Kellogg, Frederic. *Oliver Wendell Holmes Jr., Legal Theory and Judicial Restraint.* Cambridge: Cambridge University Press, 2007.

Menand, Louis. *The Metaphysical Club: A Story of Ideas in America.* New York: Farrar, Strauss and Giroux, 2001.

Nansen, Fridtjof. *Farthest North: The Norwegian Polar Expedition (1893–1896).* New York: Harper and Brothers, 1897.

Palmer, Ben W. "Holmes, Hobbes, and Hitler." *American Bar Association Journal* 31, no. 11 (November 1945): 569–73.

Peirce, Charles S. *Collected Papers of Charles Sanders Peirce*, Vol. 1 *Principles of Philosophy*; Vol. 5 *Pragmatism and Pragmaticism*, edited by Charles Hartshorne and Paul Weiss. Cambridge: Belknap Press, Vol. 1 1931; Vol. 5 1934.

Pound, Roscoe. "The Need of a Sociological Jurisprudence." *Green Bag,* 19, no. 10 (October, 1907): 607–15.

Wittgenstein, Ludwig. *Philosophical Investigations* section 201, translated by Kripke. In Saul Kripke, *Wittgenstein: On Rules and Private Language.* Oxford: Blackwell, 2007.

Wright, Chauncey. "The Philosophy of Herbert Spencer." In *Philosophical Discussions*. New York: Henry Holt and Co. 1878, 43–96

Wells, Catharine Pierce. "Situated Decision-Making." *University of Southern California Law Review* 63, no. 6 (September, 1990): 1727–47.

*Lamson v. American Axe Tool Co*, 177 Mass. 144 (Mass. 1900).

*Buck v. Bell* 274 U.S. 200 (1927).

*Lochner v. New York* 198 U.S. 45 (1905).

# *Chapter Seven*

# The Realist

Brian E. Butler

Oliver Wendell Holmes Jr. is virtually an automatic inclusion in any discussion of legal realism. And the realists took Holmes's work, especially, the "The Path of the Law," to be a central intellectual origin point of legal realism. Legal realists almost universally built their program off Holmes's prediction theory of the law and his anti-formalism. Indeed, the realists, not normally a coherent and disciplined school, were unified in looking upon Holmes as their patron saint. Jerome Frank offers Holmes as the example of his "ideal" judge, embodying the essential judicial virtues of self-mastery, overcoming of the infantile need for father authority found in the quest legal certainty. Holmes is for Frank the first "completely adult jurist," exemplifying properly realist virtues such as non-Euclidian legal thinking and an enlightened skepticism.[1] For Karl Llewellyn, Holmes was "this nation's most distinguished citizen."[2] Indeed, the godlike versions of Holmes offered by his legal realist followers seem like extreme caricature at times.[3] According to Wilfrid Rumble, "No man was more consistently or generously extolled by the legal realists. The adulation became so great, indeed, that in 1941 one scholar compared the impact of Holmes upon legal thought to that of Kant upon philosophical reflection."[4]

It is therefore quite informative to notice the aspects of Holmes's scholarship and judicial opinions that the realists admired. This chapter will trace many of these connections. But, perhaps more importantly, it will also draw distinctions between Holmes's writings and the work of the realists. Indeed, while the commonalities are important, multiple, and often quite obvious, the differences are often more enlightening. Further, the differences, while being ones of emphasis, actually tend to create a different picture of law. In order to clarify the differences, the first requirement will be to construct a clear understanding of what the legal realists generally stood for. This is no simple project. Understanding what Holmes's jurisprudence entails is complex as well.

While there are difficulties, they are not impossible to overcome as long as certain expectations are not indulged in. Most importantly, it would be most ironic to expect a conceptually complete definition of either the legal realist project or of Holmes's jurisprudence. One of the central tenets they had in common was a suspicion of the possibility or usefulness of such definitional strategies. Both Holmes and the legal realists shared a suspicion of false ideas of accuracy, completeness or determinateness. Indeed, it is one of the ironies of the literature on both Holmes and the realists that some such definition is often expected and the lack of such a definition is seen as cause for lamentation even after the skepticism towards such goals is clearly expressed. A lack of clear definitional boundaries, on the other hand, does not entail the conclusion that there is no "core" to both projects. So, in the next section the identification of a set of core attributes of legal realism will be aimed for. The list will not be offered as exhaustive or complete. Then the same strategy will be used to identify some of the most important aspects of Holmes's thought. From this an understanding of just how much of a legal realist Holmes was will be constructed.

## LEGAL REALISM

As stated above, it is a commonplace that legal realism is difficult to understand because it was not a coherent school and did not have an official creed. Indeed, the central figures of the group thought of as legal realists, Jerome Frank and Karl Llewellyn, were not fully comfortable with the label themselves. That being said, there is an extensive literature that attempts to identify what legal realism is.

Not surprisingly, contemporary scholarship is inconsistent on what legal realism was. One group, of which Brian Tamanaha can serve as an example, considers the realists to have been ultimately quite banal and anything but radical. Tamanaha ultimately sees the realist story of realists versus formalists as a distorting myth.[5] This is because, according to Tamanaha, "legal professionals regularly remarked that judges used various techniques to alter, avoid, or overrule precedents, even when they did not openly admit it."[6] Therefore, "except for the handful of realists who actually conducted social scientific studies—they were hardly distinguishable from many other law professors, judges, and legislators in the period who were busily engaged in developing substantive legal rules and doctrines in ways that adjusted to and addressed the new social, material, and economic circumstances of their vastly changed society."[7] Under this conception, then, the legal realists just highlighted an aspect of legal practice that was generally acknowledged but not foregrounded—that black letter law is not sufficient to decide many cases. But this was already understood, so such an emphasis was trivial in import.

Another quite banal interpretation of legal realism is offered in the legal realist reader, *American Legal Realism*, edited by Fisher, Horwitz, and Reed. They argue that as a matter of history, legal realism followed from Roscoe Pound's sociological jurisprudence and that the realists constructed a model of a new law school scholar that resulted in the various "law ands" that populate the legal academy today. When trying to identify important aspects beyond this historical placement they offer up an incredibly broad conception of the realist creed, "the most useful definition of legal realism is a generous one. The heart of the movement was an effort to define and discredit classical legal theory and practice and to offer in their place a more philosophically and politically enlightened jurisprudence."[8] If Tamanaha's version of legal realism is bland because it is already true to the profession, this version is bland because it is virtually devoid of any content other than progressive aspirations and a general pluralism.

If Tamanaha or Fisher, Horwitz, and Reed are correct, then legal realism is indeed a banal and largely uninteresting moment in U.S. legal history. But this view is not generally held. Indeed, a more sensitive and more nuanced understanding of the legal realist program finds important specifics that the above accounts ignore. For instance, Laura Kalman in *Legal Realism at Yale* argues that it was true the realists were banal in one sense, in that it was a palace revolution—that is, it was a fight among professional legal academics over the image of proper legal scholarship. But they offered specific content in the fight. In analyzing the evolution of case books from "cases" to a model of "cases and materials on," Kalman notes that the materials of legal education options were broadened as a result of realists. This is, of course, the move to various "law ands."

But at least as significantly, they advocated for a turn to a functionalist analysis and away from a tradition dominated by practices focused upon deductive applications of the results of conceptual analysis. Combined with this move from concept-based reasoning was a shift to temporal perspective. Kalman also brings in some further contextual analysis of legal realism's institutional location, seeing realism as located primarily at Yale and Columbia and motivated at least partially by an anti-Harvard attitude exemplifying a struggle for status within the profession. William Twining also emphasizes that legal realism was engaged in problems of professionalization and academization of legal education but that it added the foregrounding of dynamic over static aspects of law—therefore focusing on "law in action."[9]

Brian Leiter highlights another claim of legal realism as core. This is that "judges respond primarily to the stimulus of the facts."[10] That is, rather than focusing on the rules, the fact situation is claimed to be the more determinant aspect of a legal decision. He notes that this is evidence against a "postmodern" picture of legal realism where the emphasis is supposedly upon the indeterminacy of legal rules. It is rather that the legal realists claimed that a broader set of facts must be observed to find what determined judicial decision-making. In his words, some "nonlaw" facts are needed in order to actually make the determinations necessary for legal decisions. The legal realists therefore emphasized types of situations rather than categories of legal concepts. He, finally, argues that the realists turned towards a more naturalistic theory of jurisprudence because the classical account, both in legal education and in legal theory, "relies on two central argumentative devices—analysis of concepts and appeals to intuition—that are epistemologically bankrupt."[11]

Others note that for the realists law is seen not so much as a rule-based project as a social activity or institution. Morton White in *Social Thought in America* notes that the realist attack on formalism leads to "intensive study of history and theories of legislation in order to explain the meanings of certain legal terms and rules and why they emerged when they did."[12] This, of course, would be thought of as just one aspect of the naturalized jurisprudence project and the broadening of materials relevant to jurisprudential analysis. Another aspect is highlighted by Hanoch Dagan. Dagan claims that the realists' most important insight was that law was a dynamic institution that "embodies three sets of constitutive tensions" that cannot be eliminated without distorting the practice. These are tensions between power and reason, science and craft, and tradition and progress. Indeed, for Dagan what is most distinctive about law is the difficult yet necessary accommodation of these constitutive tensions.[13]

A very historically informed and subtle reading of realist thought in its social context is offered in N. E. H. Hull in *Roscoe Pound and Karl Llewellyn: Searching for an American Jurisprudence*. Therein Hull ultimately concludes that, "If the essence of twentieth-century American jurisprudence is not a set body of doctrine (or anti-doctrine), but a search based on the latitude of the bricoleurs and the proclivities of networkers, then we must stop looking for the core of realist thought or any other persuasion's thought and try to follow the human story."[14] Of course, this chapter would argue that if a "core" is thought of as a set of dominant factors the project can be continued and the human story of social bricolage can be included as one of the factors. What Hull's analysis does show is something that the realists would wholeheartedly agree with—that law seen in context, with this context including general social patterns and individual personalities, is more effectively understood than law analyzed as a domain understood best through manipulation of legal concepts.

Complementing Hull's work, another part of a legal realist thought as a story rooted in human life, individual and institutional, is highlighted in John Henry Schlegel's *American Legal Realism and Empirical Social Science*.

This tells the story of the members of the informal realist school that attempted to do empirical social science of law, such as Walter Wheeler Cook, Underhill Moore, Charles E. Clark, William O. Douglas, Herman Oliphant, Leon Marshall, and Hessel Yntema. An experimental method was adopted rather than the professionalized conception of a specifically "legal" conceptual knowledge.[15] The focus on conceptual analysis was seen as an obstructive activity of boundary maintenance practiced by a professional "union" against challenges to craft.[16] From this came a move towards emphasizing curriculum with such practice-oriented tools as the law school clinic and moot court.[17]

There was a large overlap between the legal realists and the New Deal. Marcus Curtis argues that in order to understand legal realism it must be seen in the context of the New Deal. Indeed, for him the New Deal was realism actualized. This is not only because so many of the realists were employed in the New Deal, but just as importantly because New Deal projects and Supreme Court decisions exemplified four core features of realism—rule skepticism (rules as verbal excuses), a functional approach, commitment to social science as realistic tool, and less central but still important, judicial modesty. More broadly, law was seen "as a form of socially informed expertise and as a tool for shaping social policy."[18] Curtis gives as a central example, *Wickard v. Filburn* where a functional approach was used by the Supreme Court to uphold a New Deal law under the Constitution's Commerce Clause. As opposed to the earlier categorical approach of *A. L. A. Schecter Poultry* and *Carter v. Carter Coal* which had used a categorical approach based upon definitional concepts that found essential differences between commerce, manufacturing, and production, *Wickard v. Filburn* used a functional approach that looked to systemic effects. Curtis claims in fact that the case used all four aspects of realism to get to its result.[19]

Roy Kreitner echoes Curtis's approach and also argues that a proper understanding of legal realism must include the activities of the realists in order to see realism in action.[20] The activities of governmental agencies and broader social institutions are seen as relevant, thus reinforcing earlier claims that one important core claim of legal realism is the inclusion of a much larger set of facts in analysis of the legal. Kreitner specifically gives Felix Cohen as an example of a realist that was heavily involved in Native American policy in the Department of the Interior. Thurman Arnold also is noted in that he was head of the Antitrust Division of the Justice Department. Kreitner argues that the "first lesson of realist lives for realist jurisprudence" is that, "while it is of course important to understand norms and normativity, it is at least as important to comprehend law institutionally."[21] Law must be understood as an organic enterprise. This entails a much broader picture of law jobs that is "vastly more inclusive" than the classical story.[22] Law is a mode of social ordering—but one that encompasses a great variety of institutional forms. Any tendency to seize upon one of these as essential must be suspect.

As seen from this survey of scholarship a variety of claims are attributed to the legal realists. First, and almost universally, they are thought to aim to discredit a traditional, "classical," Langdellian concept-driven and rule-based legal theory. In this they are seen as skeptical of a concept of law centered upon the application of rules. The realists emphasize the centrality of empirical facts. Further, the legal realists were engaged in a fight for professional status within the legal academy. Combine this internal fight with an emphasis on material broader than case law and you get the start of various "law ands." Also emphasized was a temporal and dynamic perspective towards law. The legal realists, according to the scholarship also demanded that law be investigated as a social institution and that the social tensions involved be faced. This allowed them to be flexible towards law as a system—thereby enabling them to help with New Deal projects and the rise of the administrative state. They also advocated a turn to a functional analysis of law and the use of the social sciences to both understand law and to make it more reliable. As will be seen in the next section, all of these traits are, indeed, aspects of the conception of law that the legal realists offered. But, as the realists were never a fully coherent group, there are also important nuances that make the human story of legal realism more challenging.

## THREE CASE STUDIES IN REALIST THOUGHT

In this section the legal theory of three realist thinkers will be investigated. Karl Llewellyn, Jerome Frank, and Felix Cohen will serve as case studies in legal realist thought. They did not always agree—as would be expected. But it is universally agreed that they were three of the most important and most representative legal realists.

As he was considered the most central figure of the legal realists, and was the most vocal in defending its legitimacy, it is appropriate to start with Karl N. Llewellyn. While his career was broad-ranging and his theoretical interests were many, in Llewellyn's writings a consistent set of attitudes can be discerned. Jerome Frank thought that Llewellyn best exemplified the legal realist stance of rule skepticism—that is, skepticism towards the idea that rules can be determinative of legal decisions. And, indeed, Llewellyn did emphasize that while lawyers talk a lot about rules, it is not always clear what this really means or what function the rules, actually as opposed to supposedly, serve. Further, Llewellyn was not sure that the application of rules was always an effective means for the ends in view.[23] And, he emphasized, if rules did function at all, this is only because they were embedded within "teamplay" and "institutional patterns."[24]

In his classic book, *The Bramble Bush*, he noted that the rule of law as ideal type involving the deduction of decisions from legal concepts dominated legal education. He claimed that, to the contrary, "students who come eager to learn the rules and who do learn them, *and who learn nothing more*, will take away the shell and not the substance. We have discovered that rules *alone*, mere forms of words, are worthless."[25] Instead for the student to learn law as it really is, they must have concrete instances. For him, law business is about solving disputes, both actual and potential. And, because disputes do not arise conveniently labelled under legal categories a study of the facts was always most important. This includes the facts of legal decision making. Indeed, "*What these officials do about disputes is, to my mind, the law itself.*"[26] Official action rather than conceptual analysis becomes central to an understanding of law.

Therefore, the main aspect that legal education should focus on is accurate description of legal practice in order to arrive at reliable predictions of what officials are going to do. As opposed to the picture of law as a set of game rules structuring behavior, Llewellyn emphasizes its dispute resolving role, where its function is "Less as *making* order than as *maintaining* order when it has gotten out of order."[27] Further, Llewellyn emphasizes the importance of the fact situation—"the facts are hardy weeds. They will not down. Whatever the theory, courts of review of 'pure law' feel the pressure of the individual case, and strain to decide it right."[28] This, in turn, creates constant tensions between rules and facts that cannot easily be harmonized: "The nature of institutions is that they grow around our needs and partly serve them. The nature of institutions is also that they almost never serve those needs to satisfaction. Hence all the detailed technique of our law procedure is not only better seen, but better judged, by following the purposes concerned. In their light and in their light only you see whether the technique is a good one or a bad, a wasteful one or an efficient, a fossil or a living organ."[29] This, of course, is the functionalism identified above, combined with a dynamic and situation-based understanding of legal institutions.

Llewellyn worries about what he describes as the "unconscious snobbery of social institutions" which embodies a "faith that the current rationalizations of the institution fit the facts and exhaust the subject."[30] In opposition to this, he argues that analysis of legal institutions requires experimental tests. Law should use an empirical, experimental, and functionalist scientific approach to prediction as far as possible.[31] Further, legal theory and education needs to be forward looking—because the real use of law, and the real tensions involved are in service of dealing with new facts and new situations.

Llewellyn's focus upon prediction of legal decisions allows him to develop a conception of law that sees the broader practices, the teamplay and institutional aspects of practice as legitimate jurisprudential material. Therefore, as opposed to a rule and application conception of law, "Law *is*, to the community, what law *does*."[32] And what law does, once again, is not to create the basic order. The basic order of society comes before law. Law's functional place is dispute resolution. Indeed, law "operates upon the fringe" and must develop changing flexible instruments to respond to newly arising legal challenges.[33] *The Cheyenne Way* brings these themes into stark relief. Therein, Llewellyn (with E. Adamson Hoebel) looks to identify the practice of "law-stuff" outside of Anglo-American assumptions of what law must look like. That is, to identify "law-stuff" and "legality" without the rigid assumptions of his specific culture keeping other options from view. He argues that instead of looking to the technical tools of law, just look at its function which is "handling trouble and of channeling behavior."[34] From this, Llewellyn distills lessons from the Cheyenne that could help overcome the unhelpful dogmas of Anglo-American legal theory.

Another telling aspect of Llewellyn's thought is a skepticism towards the attempt to define law. Law is, first, too vast and disparate a subject. Furthermore, and more broadly, "a concept, as I understand it, is built for a purpose. It is a thinking tool. It is to make your data more manageable in doing something, in getting somewhere with them.[35] Any definition of law is to be adopted given the purpose pursued. Therefore, a definition of law as a set of rules is fine, if it is used for a legitimate purpose. But if such a definition is just used to constrain the investigation of legal practice, is offered as an exhaustive and exclusive "True" definition, it becomes an obstruction. Better to note that there is some relation between law, rules, and behavior but investigate empirically just what the relationship is. Llewellyn thought the received view of law as set of rules and concepts was an inadequate description of what happens in courts of law and the result of "a drive toward narrowing the categories of description" that mistakes "the merely available, the easily seen, for all there is to see."[36] Not only that, but it is motivated by a distorting urge to simplify "by *verbal* unification."[37] But, "to leave unstudied and almost wholly implicit the ideals and traditions of the crafts is to leave unspoken and undiscussed half of the guidance and control and soundness which lies in our actual going legal scheme of things."[38]

One recurring aspect of Llewellyn's legal theorizing is a suspicion of legal philosophy. This makes perfect sense when it is realized that for him "philosophical analysis" was a search for a true, totalizing theory based upon conceptual analysis and deductive form. In this case legal philosophy is the philosophical or academic analogue to Christopher Langdell's science of law. If this is what legal philosophy must be, then Langdell was properly suspicious. This is why he states that, "Realism was never a philosophy." Instead it is a research agenda, or as he puts it, a technology. Most basically, for him legal realism aims to ensure that "'see it fresh,' 'see it clear' and 'come back to make sure' are of the essence." These aims, "go to method. *That method is eternal*"—"*Realism* is *not* a philosophy. But a *technology*.

That is why it is eternal. The fresh look is always the fresh hope. The fresh inquiry into results is always the needed check-up."[39]

Llewellyn's understanding of the "working constitution" is a striking example of his theory in practice. He claims that the existing theory of constitution is misrepresentation of facts because in reality when dealing with the U.S. Constitution it is not language that controls, but rather institutional actions. Therefore, the language of the constitution and official doctrine are actually both "misdescriptive" and reference to them as controlling acts as "a refuge from responsibility."[40] To prove this claim, he notes the central and unavoidable fact that while judicial review is accepted practice, it is nowhere in the text of the document. Rather the practice is so habitual and accepted that any arguing against it is thought overtly radical.

Further, Llewellyn notes that conceptualizing the rule of law as rules is orthodox but absurd. If the law as a set of rules theory was accurate the quality of a judge would not matter, law would be static, and lawyers and judges would always agree.[41] Of course, this is all contrary to fact. Indeed, to hold to this theory in spite of the facts is an exercise in willful blindness—"The concentration of unseeingness which has made this possible must be regarded as a notable intellectual achievement."[42] The constitution rightly seen is more like a code, and therefore must be seen as an experiment that almost immediately needs the ability to grow and change. The problem is solved not through a literal reading of what the text says but rather by a proper understanding of what existing institutional practices allow at any moment. This only can be understood through an understanding of institutional habits which include ideals of what an institution should do. This is, in turn, a problem of "leeway and give" and must be understood through observation of habits.[43] Therefore, "A 'written constitution' is a system of unwritten practices in which the Document in question, by virtue of men's attitudes, has *a little influence*."[44]

Like Llewellyn, Jerome Frank also contrasted his legal theory from Langdellian formalism. In response to a claim like Tamanaha's that legal realism is banal because everybody in the legal profession knows that formalism is not sufficient, Frank notes, "The undiluted Langdell principles are nowhere in good repute today. But they are still the basic ingredient of legal pedagogy, so that, whatever else is mixed with them, the dominant flavor is still Langdellian. Our leading law schools are still library-law schools, book-law schools. They are not, as they should be, *lawyer-schools*."[45] And Frank thinks that even though the profession tries to distance itself from any admission of formalism, the underlying dominance of formalist assumptions creates a false picture, encourages "dupery" about how law really functions. Frank believes that it is better to look at law in terms of what the client worries about—and that is what the court will do. Therefore, at least a large part of legal education should focus upon the art of predicting court decisions. This goes against Langdellian claims and against its manifestation for Frank in "Bealism" where law is seen as "extra-experimental" and a "brooding omnipresence in the sky."[46] Frank identifies this as a hope for certainty based upon a "compensatory metaphysics" rooted in childish thought-ways. Further, Frank believes that, "The concealment of the human element in the judicial process allows that element to operate in an exaggerated manner; the sunlight of awareness has an antiseptic effect on prejudices."[47] Interestingly, according to Frank the basic myth aims at certainty, but, uncertainty in the law is often more desirable because socially valuable.[48] Therefore, legal practice should aim for "dynamic security" rather than replicable deductions.[49]

Famously, Frank described law as at least partially constructed as a father substitute standing in for the infant's need for certainty and safety. This infantile need for certainty manifests itself in various ways within legal thought. For instance, there is the desire for verbal certainty. As opposed to a static realm of certainty, though, the lawyer's real task is to "reconcile incompatibles" and bring about "practical adjustment." Because of this, "Realistic recognition of novel circumstances, tentativeness, adaptation, are of the very essence of the lawyer's invaluable technique."[50] Judges, therefore, are not oracles of law but creators of law, constructors of court decisions. In this process, "the judge's innumerable unique traits, dispositions and habits often get in their work in shaping his decisions not only in his determination of what he thinks is fair or just with reference to a given set of facts, but in the very processes by which he becomes convinced what those facts are."[51] The personality of the judge is, therefore, "the pivotal factor."[52] Of course, this is the theory that gets caricatured as the stance that what the judge had for breakfast becomes determinative of the decision. Frank's theory is much more nuanced than this and is more charitably described as pointing out that social factors, training, and psychological factors do have some predictive force in legal decision making, more predictive force than various formalist strategies would want to admit.

For instance, there is the current favorite of originalism. Frank finds the quest for originalist thought another version of father substitution. He also shows a strong skepticism towards the accuracy of historical explanation—such explanations he labels "Twistory."[53] As he puts it, "If there ever was an art calling for humility on the part of its practitioners, it is history writing. The first sentence of almost every history book should read, 'What follows consists of a series of guesses most of which are based on highly doubtful evidence—so doubtful that the reader is warned to take little of this book very seriously."[54] In his theory, an appeal to a determinant history in order to find meaning is one obvious example of the construction of false certainty in order to have a father surrogate. Originalism, that is, is a form of compensatory metaphysics.

Another important claim of Frank's, related to the problem of twistory, was that the "rule skepticism" of Llewellyn and other legal realists missed the major cause of legal uncertainty—the difficulty of ascertaining the actual facts of any legal controversy. Frank thought a very telling distinction was between the rule skeptics such as Llewellyn, who focused upon the difficulty of living up to a rule-based legal process, and the fact skeptics which, though agreeing with rule skepticism, found that the problem of legal facts was much more important and intractable. Frank saw this latter fact skepticism as being advocated for by a group of theorists, including "Dean Leon Green, Max Radin, Thurman Arnold, William O. Douglas (now Mr. Justice Douglas), and perhaps E. M. Morgan."[55] This group believed that the accurate identification of facts is the chief impediment to prophesying a court decision. Indeed, the court needs an accurate account of the relevant facts to decide which legal rule is applicable. Of course, an inability to determine the actual facts makes following precedent more difficult. Even assuming that there were clear rules, if the facts are unclear it is difficult to know how the rules should operate. Frank concludes that in current legal proceedings, "facts are guesses."[56]

He saves his most direct skepticism in this regard for the jury—claiming that at least the trial judge has a chance to become more able to detect facts through bench experience.[57] Here he thinks judicial expertise can control for some of the facts in a more systematic manner. The jury, by contrast, is portrayed as an exercise in arbitrariness, exemplifying unpredictable and arbitrary results because of consistent incompetence in the identification of facts. Another problem here is appellate court bias—a bias towards theory and doctrine rather than the determination of facts that fits very comfortably with Langdell's theory. Instead, Frank emphasizes the trial court and notes that the trial court is the virtually ignored real center of legal proceedings. Further aspects are in need of investigation. It is in this trial court realm that emphasis should be made towards the identification of truth instead of "sporting theory of justice" and where the "belief in an angelic community which can and will obey laws merely because they are enacted" can be challenged with accurate analysis.[58]

It is important to note that for Frank skepticism was not a stopping point but rather a starting point for a positive program. This program aimed to add a "fourth dimension to legal theory" wherein law would utilize "not mere intellectual but also artistic insights."[59] It would also note that "the leaky character of words is not *always* an unmixed evil. Isn't it, perhaps, lucky that 'democracy' was not frozen in meaning in 1800? Where would we be if the words in our Constitution had been given inflexible definitions?"[60] And once this quest for complete definition was discarded, with certainty and self-evident truth being lost, law could be regarded as an experimental and dynamic project.

It is important to note that Frank, like most of the so-called legal realists, was uncomfortable with that name. He noted that the term "legal realism" was borrowed from Llewellyn but that the problems with terminology made it not worth keeping.[61] He thought it better to describe his project as "constructive skepticism," "experimental jurisprudence," or theorists like him as "experimentalists."[62] These terms were meant to emphasize experimentation, adaptation, and novelty combined with a "zeal to reform."[63] Therefore, he wanted to focus upon the positive project rather than any specific content of the real. In this sense his descriptive critique was not an end but only the first step in a constructive forward-looking legal project.

Part of this project, the part most emphasized by readers of Frank (especially those that don't read past *Law and the Modern Mind*) is a focus upon creating better judges. He notoriously prescribes an agenda of "self discovery" for judges that includes psychoanalysis, though he concedes that this is a young and not fully developed science. More important is the much broader realization that the legal decision is "the thing" and the rules somewhat "incidental."[64] That is, the case is more important than the purported rules. In his opinion, fixating on rules and traditional legal ideology creates "judicial somnambulism" and "rule-fetishism." Realism, in contrast, holds that "Past decisions are experimental guides to prognostications of future decisions. And legal rules are mental devices for assembling, in convenient form, information about past cases to aid in making such prognostications."[65]

He thought good judicial models to start with were Marshall, Story, and Holmes because they were more aware of own thinking processes. Indeed, he claimed that to create a government of laws and not of men "legal machinery" is not enough—needed were operators who are conscious of their own limitations and these three were good models to start with.[66] But of these Holmes was thought closest to the ideal judge. Holmes was "the completely adult jurist."[67] This is because, first, Holmes emphasized the consequences of specific decisions. Most famously, this was centered in his "bad man" theory of law. Indeed, Frank relates that he was inspired by Holmes to look at what lawyers and courts actually do—actual decisions—in a chapter entitled "Holmes' 'Bad Man' Starts Something." Further, Holmes "began naturalistic thinking on the subject"; his aim was observation of legal activity, not a definition of law.[68] Because of Holmes's influence, the investigation of law looked at enforceable judgments—what courts do "in fact".[69] Importantly, Holmes held that rules are "embodiments of social policies, values, ideals" and therefore should be constantly re-examined.[70] In addition, Holmes was non-Euclidian in that he knew that certitude was not the test of certainty. This was seen in Holmes's use of history which helped develop enlightened skepticism towards the past, precedent, legal conceptions, etc.[71] Finally, Holmes properly observed that democracy is the only form of political organization open to experiment.[72]

The third case study in this chapter is of Felix S. Cohen. His version of realism, unsurprisingly, offers a different yet overlapping set of claims with those of Llewellyn and Frank. Cohen claimed, most importantly, that law had an implicit ethics, and that, "An Ethics, like a metaphysics, is no more certain and no less dangerous because it is unconsciously held."[73] Further, Cohen was trained in the philosophical tradition of the philosophy of language. He advocated for a stance whereby "A verbal definition is neither true nor false—it is convenient or misleading."[74] He combined this emphasis upon ethics and attention to language with an emphasis upon a science-inspired experimental program: "although some simple principle of legal criticism may be correct, we cannot be sure that it is correct without solving all the problems of positive science the consideration of which it proposed to avoid."[75] Therefore, empirical knowledge is key. Indeed, "'Realistic jurisprudence' has sprung in great measure from the recognition that principles enunciated by courts as grounds of decision often represented nothing more objective than a resolution to use sanctified words wherever specified results are dictated by undisclosed determinants."[76] Cohen contrasts realism with the fallacious practice of abstracting verbal rules out of empirical context and treating them as legally determinative and prior to the facts at hand. This practice is what he calls "transcendental nonsense."

Along the same lines, Cohen emphasizes the danger of an "aesthetic evaluation" of law.[77] Law, he claims, is always in danger of being dominated by a craftsman ethos, and this emphasizes aesthetic determinants internal to the practice rather than social results. Especially in academic analysis judgments are passed upon legal rules and cases in our law due to a broadly defined aesthetic appeal rather than empirical fact. Law reviews, he notes, bear most clearly the imprint of the aesthete. This can be seen when the rule or holding is judged not in terms of "What are its effects likely to be, in practice, and are these effects good or bad?" but rather in terms of "Does this rule or holding fit smoothly into some lovely pattern which some law teacher has found in the past cases, does it perhaps give a pleasing new turn to this pattern, or does it spoil the pattern?"[78] Instead of this Cohen emphasizes the need to look at all social forces, including social habits, institutional practices and how power is distributed. Formalism for Cohen is one of the most ubiquitous aesthetics in law. And formalism as an aesthetic is, Cohen admits, economical. But the problem of this aesthetic appeal for him is that it helps legal analysis avoid all the difficulties of law in the empirical world in favor of word-magic. Indeed, such formalist "Made-to-order legal philosophies make a virtue of judicial fatigue, bless judicial ignorance, and sanctify the impotence of law."[79]

As stated above, Cohen claimed that a scientific ethics should underlie legal decision making. This is because without an appeal to transcendental nonsense it is not logic but ethical judgment that underlies any but the most obvious legal decision. And, Cohen claims, an ethic is not informed without a proper understanding of the facts involved. Therefore, the concrete context of moral facts must be known to the court for the court to make an informed decision. As opposed to the idea that black letter law determines cases, Cohen claims that properly understood, traditional legal language and rules are "poetical or mnemonic devices for formulating decisions on other grounds."[80]

An example he gives of this is the legal personhood of specific social institutions. As he puts it, "The Supreme Court argued, 'A labor union can be sued because it is, in essential aspects, a person, a quasi-corporation.'" The realist will say, "A labor union is a person or quasi-corporation because it can be sued; to call something a person in law is merely to state, in metaphorical language, that it can be sued."[81] For him, the court's argument is as circular as Molière's physician's famous appeal to dormitive virtue.[82] Instead, a functional method must be adopted. In practice, this means that the analysis must first eliminate terms that cannot be translated into a functional test. Cohen notes that that will be very much like the elimination of philosophical pseudo-problems as practiced by Wittgenstein.[83]

Concepts should be redefined experimentally for technical use. Cohen cites Charles Sanders Peirce for this practice. He also gives credit to William James and thinks the courts should always look to the cash value of each concept. This means, most simply put, to investigate law and legal concepts in terms of consequences as opposed to "ceremonial adequacy."[84] This in turn requires constant attention to "non-legal" facts.

For Cohen it is most important to emphasize that through all of this analysis the centrality of ethical considerations must be faced. Decisions require some standard of value. Functionalists cannot just remain in the realm of cause and effect but must have some idea of import and value; otherwise, what is offered is just an infinite mass of trivial facts.[85] But, on the other hand, any standard of value is not separate from the facts but is tested and justified by its deep immersion in the facts.

Cohen ultimately offers a very concise description of realism: "realist jurisprudence, in essence, is the idea that rules, principles, and opinions do not exhaust or explain actual judicial decisions."[86] As Llewellyn and Frank also noted, Cohen claims that judges rest their decisions largely on unconscious values and unconscious metaphysics. Because of this, "Judges and non-judges who denounce metaphysics do not thereby escape from metaphysics" just because their metaphysics are uncritically accepted.[87] All judging requires a metaphysics and just because "inarticulate," the metaphysical is not avoided, but rather just dogmatically held. Indeed, Cohen states that if a judge argues against philosophy or theology, then actually the judge is just ignorant of his or her own theological/philosophical assumptions.

This stance he opposes to that of Holmes who explicitly acknowledges his assumptions.[88] Further, Holmes's description of law as prophecy is thought central to realism.[89] As is the skepticism of any attempts at a definition of law other than for a forward-looking research agenda. Most importantly, Cohen quotes Holmes's thought that, "I know of no point at which the scientific search for facts needs to stop short of complete understanding of all the relevant factors in any problem situation."[90]

While Llewellyn, Frank, and Cohen are legal realists by any account, there are other realists that could just as easily have been used as subjects. Generally, they show a lot of similarities with the differences being one of emphasis. For instance, Hessel Yntema attacks the hornbook writer for the "intransigent in his conceptualism."[91] William O. Douglas attacks legal reasoning's focus upon form—"The analysis took the form of rules; the rules became the theology. . . . The theology obscured thinking. It instituted an endless process of refinement. It continued by its own momentum."[92] Thurman W. Arnold emphasizes with Cohen that legal reasoning rests unduly upon its internal symbolism, and that the great need is a more scientific approach: "Principles have been obstacles, and not aids."[93] An example he gives is that of the Supreme Court and its ossified conception of the Constitution versus the flexibility and fact-intensive work of the administrative process. Arnold points out that because the latter is not burdened by a principled theology of virtue and sin, in its practice the administrative agency can look to facts and experiment and therefore can learn.

Walter W. Cook, as does Frank, offers an anti-rationalistic approach that moves from Euclidian thought based upon unquestioned axioms and deduction to non-Euclidian thought based upon experiment and induction.[94] Joseph C. Hutcheson wrote on his infamous hunch theory of legal reasoning wherein lawyers develop intuitive faculties through training.[95] Herman Oliphant argues against the problematic shift from *stare decisis* to *stare dictis*, that is, from the common law and precedent to principled reasoning. This he sees as a retreat to abstraction, that is, "stare dictis." As opposed to stare dictis, for him stare decisis keeps legal practice close to experience and only uses principles to orient social experimentation—but always after letting experiments run process.[96] Max Radin, in *Law as Logic and Experience* emphasizes the use of precedent as information, not duty. This is because, "Prospective application has advantages of a kind that commend themselves to science. It permits experimentation, which must be assumed to be dear to scientists."[97] And Edward Stevens Robinson, in *Law and the Lawyers* emphasized that "the New Deal has sought to popularize the idea that the experimental, fact-dominated, forward-looking view of natural science is relevant to the process of social adjustment" where natural science serves as a model because of its greater "responsibility to fact."[98]

While the descriptions of legal realism offered above are disparate, they do exhibit a bundle of recurring themes. There is a skepticism of a case-based concept and rule-based approach, an emphasis on the centrality of empirical facts, the willingness to embrace pluralist methodologies and a temporal and dynamic approach to law that foregrounds functional analysis and experiment. This set of themes is then often associated with an embrace of new possibilities in law, such as those seen in the rise of the administrative state.

What the case studies offered was a more nuanced picture of three different realist views. Llewellyn offers the classical realist example of rule skepticism. In contrast to a text-based picture of law he argues that to understand law there needs to be analysis of law as a social institution with an emphasis on what legal actions do in the world. Descriptive analysis is contrasted with the official story of law offered by the profession which is seen as a distortion of the facts. Further, law practice is decentered and described not as rule setter, after the model of game rules, but rather as an institution aimed at dispute resolution. Indeed, law is best seen as an open-ended project and not a natural type to be identified so to be true to its essence. This is seen clearly in Llewellyn's investigations into Cheyenne "law stuff." Therein he identifies alternate ways to do law-like activities emphasizing function over type-based description.

Jerome Frank was the second theorist studied. As with Llewellyn, he was highly suspicious of formalism which is seen as dupery based upon a compensatory metaphysics constructed as a father substitute. One of his examples of this father substitute is the reliance on historical analysis which, he claimed, was so dubious that it should be described as "twistory." Not that history does not have a use, but that it is to encourage enlightened skepticism not present certainly. Frank emphasizes the perspective of the client. That is, to see law as predicting what the court's actions will mean to the client, not to the judge or attorney. Further, Frank argues that legal theory shows an overemphasis upon stability, and he highlight the virtues, and the necessity, of a legal system that offers flexibility and the ability to handle novelty through adaptation. Infamously, Frank also argued that the judge's personality matters. Legal decisions, that is, are influenced by personal and social aspects of the judge. In addition to Llewellyn's rule skepticism, which he agreed with, Frank emphasized fact skepticism. If rules were unclear, facts were even more unclear, and because rules are only employed given identified fact patterns, this showed just how uncertain the legal process could be. The emphasis upon fact skepticism and the tenuousness of fact identification in law was a part of Frank's argument against appellate court bias in analysis. If law is seen from the perspective of the client, the lower courts become much more important.

Finally, Felix Cohen offers a slight variation on these themes. He is equally suspicious of verbal definitions—which he characterizes as the use of sanctified words based upon transcendental nonsense. He diagnoses this as partially an aesthetic bias towards form over content often based upon avoidance of real world problems. Further, he claims that while all legal thought rests upon ethical and metaphysical assumptions, an implicit ethics and metaphysics is usually operative. But because these assumptions are not explicit they are not avoided, but rather become more dangerous because theyhelp as dogma, not as examined positions. Ultimately he argues for a clear ethical foundation for law, an ethics based in fact and developed though a legal system that explicitly is founded upon words defined operationally and tested through experiment.

## REALIST THOUGHT AND THE JURISPRUDENCE OF OLIVER WENDELL HOLMES JR.

So, was Holmes a legal realist? Clearly the central realists thought so. But, of course, Holmes developed his theories well before the realists arrived. Further, Holmes notoriously did not like "fighting tags" such as legal realism or pragmatism.[99] More directly, was Holmes a realist in the sense of having enough of the same assumptions to count as one of the group?

First, as for the skepticism toward formalism, Holmes certainly fits into the legal realist family. This is true even though his attitude towards Langdell and the case method was much more ambiguous than the realists'. Indeed, he praised Langdell's casebook method.[100] But this cannot obscure his negative attitude towards formalist thought in law. Famously, in *The Common Law* he wrote:

> The life of the law has not been logic: it has been experience. The felt necessities of the time, the prevalent moral and political theories, intuitions of public policy, avowed or unconscious, even the prejudices which judges share with their fellow-men, have had a good deal more to do than the syllogism in determining the rules by which men should be governed. The law embodies the story of a nation's development through many centuries, and it cannot be dealt with as if it contained only the axioms and corollaries of a book of mathematics.[101]

Indeed, he had little shrift with essentialist ideas of law in general, writing that, "in substance the growth of law is legislative."[102]

He thought that because lawyers get trained in formalist logic they tend to overemphasize its importance. In a manner that sounds a lot like Frank, he noted:

> Logical method and form flatter that longing for certainty and for repose which is in every human mind. But certainty generally is illusion, and repose is not the destiny of man. Behind the logical form lies a judgment as to the

> relative worth and importance of competing legislative grounds, often an inarticulate and unconscious judgment, it is true, and yet the very root and nerve of the whole proceeding.[103]

In his famous *Lochner* dissent, he wrote that any legal "decision will depend upon a judgment or intuition more subtle than any articulate major premise."[104] And in his *Truax* dissent he noted that "Delusive exactness is a source of fallacy throughout the law."[105] Certainly Holmes had a suspicion of the formalist tendencies in law in common with the realists.

Following from his critique of formalism, Holmes also had in common with realists a functionalist theory of law. Indeed, Holmes's work was one of the main sources of the legal realists' emphasis upon a functionalist theory of law. His favorite analytical tools such as the aim of pushing law towards "objective" external factors, recourse to the average man or prudent man as well as the famous bad man theory of the law all were in the service of a functionalist approach. Most famous is, of course, his "bad man" description of how to investigate the law: "If you want to know the law and nothing else, you must look at it as the bad man, who cares only for the material consequences which such knowledge enables him to predict, not as a good one, who finds his reasons for conduct, whether inside the law or outside of it, in the vaguer sanctions of conscience."[106]

This theory has been ridiculed as a complete theory of law. But along with the realists, Holmes did not offer a complete theory of law, but a theory of law for specific purposes. So, in fact, it is the taking of the theory as a complete theory that is ridiculous. When its purpose is kept in view—to make the practice of law clearer as to goals and the investigation of law more clear as to content—the theory makes perfect functionalist sense. Understanding law from the point of view of the bad man focuses the investigation on what courts do in fact. As he stated in *American Banana Co.*, "Law is a statement of circumstances in which the public force will be brought to bear upon men through the courts."[107] As with the legal realists, therefore, Holmes wanted to get a better take on prediction, specifically, "prediction of the incidence of the public force through the instrumentality of the courts."[108]

While a functionalist analysis was emphasized, Holmes also used historical analysis to make visible the underlying evolution of law. As he said in *Gompers*, "the provisions of the Constitution are not mathematical formulas having their essence in their form; they are organic, living institutions transplanted from English soil. Their significance is vital not formal; it is to be gathered not simply by taking the words and a dictionary, but by considering their origin and the line of their growth."[109] He used the description of the historical evolution of legal concepts as a way to "burst inflated explanations."[110] Famously, he wrote that, "In form its growth is logical. The official theory is that each new decision follows syllogistically from existing precedents. But just as the clavicle in the cat only tells of the existence of some earlier creature to which a collarbone was useful, precedents survive in the law long after the use they once served is at an end and the reason for them has been forgotten."[111] This might not be as skeptical towards history as Frank's "twistory," but Holmes uses history not as a foundation but rather as a tool to induce modesty in claims. Indeed, he explains that, "The past gives us our vocabulary and fixes the limits of our imagination; we cannot get away from it. There is, too, a peculiar logical pleasure in making manifest the continuity between what we are doing and what has been done before. But the present has a right to govern itself so far as it can; and it ought always to be remembered that historic continuity with the past is not a duty, it is only a necessity."[112] Therefore Holmes noted the historical evolution of law, its dynamic quality, while critiquing any conception of this evolution as logically determined.

Holmes also shares with the legal realists an emphasis upon scientific methodology. He believed that law, "should draw its postulates and its legislative justification from science."[113] For him, "the man of the future is the man of statistics and the master of economics."[114] Against an autonomous and formalist view of law, he contrasted "a time when the part played by history in the explanation of dogma shall be very small, and instead of ingenious research we shall spend our energy on a study of the ends sought to be attained and the reasons for desiring them."[115] Instead of logical or legal form and historical precedent being emphasized, rather the future legal practitioner should study the ends of legislation, the effectivity of the means chosen, and the costs.[116] This study includes a specific interest in values. Holmes thought that judges could not avoid considerations of value because, "The duty is inevitable, and the result of the often proclaimed judicial aversion to deal with such considerations is simply to leave the very ground and foundation of judgments inarticulate, and often unconscious."[117]

While less emphasized, Holmes also saw law as an experimental enterprise. This is seen most clearly in his *Abrams* dissent where he describes the underlying theory of the U.S. Constitution as experimental:

> That at any rate is the theory of our Constitution. It is an experiment, as all life is an experiment. Every year if not every day we have to wager our salvation upon some prophecy based upon imperfect knowledge. While that experiment is part of our system I think that we should be eternally vigilant against attempts to check the expression of opinions that we loathe and believe to be fraught with death, unless they so immediately threaten immediate interference with the lawful and pressing purposes of the law that an immediate check is required to save the country.[118]

Yet this version of experimentalism shows a slight variation between Holmes's thought and that of the legal realists. Here the court isn't adopting a technocratic position of expert, but rather placing the location of experiment in public discourse. Arguably, Holmes is more "democratic" and less enamored with the position of legal authority whether or not it adopts all the above aspects of realism. Law, as he characterizes it, is "a conscious reaction upon itself of organized society knowingly seeking to determine its own destinies."[119] It is not one driven by lawyers, but by society. This is seen in his famous *Lochner* dissent where he argues, "a constitution is not intended to embody a particular economic theory, whether of paternalism and the organic relation of the citizen to the state or laissez-faire. It is made for people of fundamentally differing views, and the accident of our finding certain opinions natural and familiar or novel and even shocking ought not to conclude our judgment upon the question whether statutes embodying them conflict with the Constitution of the United States."[120] He made this statement in response to a court majority that in his opinion read their own authoritative preferences in to the Constitution. Importantly, he did not argue for a different official economic theory, but rather against the court's authority in making any economic theory official. This social and democratic focus is also seen in the difference between Frank's overt contempt for the jury and Holmes's conception of the "democratic verdict of the jury" that he used to find issues of mixed fact and law as a better way to find social criteria.[121] Frank hoped for the expertise of an adult judge; Holmes looked to the jury as a way to keep "the administration of law in accord with the wishes and feelings of the community."[122]

This difference also shows in relationship to Llewellyn's conception of common law. Llewellyn emphasizes lawyerly craft, whereas Holmes emphasizes common law's rootedness in society and its specificity to context: "while opposite convictions still keep a battle front against each other, the time for law has not come; the notion destined to prevail is not yet entitled to the field. It is a misfortune if a judge reads his conscious or unconscious sympathy with one side or the other prematurely into the law, and forgets that what seem to him to be first principles are believed by half his fellow men to be wrong."[123] Once again, deference is to society, not to legal expertise. Indeed, the judge should "learn to transcend our own convictions and to leave room for much that we hold dear to be done away with short of revolution by the orderly change of law."[124] This attitude is not surprising with the example of *Dred Scott* and the Civil War as part of his life. It is important to emphasize that this deference to social discourse or democracy does not entail an optimistic view of social decision making as much as a very skeptical view of the court's ability to solve contentious social issues. Judicial modesty might seem a moral obligation in light of the anti-precedential qualities following from the judicial certainty shown in *Dred Scott*.

Frederic Kellogg's work on Holmes identifies this aspect of his thought most effectively. Kellogg characterizes Holmes's picture of law as one where "law is a process of inquiry, not a static body of logic or obligation."[125] Indeed, given this conception of law, any analytical attempt at boundaries fossilizes law's ability to adapt and change. Further, this is not a value-free picture of law, indeed, does not entail a moral skepticism at all. But, as opposed to Cohen, the primary location of moral reasoning is in the public realm rather than the judge. Preservation of democratic debate entails judicial restraint. Therefore, law is constructed as much as possible through evolving and embedded patterns of social life—"a community-based deference to on-going transgenerational consensus."[126] Interestingly, Kellogg notes that given this theory, "appeal to "principle" is an aggressive dereliction of the judicial role."[127] Further, if this is correct, then the idea of law as a set of game rules and applied concepts is hopelessly naïve.

Therefore, the legal realists were generally not as rooted in community values as Holmes. As a tendency, Holmes looked to community, whereas the realists were generally more focused upon the conduct of legal officials.[128]

## CONCLUSION

The legal realists and Holmes had many aspects of commonality. This is not surprising given the canonized status of Holmes in their scholarship. No other legal thinker was even close in strength of influence for legal realist theory. As Holmes did, the realists aimed to critique and discredit the traditional, "classical," Langdellian concept-driven and rule-based version of legal theory, were skeptical of a concept of law centered upon the application of rules, and rather emphasized the centrality of empirical facts. Anti-essentialism towards law was common to both. Further, both Holmes and the realists adopted a dynamic perspective towards law, and argued that law should be investigated as a social institution and that actual effects in the world should be foregrounded in the investigation. In common also was an emphasis upon forward-looking policy and the use of the social sciences to both understand law and to make it more reliable.

As opposed to Holmes, the legal realists were engaged in a fight for professional status within the legal academy, and were much more willing to see legal professionals as experts in positions of decision-making power. The technocratic stance found in the New Deal attributes of the legal realists were not nearly so prevalent in Holmes. For instance, Holmes advocated judicial deference where the realists aimed more towards judicial expertise and transparency. Further, Holmes was much more ambivalent towards social process. In this sense Holmes was more democratic, but only in the sense of being more skeptical of legal solutions and legal expertise. Holmes was certainly not an advocate of any optimistic version of democratic progress. All these contrasts are, of course, as Holmes would say "a matter of degree." But that is as it should be in reasoning that is wary of trying to draw sharp boundaries where none are properly found. After all, it is a matter of experience and analysis, not of "logic."

## NOTES

1. Jerome Frank, *Law and the Modern Mind* (Garden City: Anchor Books, 1963), 270. See also Jerome Frank, *Fate and Freedom: A Philosophy for Free Americans* (New York: Simon and Schuster, 1945), 31, 307.
2. Karl N. Llewellyn, *Jurisprudence: Realism in Theory and Practice* (Chicago: The University of Chicago Press, 1962), 513.
3. Morton White, *Social Thought in America: The Revolt against Formalism* (Oxford: Oxford University Press, 1976), 177.
4. Wilfrid E. Rumble, *American Legal Realism: Skepticism, Reform, and the Judicial Process* (Ithaca: Cornell University Press, 1968), 39.
5. Brian Z. Tamanaha, *Law as a Means to an End* (Cambridge: Cambridge University Press, 2006), 228.
6. Brian Z. Tamanaha, *Beyond the Formalist–Realist Divide: The Role of Politics in Judging* (Princeton: Princeton University Press), 39.
7. Tamanaha, *Beyond the Formalist–Realist Divide*, 103.
8. William W. Fisher III, Morton J. Horwitz, and Thomas A. Reed, *American Legal Realism* (New York: Oxford University Press, 1993), xiii–xiv.
9. William Twining, *Karl Llewellyn and the Realist Movement* (Norman: University of Oklahoma Press, 1973), 7, 74.
10. Brian Leiter, *Naturalizing Jurisprudence: Essays on American Legal Realism and Naturalism in Legal Philosophy* (Oxford: Oxford University Press, 2007), 16.
11. Leiter, *Naturalizing Jurisprudence*, 175.
12. White, *Social Thought*, 17.
13. Hanoch Dagan, "The Realist Conception of Law," *University of Toronto Law Journal* 57, no. 3 (2007): 610.
14. N. E. H. Hull, *Roscoe Pound and Karl Llewellyn: Searching for an American Jurisprudence* (Chicago: The University of Chicago Press, 1997), 15.
15. John Henry Schlegel, *American Legal Realism and Empirical Social Science* (Chapel Hill: University of North Carolina Press, 1995), 36.
16. Schlegel, *American Legal Realism and Empirical Social Science*, 213.
17. Rumble, *Realism*, 23–24.
18. Marcus J. Curtis, "Realism Revisited: Reaffirming the Centrality of the New deal in Realist Jurisprudence," *Yale Journal of Law & the Humanities* 27, vol. 1 (2015): 173.
19. Curtis, *Realism Revisited*, 184.
20. Roy Kreitner, "Biographing Realist Jurisprudence," *Law & Social Inquiry* 5, vol. 3 (2010): 766.
21. Kreitner, "Biographing Realist Jurisprudence," 778.
22. Kreitner, "Biographing Realist Jurisprudence," 780.
23. Karl N. Llewellyn, *The Theory of Rules* (Chicago: The University of Chicago Press, 2011), 43.
24. Llewellyn, *The Theory of Rules* 44.
25. Karl N. Llewellyn, *The Bramble Bush* (Oxford: Oxford University Press, 2009), 4.
26. Llewellyn, *The Bramble Bush*, 5.
27. Llewellyn, *The Bramble Bush*, 15.
28. Llewellyn, *The Bramble Bush*, 32.
29. Llewellyn, *The Bramble Bush*, 36.
30. Llewellyn, *The Bramble Bush*, 40.
31. Llewellyn, *The Bramble Bush*, 50.

32. Llewellyn, *The Bramble Bush*, 96.
33. Llewellyn, *The Bramble Bush*, 120.
34. Karl N. Llewellyn and E. Adamson Hoebel, *The Cheyenne Way* (Norman: University of Oklahoma Press, 1941), 42.
35. Llewellyn, *Jurisprudence*, 3.
36. Llewellyn, *Jurisprudence*, 68–69, 82.
37. Llewellyn, *Jurisprudence*, 83.
38. Llewellyn, *Jurisprudence*, 136–37.
39. Karl N. Llewellyn, *The Common Law Tradition: Deciding Appeals* (Boston: Little, Brown and Company, 1960), 509–510.
40. Karl N. Llewellyn, "The Constitution as an Institution," *Columbia Law Review* 34, no. 1 (1934): 4.
41. Llewellyn, "The Constitution as an Institution," 7.
42. Llewellyn, "The Constitution as an Institution," 10.
43. Llewellyn, "The Constitution as an Institution," 28, 31.
44. Llewellyn, "The Constitution as an Institution," 39.
45. Jerome Frank, *Courts on Trial: Myth and Reality in American Jurisprudence* (Princeton: Princeton University Press, 1950), 230.
46. Frank, *Modern Mind*, 60.
47. Frank, *Modern Mind*, xxiii.
48. Frank, *Modern Mind*, 7.
49. Frank, *Modern Mind*, 1.
50. Frank, *Modern Mind*, 33.
51. Frank, *Modern Mind*, 119.
52. Frank, *Modern Mind*, 120.
53. Frank, *Fate and Freedom*, 18.
54. Frank, *Fate and Freedom*, 23–24.
55. Frank, *Modern Mind*, xi.
56. Frank, *Courts on Trial*, 14.
57. Frank, *Courts on Trial*, 111.
58. Jerome Frank, *If Men Were Angels: Some Aspects of Government in a Democracy* (New York: Harper & Brothers, 1942), 123, 159.
59. Frank, *Courts on Trial*, 183.
60. Frank, *Angels*, 313.
61. Frank, *Modern Mind*, ix.
62. Frank, *Modern Mind*, ix, See also Jerome Frank, "Experimental Justice and the 'New Deal,'" *Constitutional Record* 78 (June 18, 1934), 1.
63. Frank, *Modern Mind*, x.
64. Frank, *Modern Mind*, 136.
65. Frank, *Modern Mind*, 297.
66. Frank, *Angels*, 7.
67. Frank, *Modern Mind*, 270.
68. Frank, *Angels*, 56.
69. Frank, *Angels*, 307.
70. Frank, *Modern Mind*, xxvii.
71. Frank, *Fate and Freedom*, 31.
72. Jerome Frank, *Save America First: How to Make Our Democracy Work* (New York: Harper & Brothers, 1938), 228.
73. Felix S. Cohen, *Ethical Systems and Legal Ideals: An Essay on the Foundations of Legal Criticism* (Ithaca: Cornel University Press, 1959), 3.
74. Cohen, *Ethical Systems and Legal Ideals*, 9.
75. Cohen, *Ethical Systems and Legal Ideals*, 53.
76. Cohen, *Ethical Systems and Legal Ideals*, 237.
77. Ibid. Cohen, *Ethical Systems and Legal Ideals*, 2.
78. Lucy Kramer Cohen (ed.), *The Legal Conscience: Selected Papers of Felix S. Cohen* (New Haven: Yale University Press, 1960), 31.

79. Cohen, *Ethical Systems*, 271.
80. Cohen, *Legal Conscience*, 37.
81. Cohen, *Legal Conscience*, 38.
82. Cohen, *Legal Conscience*, 45.
83. Cohen, *Legal Conscience*, 49.
84. Cohen, *Legal Conscience*, 59.
85. Cohen, *Legal Conscience*, 79.
86. Cohen, *Legal Conscience*, 113.
87. Cohen, *Legal Conscience*, 145.
88. Cohen, *Legal Conscience*, 167.
89. Cohen, *Legal Conscience*, 182.
90. Cohen, *Legal Conscience*, 401.
91. Hessel E. Yntema, "The Hornbook Method and the Conflict of Laws," *Yale Law Journal* 37, no. 4 (1928): 480.
92. William O. Douglas, "Functional Approach to the Law of Business Associations," *Illinois Law Review* 23 (1928–29): 674.
93. Thurman W. Arnold, *The Symbols of Government* (New Haven: Yale University Press, 1935), 3.
94. Walter W. Cook, "Scientific Method and the Law," *American Bar Association Journal* 13, no. 6 (1927): 309.
95. Joseph C. Hutcheson, Jr., "Judgment Intuitive: The Function of the 'Hunch' in Judicial Decision," *Cornell Law Review* 3 (1929): 276.
96. Herman Oliphant, "A Return to Stare Decisis," *American Bar Association Journal* 14, no. 2 (1928), 75.
97. Max Radin, *Law as Logic and Experience* (New Haven: Yale University Press, 1940), 101.
98. Edward Stevens Robinson, *Law and The Lawyers* (New York: The Macmillan Company, 1935), 6, 21.
99. Seth Vannatta, *Conservatism and Pragmatism: In Law, Politics and Ethics* (New York: Palgrave Macmillan, 2014), 127.
100. Oliver Wendell Holmes Jr., *Collected Legal Papers* (New York: Harcourt, Brace and Co., 1921), 44.
101. Oliver Wendell Holmes Jr., *The Common Law* (New York: Dover Publications, 1991), 1.
102. Holmes, *The Common Law*, 35.
103. Holmes, *Collected Legal Papers*, 181.
104. *Lochner v. New York* 198 U.S. 45 (1905)
105. *Truax v. Corrigan* 257 U.S. 312 (1921).
106. Holmes, *Collected Legal Papers*, 171.
107. *American Banana Co. v. United Fruit Co.* 213 U.S. 347 (1909).
108. Holmes, *Collected Legal Papers*, 167.
109. *Gompers v. United States* 233 U.S. 604 (1914).
110. Holmes, *Collected Legal Papers*, 225.
111. Holmes, *The Common Law*, 35.
112. Holmes, *Collected Legal Papers*, 138, 139.
113. Holmes, *Collected Legal Papers*, 139.
114. Holmes, *Collected Legal Papers*, 187.
115. Holmes, *Collected Legal Papers*, 195.
116. Holmes, *Collected Legal Papers*, 195.
117. Holmes, *Collected Legal Papers*, 184.
118. *Abrams v. United States* 250 U.S. 616 (1919).
119. Holmes, *Collected Legal Papers*, 129–30.
120. *Lochner v. New York* 198 U.S. 45 (1905).
121. Holmes, *Collected Legal Papers*, 212, 234.
122. Holmes, *Collected Legal Papers*, 238.
123. Holmes, *Collected Legal Papers*, 295.

124. Holmes, *Collected Legal Papers*, 29.
125. Frederic R. Kellogg, *The Formative Essays of Justice Holmes: The Making of an American Legal Philosophy* (Westport: Greenwood Press, 1984), xi.
126. Frederic R. Kellogg, *Oliver Wendell Holmes Jr., Legal Theory and Judicial Restraint* (Cambridge: Cambridge University Press, 2007), 39.
127. Kellogg, *Judicial Restraint*, 45.
128. Frederic R. Kellogg, emphasizes this in his forthcoming book, *Oliver Wendell Holmes Jr., and Legal Logic* (University of Chicago Press).

## BIBLIOGRAPHY

Arnold, Thurman W. *The Folklore of Capitalism*. New Haven: Yale University Press, 1937.
———. "The New Deal is Constitutional." *New Republic* 1933.
———. *The Symbols of Government*. New Haven: Yale University Press, 1935.
Baker, Liva. *The Justice from Beacon Hill: The Life and Times of Oliver Wendell Holmes*. New York: Harper Collins, 1991.
Cardozo, Benjamin N. *The Nature of the Judicial Process*. New Haven: Yale University Press, 1921.
Cohen, Felix S. *Ethical Systems and Legal Ideals: An Essay on the Foundations of Legal Criticism*. Ithaca: Cornell University Press, 1959.
Cohen, Lucy Kramer (ed.). *The Legal Conscience: Selected Papers of Felix S. Cohen*. New Haven: Yale University Press, 1960.
Cohen, Morris R., and Felix S. Cohen (eds.). *Readings in Jurisprudence and Legal Philosophy*. Boston: Little, Brown and Company, 1951.
Cook, Walter W. "Scientific Method and the Law." 13 *American Bar Association Journal* 6 (1927): 303–309.
Curtis, Marcus J. "Realism Revisted: Reffirming the Centrality of the New Deal in Realist Jurisprudence." 27 *Yale Journal of Law & the Humanities* 1 (2015): 157–200.
Dagan, Hanoch. "The Realist Conception of Law." 57 *University of Toronto Law Journal* 3 (2007): 607–660.
Douglas, William O. "Functional Approach to the Law of Business Associations." 23 *Illinois Law Review* (1928–29): 673–682.
Dowling, Noel T., Edwin W. Patterson, and Richard R. Powell (eds.). *Materials for Legal Method*. Chicago: The Foundation Press, 1946.
Fisher, William W., III, Morton J. Horwitz, and Thomas A. Reed. *American Legal Realism*. New York: Oxford University Press, 1993.
Frank, Jerome. *A Man's Reach: The Philosophy of Judge Jerome Frank*. New York: Macmillan, 1965.
———. *Courts on Trial: Myth and Reality in American Justice*. Princeton: Princeton University Press, 1950.
———. "Experimental Jurisprudence and the 'New Deal.'" *Constitutional Record* 78 (June 18, 1934): 12412–12414.
———. *Fate and Freedom: A Philosophy for Free Americans*. New York: Simon and Schuster, 1945.
———. *If Men Were Angels: Some Aspects of Government in a Democracy*. New York: Harper & Brothers, 1942.
———. *Law and the Modern Mind*. Garden City: Anchor Books, 1963.
———. "Mr. Justice Holmes and Non-Euclidean Legal Thinking." 17 *Cornell Law Review* 4 (1932): 568–603.
———. *Save America First: How to Make Our Democracy Work*. New York: Harper & Brothers, 1938.
Fuller, L. L. "American Legal Realism." 82 *University of Pennsylvania Law Review* 82 (1934): 429–462.
Glennon, Robert Jerome. *The Iconoclast as Reformer: Jerome Frank's Impact on American Law*. Ithaca: Cornell University Press, 1985.

Green, Michael Steven. "Legal Realism as Theory of Law." 46 *William & Mary Law Review* 6 (2005): 1915–2000.

———. "Legal Realism, Lex Fori, and the Choice-of-Law Revolution." 104 *Yale Law Journal* (1995): 967–967.

Hall, Jerome (ed.). *Readings in Jurisprudence.* Indianapolis: The Bobbs-Merrill Company, 1938.

Hart, H. L. A. *The Concept of Law.* Oxford: Oxford University Press, 1961.

Holmes, Oliver Wendell, Jr. *Collected Legal Papers.* New York: Harcourt, Brace and Co., 1921.

———. *The Common Law.* New York: Dover Publications, 1991.

Howe, Mark DeWolfe. *Justice Oliver Wendell Holmes: The Proving Years 1870–1882.* Cambridge: Harvard University Press, 1963.

Hull, N. E. H. *Roscoe Pound and Karl Llewellyn: Searching for an American Jurisprudence.* Chicago: The University of Chicago Press, 1997.

Hutcheson, Joseph C., Jr. "Judgment Intuitive: The Function of the 'Hunch' in Judicial Decision." 3 *Cornell Law Review* (1929): 274–288.

Kalman, Laura. *Legal Realism at Yale, 1927-1960.* Chapel Hill: The University of North Carolina Press, 1986.

Kellogg, Frederic R. *The Formative Essays of Justice Holmes: The Making of an American Legal Philosophy.* Westport: Greenwood Press, 1984.

———. *Oliver Wendell Holmes, Jr. and Legal Logic.* Forthcoming, Chicago: University of Chicago Press, 2018.

———. *Oliver Wendell Holmes, Jr., Legal Theory, and Judicial Restraint.* Cambridge: Cambridge University Press, 2007.

Kreitner, Roy. "Biographing Realist Jurisprudence." 5 *Law & Social Inquiry* 3 (2010): 765–791.

Leiter, Brian. *Naturalizing Jurisprudence: Essays on American Legal Realism and Naturalism in Legal Philosophy.* Oxford: Oxford University Press, 2007.

Llewellyn, Karl N. *The Bramble Bush.* Oxford: Oxford University Press, 2008.

———. *The Common Law Tradition: Deciding Appeals.* Boston: Little, Brown and Company, 1960.

———. "The Constitution as an Institution." 34 *Columbia Law Review* 1 (1934): 1–40.

———. *Jurisprudence: Realism in Theory and Practice.* Chicago: The University of Chicago Press, 1962.

———. *The Theory of Rules.* Chicago: The University of Chicago Press, 2011.

———., and E. Adamson Hoebel. *The Cheyenne Way.* Norman: University of Oklahoma Press, 1941 .

Mendenhall, Allen. *Oliver Wendell Holmes Jr., Pragmatism, and the Jurisprudence of Agon: Aesthetic Dissent and the Common Law.* Lewisburg: Bucknell University Press, 2017.

Mentschikoff, Soia, and Irwin P. Stotzky (eds.). *The Theory and Craft of American Law—Elements.* New York: Matthew Bender, 1981.

Mills, C. Wright. *Sociology and Pragmatism: The Higher Learning in America.* Oxford: Oxford University Press, 1969.

Moore, W. Underhill. "Rational Basis of Legal Institutions." 23 *Columbia Law Review* 7 (1923): 609–617.

Novick, Sheldon M. *Honorable Justice: The Life of Oliver Wendell Holmes.* Boston: Little, Brown and Company, 1989.

Oliphant, Herman. "A Return to Stare Decisis." 14 *American Bar Association Journal* 2 (1928): 71–76.

———. "Stare Decisis—Continued." 14 *American Bar Association Journal* 3 (1928): 159–162.

Posner, Richard A. *Cardozo: A Study in Reputation.* Chicago: University of Chicago Press, 1990.

———. (ed.). *The Essential Holmes: Selections from the Letters, Speeches, Judicial Opinions, and Other Writings of Oliver Wendell Holmes, Jr.* Chicago: The University of Chicago Press, 1992.

Postema, G. J. *Legal Philosophy in the Twentieth Century: The Common Law World.* Dordrecht: Springer, 2011.

Pound, Roscoe. *The Formative Era of American Law.* Boston: Little, Brown and Company, 1938.

Radin, Max. *Law as Logic and Experience.* New Haven: Yale University Press, 1940.

———. "The Theory of Judicial Decision: Or How Judges Think." 11 *American Bar Association Journal* 6 (1925): 357–362.

Robinson, Edward Stevens. *Law and the Lawyers.* New York: The Macmillan Company, 1935.

Rumble, Wilfrid E. *American Legal Realism: Skepticism, Reform, and the Judicial Process.* Ithaca: Cornell University Press, 1968.

Schlegel, John Henry. *American Legal Realism and Empirical Social Science.* Chapel Hill: University of North Carolina Press, 1995.

Singer, Joseph William. "Legal Realism Now." 76 *California Law Review* 2 (1988): 465–544.

Stone, Julius. *Law and the Social Sciences in the Second Half Century.* Minneapolis: University of Minnesota Press, 1966.

Tamanaha, Brian Z. *Beyond the Formalist–Realist Divide: The Role of Politics in Judging.* Princeton: Princeton University Press, 2010.

———. *Law as a Means to an End: Threat to the Rule of Law.* Cambridge: Cambridge University Press, 2006.

———. *On the Rule of Law: History, Politics, Theory.* Cambridge: Cambridge University Press, 2004.

Twining, William. *Karl Llewellyn and the Realist Movement.* Norman: University of Oklahoma Press, 1973.

Vannatta, Seth. *Conservatism and Pragmatism: In Law, Politics, and Ethics.* New York: Palgrave Macmillan, 2014.

White, G. Edward. *Justice Oliver Wendell Holmes: Law and the Inner Self.* Oxford: Oxford University Press, 1993.

White, Morton. *Social Thought in America: The Revolt Against Formalism.* Oxford: Oxford University Press, 1976.

Wiener, Philip P. *Evolution and the Founders of Pragmatism.* Cambridge: Harvard University Press, 1949.

Yntema, Hessel E. "The Hornbook Method and the Conflict of Laws." 37 *Yale Law Journal* 4 (1928): 468–483.

Zaremby, Justin. *Legal Realism and American Law.* New York: Bloomsbury, 2014.

# *Chapter Eight*

# The Pragmatist

Susan Haack

Holmes has been described as a great liberal,[1] a legal realist *avant la lettre*,[2] a precursor of the "law and economics" movement,[3] a moral skeptic or nihilist,[4] and even as a proto-Nazi[5] and, by one exasperated critic, a "cynical . . . brutalitarian";[6] but all these descriptions are, in one way or another, unsatisfactory. Historian of philosophy Max Fisch was much more illuminating when he wrote in 1942 that, while "[i]t would be generally agreed . . . that pragmatism is America's most distinctive contribution to philosophy," and that "Oliver Wendell Holmes Jr. had the ablest philosophical mind that has been devoted to law in this country," it had "not yet been shown how close [Holmes] stood to pragmatism."[7] Showing just how thoroughly pragmatist Holmes's thought was, however, requires more evidence and more argument than Fisch could provide in his short paper. My goal in what follows is to supply that further evidence and further argument.

I begin, in the first section, by telling the story of the origin and evolution of the pragmatist tradition, and Holmes's part in that story—which, as we'll see, was very far from straightforward. Next, in the second section, I argue that what united the philosophers of this tradition was, not a body of doctrine, but a congeries of themes, attitudes, and predilections that, despite their great diversity and their many disagreements, they all shared. Then, in the third section, I'll show that the shared themes and attitudes found in Peirce, James, and Dewey[8] can also be seen at work, in a distinctively legal form, in Holmes; and finally, in the concluding section, that, once we recognize the pragmatist character of Holmes's multi-faceted legal thinking, it's easier to see what's true but misleading, what's half-true, and what's just plain false in that litany of discrepant, one-dimensional classifications with which I began.

## "A KNOT OF YOUNG MEN IN OLD CAMBRIDGE"

"The conscious adoption of [pragmatism] . . . in the discussion of dark questions, and the elaboration of it into a method in aid of philosophical inquiry," Charles Sanders Peirce would write in a much later reminiscence, came initially from "the humblest *souche* imaginable": meetings of "a knot of young men in old Cambridge," calling themselves the "Metaphysical Club."[9] And Holmes, we know, was involved even before the beginning. In 1868, evidently hankering for the stimulation of his friend's intellectual company, William James had written to him from Berlin: "When I get home, let's establish a philosophical society to have regular meetings and discuss none but the very tallest and broadest questions . . . to be composed of none but the very topmost cream of Boston manhood"—a society, James continued, that might "grow into something very important after a sufficient number of years."[10]

Holmes was certainly among the topmost of young Boston manhood: his father, Boston physician Oliver Wendell Holmes, Sr., was celebrated both in the U.S. and in Britain for the essays and poems he published in the *Atlantic Monthly* under the title "The Autocrat of the Breakfast Table"; his mother, Amelia Lee Jackson, was the daughter of a prominent judge, Charles Jackson.[11] From 1861–1864 Holmes served on the Union side in the Civil War; in 1864–1865 he attended Harvard Law School; and in 1866 he traveled in Britain and Europe. After his return in 1867, he was admitted to the bar, and briefly practiced with a Boston law firm. But by the early 1870s, when the Metaphysical Club was getting going, he had resigned from the firm to write articles and book reviews for the *American Law Review*, and to edit James Kent's *Commentaries on American Law*.[12]

Among the members of the Metaphysical Club—besides Peirce and James, out of whose discussions the pragmatist movement in philosophy would arise—were Chauncey Wright, then working on the application of the theory of evolution to psychology; historian John Fiske; occasionally the metaphysically-inclined Unitarian clergyman Francis Ellingwood Abbot; and, besides Holmes, attorney Nicholas St. John Green and Joseph Warner, who was still in law school.[13] Peirce would write in his memoir of Green's "marvelously strong intelligence," his "extraordinary power of disrobing warm and breathing truth of the draperies of long worn formulas," and his vital role in the origin of pragmatism.[14] But he was much more reticent about Holmes's contribution, saying only that "Mr. Justice Holmes will not, I believe, take it ill that we are proud to remember his membership."[15]

No doubt this was in part because by the winter of 1872, after his marriage to Fanny Dixwell, Holmes had set aside his scholarly pursuits, joined another law firm,[16] and—"sinking ever deeper into the sloughs of the law," to borrow a phrase from that letter of James's[17]—dropped out of the Club.[18]

And by 1906, when Peirce wrote his memoir, Holmes had reached the highest ranks of the legal profession. In 1881, after the publication of *The Common Law*[19] and one semester teaching at Harvard Law School, he had become associate justice of the Massachusetts Supreme Court, and in 1899, chief justice; and in 1902 he had taken his seat on the U.S. Supreme Court,[20] where he served until his retirement in 1932.[21]

Moreover, Holmes's reaction to what he later read of the pragmatists' philosophical work was by no means uniformly favorable. He was much impressed by Dewey's *Experience and Nature*:[22] "[Dewey's] view of the universe came home closer to me than any other that I know. . . . So methought God would have spoken had he been inarticulate but keenly desirous to tell you how it was."[23] But he was dismissive of James's doctrine of the Will to Believe;[24] and, when the first anthology of Peirce's work appeared in 1923,[25] disappointed by what he saw as his weakness for religious speculation, "in spite of his devotion to logic."[26] And in 1927, when one of the editors of Peirce's *Collected Papers*, Charles Hartshorne, asked Holmes—by then the only member of the Metaphysical Club still alive—for his recollections of the group, he replied that he learned more from Chauncey Wright and St. John Green than from Peirce, "as I saw him very little"; and expressed "misgivings" about Hartshorne's prediction that Peirce's papers would prove philosophically important.[27]

So if Holmes's approach to law really *is* appropriately classified as pragmatist, it can't be in virtue of his membership in the Metaphysical Club (too brief), or his attitude to the work of the philosophers of the classical pragmatist tradition (too ambivalent); the reasons must lie, rather, in affinities between his approach to the law and the themes and attitudes characteristic of pragmatism. But we can't see these affinities until we first identify those characteristically pragmatist themes and attitudes; and this is no easy task, because the pragmatists were a heterogeneous bunch, with different philosophical backgrounds, diverse philosophical interests, and divergent intellectual paths.

## "THE SPIRIT OF PRAGMATISM"

Pragmatism, its founders agreed, was nothing like a body of philosophical theory; it was a *method*, a way of tackling philosophical questions—the method embodied in the pragmatic maxim of meaning.[28] Though he had already expressed some pragmatist ideas, Peirce first formulated the pragmatic maxim explicitly in talks given at the Metaphysical Club, and later put it in print in "How to Make Our Ideas Clear" (1878).[29] But nowhere in the published piece did he use the word "pragmatism";[30] as he later wrote, he *dared not* use it, for fear his technical usage might be confused with its meaning in ordinary speech.[31] And it would not be Peirce but James who first used "pragmatism" in print as a philosophical term of art,[32] and who launched the pragmatist movement.

Peirce had come to pragmatism by way of an intensive study of Kant;[33] James, who hadn't much time for Kant,[34] was more influenced by the British empiricists;[35] while John Dewey, who would carry the pragmatist tradition forward, came to pragmatism via Hegel.[36] Peirce wrote extensively on logic, theory of inquiry, semeiotics, philosophy of science (and much more besides); James concentrated on philosophy of religion, philosophy of mind, and ethics; and Dewey, working in just about every branch of the subject, added social and political philosophy, philosophy of education, aesthetics, and even legal philosophy to the list.

Moreover, there were somewhat different versions of the pragmatic maxim from the beginning. In the 1898 lecture that introduced pragmatism to the philosophical world, recognizing that it had been Peirce who first formulated the maxim, James explained that he would express the idea "more broadly."[37] In fact, the difference between Peirce's understanding of the maxim and James's understanding was deeper, and subtler, than this might suggest: while Peirce had tied the meaning of a concept to the consequences for conduct of *that concept's truly applying*, James tied the meaning of a proposition to the consequences for action of *belief in that proposition*.[38]

So it's hardly surprising that there were substantive disagreements in the philosophical theories the pragmatists developed: e.g., that Peirce's realistic pragmaticism[39] diverged markedly from James's nominalist pragmatism;[40] that Peirce was uneasy with James's doctrine of the Will to Believe[41] and dismissive of Dewey's idea that knowing a thing somehow changes the object itself;[42] or that Peirce's conception of truth was significantly different both from James's and from Dewey's,[43] and Dewey's understanding of ethics significantly different from James's.[44]

You might be tempted to conclude that the pragmatists really had nothing in common except the name and their shared but diverging history; but this would be a mistake. What they had in common wasn't, however, a shared theory of truth, a shared metaphysical position, shared ethical ideas, or anything of that nature; it was, rather, a skein of shared themes, predilections, and attitudes woven through the whole rich tapestry of their thought:

- *A distaste for verbalism, and an approach to meaning in terms of "practical" or "pragmatic" consequences.*
- *The idea that meaning shifts and changes, growing as our knowledge grows.*
- *A disinclination to philosophize in an a priori way, and an understanding of philosophy as about the world, not exclusively about our concepts or our language.*

- *A distaste for dogmatism and, correspondingly, a robust and thoroughgoing fallibilism.*
- *A repudiation of false dichotomies, and (to use Peirce's word) a synechistic stress on continuity.*
- *A concern with the social character both of language and of inquiry.*
- *A willingness to draw on results from the sciences and, in particular, to take the theory of evolution seriously.*
- *An acknowledgment of contingency, of the role of chance, both in the cosmos and in human affairs.*
- *An inclination to look to the future, and a distinctive way of knitting future and past.*[45]

It is these shared themes, attitudes, and predilections that are the real heart of pragmatism, its spirit. And as we'll soon see, they are all found not only in Peirce, James, and Dewey, but also in Holmes.

## "THE COMPLETELY ADULT JURIST"

Holmes was a complicated man. He was extraordinarily well-read in law, in the history of law, and in legal theory; he conducted a voluminous correspondence, notably with Sir Frederick Pollock in England, but also with many others; and he had long experience of the courts, first as an attorney and then as a judge. He had also, as a young man, endured the horror, dislocation, and social breakdown of the Civil War.[46] No doubt all this—his reading, his correspondence, the experiences of his long life—influenced his thinking in innumerable ways. Probably, for example, his Civil War experience partly explains his sense of the importance of a functioning legal system in holding a society together, preventing its falling into violent internecine conflict. What I will emphasize here, however, is how thoroughly Holmes's legal thought is imbued with those pragmatist attitudes, how "full of the spirit of pragmatism,"[47] as Fisch puts it.

The most obviously pragmatist theme in Holmes, probably, is what has come to be called his "prediction theory of law"—which, indeed, Fisch described as "the only systematic application of pragmatism that has yet been made."[48] The key sentence is this, from early in Holmes's famous 1897 lecture, "The Path of the Law": "A legal duty so called is nothing but a prediction that if a man does or omits certain things he will be made to suffer in this or that way by judgment of the court;—and so of a legal right."[49]

Fisch sees this as the legal analogue of the pragmatic maxim; and it is certainly strikingly akin to Peirce's observation that "there is no distinction of meaning so fine as to consist in anything but a possible difference of practice,"[50] and James's that "there can *be* no difference anywhere that *makes* no difference elsewhere."[51] Noting that Holmes had suggested something closely akin to the law-as-prediction idea in early 1871, Fisch even speculates that, rather than Holmes's having drawn his prediction idea from the pragmatic maxim, Peirce may have drawn the pragmatic maxim from Holmes.[52] This, however, is a stretch; after all, Peirce had offered a clearly-pragmatist account of the concept of reality as early as 1868, in "Some Consequences of Four Incapacities."[53]

In any case, a closer look at the opening pages of "The Path of the Law" suggests that it may not be wise to put too much weight on this affinity; for you soon see that, when he spoke of law as prediction, Holmes wasn't so much offering a systematically worked-out theory of law as insisting on the difference between law and morality: "[T]he vague circumference of the notion of duty shrinks and at the same time becomes more precise when we wash it in cynical acid and expel everything except the object of our study, the operation of the law."[54] Holmes's strategy was to begin by disabusing his audience of any romantic illusion that the law is about what's right, in a moral sense, before he goes on to inspire them with the sweeping socio-historical vistas to which study of the legal system and its history could open their eyes. That's why the idea of law as prediction, so prominent in the first part of his lecture, is left behind in the latter, more theoretical part.[55]

Still, Holmes seems always to have been concerned with what James might have described as the "particular go"[56] of the law, with legal systems in all their messy specificity. When, in "The Path of the Law," he criticizes Sir James Stephen for seeking a "useless quintessence of all legal systems, instead of an accurate anatomy of one,"[57] we hear a characteristically pragmatist empiricism, a distaste for abstract legal philosophizing reminiscent both of Peirce's critique of the A Priori method of inquiry[58] and of James's repudiation of rationalist abstractions and "solving words."[59] And we hear it again in Holmes's dissent in *Southern Pacific v. Jensen*, when he insists that "the common law is not some brooding omnipresence in the sky, but the articulate voice of some sovereign or quasi-sovereign,"[60] always the law in some particular place at some particular time.

Fisch also drew our attention specifically to the "ringing sentences" with which Holmes opens *The Common Law*:[61] "The life of the law has not been logic; it has been experience," Holmes writes. "It is something," he continues, "to show that the consistency of a system requires a particular result, but it is not all."[62] And as we explore his reasons for stressing the limited usefulness of logic in the law we find two other pragmatist themes at work: the growth of meaning, and fallibilism.

Rather as Peirce had pointed out that the meanings of scientific terms and concepts shift and expand with the growth of our knowledge, Holmes points out that the meanings of legal terms shift and change over time, as society changes.[63] In 1880, he had reviewed Christopher Columbus Langdell's book on contracts.[64] Langdell had argued that the essential definition of the legal concept of contract—which he thought could be distilled from previous cases—could serve as axiom for this area of law, enabling judges to deduce the correct result "syllogistically." Holmes doesn't buy it: judges may write as if they were arriving at their legal conclusions by deduction, but much of the time this is only "the evening dress the newcomer puts on to appear respectable."[65] In fact, legal concepts are constantly adapting in response to changing social needs, "old form tak[ing] on new content."[66] And the next year, in the first lecture of *The Common Law*, "Early Forms of Liability," he describes how older conceptions, according to which animals or even inanimate objects could be held legally responsible for the injuries they caused, gradually gave way to the much more restricted conceptions of his own day[67]—bringing to mind Peirce's observation that "in use and in experience, . . . meaning grows."[68]

Closely related themes appear in some of Holmes's legal opinions. For example, in *Gompers* (1914) he writes that "the provisions of the constitution are not mathematical formulas. . . . Their significance is vital not formal; it is to be gathered not simply by taking the words and a dictionary, but by considering their origin and their line of growth";[69] and in *Missouri v. Holland* (1920) that the issues "must be considered in the light of our whole experience and not merely in that of what was said a hundred years ago."[70]

Also behind Holmes's distaste for legal formalism is another characteristically pragmatist attitude: fallibilism. As he writes in "The Path of the Law":

> The language of judicial decision is mainly the language of logic. And the logical method and form flatter that longing for certainty and for repose which is in every human mind. But certainty generally is illusory, and repose is not the destiny of man. Behind the logical form lies a judgment as to the relative worth and importance of competing legislative grounds, often an inarticulate and unconscious judgment, it is true, and yet the very root and nerve of the whole proceeding.[71]

And this is by no means Holmes's only expression of fallibilism. "Certitude is not the test of certainty," he writes; "[w]e have been cock-sure of many things that were not so"[72]—a thought reminiscent of Peirce's avowal of "contrite fallibilism"[73] and his pointed warnings against "the blight of cock-sureness"[74] and the "vanity of cleverness";[75] of James's acknowledgement of the "patience and postponement, the choking down of preferences built into the very stones and mortar" of the sciences;[76] and of the central theme of Dewey's *Quest for Certainty*. Holmes warns, also, against a kind of *moral* over-confidence, the dangers of a judge's "forget[ting] that what seem [to him] to be first principles are believed by half his fellow-men to be wrong"[77]—a thought reminiscent of James's and Dewey's moral fallibilism, their conception of ethical principles as needing to be worked out through experience, not something we can intuit a priori.

Also thoroughly fallibilist in tone and tenor is the defense of freedom of thought and speech in Holmes's celebrated dissent in *Abrams* (1919):

> When men have realized that time has upset many fighting beliefs, they may come to believe even more than they believe the very foundations of their own conduct that the ultimate good desired is better reached by free trade in ideas—that the best test of truth is the power of the thought to get itself accepted in the competition of the market, and that truth is the only ground upon which their wishes safely can be carried out.[78]

Years later, Dewey will cite this passage as summing up Holmes's intellectual temper.[79]

Again like the pragmatist philosophers, Holmes is ready to call on the work of the sciences where it's relevant. In "The Path of the Law" he writes that "for the rational study of the law the blackletter man may be the man of the present; but the man of the future is the man of statistics and the master of economics";[80] and goes on to urge that, if we want to know "whether the criminal law does more harm than good," we look to the then-emerging science of criminology to tell us:

> Does punishment deter? . . . If the typical criminal is a degenerate, bound to swindle or to murder by as deep-seated an organic necessity as that which makes the rattlesnake bite, . . . he must be got rid of. . . . If, on the other hand, crime, like normal human conduct, is mainly a matter of imitation, punishment may fairly be expected to keep it out of fashion.[81]

And in Holmes, as in the other pragmatists, we also hear the influence of Darwin. Of course, he doesn't engage in the kind of ambitious metaphysical theorizing that leads Peirce to his agapism, the "doctrine of evolutionary love,"[82] nor write, as Dewey does, of "the influence of Darwinism on philosophy."[83] But not only does he speak of the law as evolving, he even goes so far as to describe each generation as "taking the inevitable next step, mind, like matter, simply obeying a law of spontaneous growth."[84] Here, perhaps, he goes *too* far; at any rate, it's clear he doesn't really think the evolution of law is a deterministic process.[85] In fact, he seems well aware the legal systems are social institutions; that, like all such institutions, they are brought into being by things people do; and that they are shaped in part by the contingencies of their place and their time.

He also took for granted that an important function of a legal system is to adjudicate disputes between individuals, groups, classes, etc., in a way that allows people with very different ideas and very different interests to live peaceably together. And so we find in his constitutional opinions an analogue of the pragmatist reliance on the *methods* of science, in the form of a conception of law as experiment. In his dissent in *Lochner* (1905), and again in his dissent in *Truax v. Corrigan* (1921), stressing that the Constitution is "made for people of fundamentally differing views,"[86] he argues for "the making of social experiments that an important part of the community desires, in the insulated chambers afforded by the several states."[87] He took for granted that only by trial and error can we figure out what legal arrangements best accommodate competing social interests: the interests of employers and employees, for example, of manufacturers and consumers, of the religious and the secular,[88] and (Holmes might have added) states' rights and national unity. There is a more than passing resemblance to James's idea of ethical theorizing as a matter of gradually figuring out how best to satisfy the most demands.[89] This trial-and-error process, Holmes recognizes, carries real costs; indeed, the history of law vividly reveals "every painful step and world-shaking contest by which mankind has fought and worked its way from savage isolation to organic social life."[90] He is well aware, too, that there will be losers as well as winners; though—unlike James, who is acutely conscious that, since not all demands can be satisfied, "there is always a *pinch*"[91]—he can seem detached to the point of harshness about the fate of the losers.[92]

When Holmes uses the phrase, "rule of law" it is always to refer to some legal rule, never to the principle that government should be by laws, rather than by men.[93] But he seems well aware of the importance of a functioning legal system in making the social world predictable and orderly enough to be livable; and he sees the law as an engine of moral progress. The history of law, he writes, "is the history of the moral development of the race"; moreover, "in spite of popular jests," the practice of law "tends to make good citizens and good men."[94]

When Holmes writes of the history of law, we sometimes hear that characteristically pragmatist recognition of the role of chance, of contingency—not, to be sure, in the metaphysical form of Peirce's tychism,[95] but rather in the form of a keen awareness that many legal provisions have their origin in very specific past circumstances, often past circumstances that no longer obtain. Once upon a time, for example, a bond was nothing but the actual piece of parchment on which the relevant words were written, so that, if the document was destroyed or the seal torn off, the bond no longer existed, and there could be no recovery; and this idea gradually came to apply to contracts generally.[96] In fact, many legal procedures and provisions are, in whole or in part, surviving remnants of past contingencies. But, Holmes avers, "this is how we have long done it" is no reason to continue a legal rule when the circumstances that prompted it "have vanished long since."[97] The intelligent appraisal of the law requires, rather, an understanding of "the ends which [legal] rules seek to accomplish, the reasons why those ends are desired, what is given up to gain them, and whether those ends are worth the price."[98]

The need to balance past and future is, in a way, built into the job-description of a common-law judge: he must apply the law to the case at hand in a way that is consistent with how it was written and with how it has been interpreted in the past, but also with an eye to the future consequences of interpreting it this way rather than that. In 1881, Holmes writes that, to know what the law is, "we must know what it has been, and what it tends to become."[99] In a speech of 1895, he writes that the past "gives us our vocabulary and fixes the limits of our imagination . . . [b]ut the present has a right to govern itself so far as it can." And a few lines later, we find this remarkable expression of the pragmatist style of knitting past and future: "[T]he eternal procession [of many generations of lawyers, judges, and legal thinkers] moves on, we in the front for the moment; and stretching away against the unattainable sky, the black spearheads of the army that has been passing in unbroken line already for over a thousand years."[100] This bears more than a passing resemblance to Peirce's metaphor of inquirers as "storming the stronghold of truth";[101] moreover, it is notably synechistic in spirit.

Meaning and consequences, the growth of meaning, empiricism, fallibilism, the role of the sciences, law as social institution, the past and the future, continuity: all are found in Holmes. But what about the pragmatist sensitivity to false dichotomies? Isn't the law inherently binary, obliged to make sharp distinctions: e.g., to specify a precise point at which a child becomes an adult,[102] draw a sharp line between the mentally normal and the retarded,[103] make a clear distinction between a genuinely religious objection to military service and an objection that is a matter merely of personal philosophy,[104] and so on? Indeed. But Holmes was pragmatist enough to understand that such bright-line distinctions are usually artificial: "most differences, when nicely considered, are really matters of degree";[105] and he realized the dangers of this artificial precision, writing in *Truax v. Corrigan* that "delusive exactness is a source of fallacy throughout the law."[106]

In the first chapter of *Law and the Modern Mind* (1930), Jerome Frank observed that "the law deals with human relations in their most complicated aspects. The whole confused, shifting helter-skelter of life parades before it—more confused than ever in our kaleidoscopic age."[107] And in the final chapter of the book he wrote that "whatever clear vision of legal realities we have attained in the past twenty-five years is in large measure due to [Holmes]," "the completely adult jurist."[108] But as we saw, not all have agreed with this assessment, or with the classification of Holmes as pragmatist.

## "TWISTING OUR PURPOSE AND PURPORT ALL AWRY"

The pragmatist spirit of Holmes's thinking is *so* marked that there's some temptation—perhaps recalling Peirce's complaint that, "in spite of pragmatists' declarations, unanimous, reiterated, and most explicit," many "persist in twisting our purpose and purport all awry"[109]—to dismiss those who classify him as legal-realist, moral skeptic, etc., out of hand. But it's worth taking the time to distinguish those are simply mistaken from those that can help us understand Holmes a little better because, though they are partial and misleading, they also contain a grain of truth.

Legal realist Karl Llewllyn wrote in 1930 that "*rules* . . . are important so far as they help you . . . predict what judges will do, or so far as they help you get judges to do something."[110] The same year, in a passage reminiscent of Peirce's critique of Descartes's "paper doubts,"[111] he contrasted "real" rules, rules that will actually be enforced, with mere "paper" rules; and rather than offering a definition of "law," in a passage reminiscent of Peirce's synechism envisaged a continuum of normative systems, with no sharp line demarcating the legal from the rest. Reflecting on the many interconnections of law with the social sciences, he acknowledged that "Holmes's mind had traveled most of the road two generations back."[112] Fair enough. But to imagine, as many subsequent commentators have done, that this justifies classifying Holmes as a legal realist is to commit an unfortunate anachronism. Yes, some themes found in Holmes are also found in legal realism; and yes, in the ordinary-language sense of the term, Holmes was "realistic"—anxious, that is, to avoid idealistic misconceptions of law, to understand how the legal system really works. But to suppose that this justifies classifying Holmes as proto-legal-realist is to get things exactly backwards; one might more appropriately classify Llewellyn as post-Holmesian.

In 1931 Dewey praised Holmes's commitment to "[l]iberalism as a method . . . the adoption of the scientific attitude of mind in application to social affairs," and described his judicial writings as "a pattern of the liberal mind in operation";[113] on Holmes's death in 1935, the *New York Times* hailed him as "the chief liberal of the supreme bench for 29 years."[114] What Dewey had in mind, obviously, was Holmes's willingness to allow the states to make legal experiments. By now, however, the meaning of "liberal" has shifted significantly:[115] any association with "liberty" and "libertarian" is fading into the background, and the word has come vaguely to connote "socially progressive" as opposed to "socially conservative." So for readers today Dewey's description is, not false exactly, but potentially misleading.

Holmes's well-known dissent in *Lochner* (1905) illustrates the point. The majority had held that a New York statute limiting the hours of work in bakeries to sixty a week was an unconstitutional violation of bakers' right to contract as they chose. In dissent, Holmes argued that many precedents allowed states to "regulate life in . . . ways which we as legislators might think injudicious. . . ."[116] The *result* for which Holmes argued (allowing the regulation of bakers' hours of work) would today be seen as liberal, progressive. His *reasoning*, however (that states have been and should be allowed to make such experiments), might today be perceived as profoundly conservative—like Justice Thomas's essentially similar argument in a 2005 medical-marijuana case, *Gonzales v. Raich.*[117]

The perception of Holmes as precursor of the law-and-economics movement is perhaps best described as an exaggeration. As we saw, Holmes certainly acknowledges the potential importance of economics to the law. But this is just one element of his larger theme of the potential relevance of the full range of the social sciences generally; moreover, so far as I know Holmes never suggests anything like the more imperialist ambitions of the modern movement to give economic values primary importance in legal decisions.[118]

The description of Holmes as moral skeptic or nihilist, however, is best described not as misleading, anachronistic, or exaggerated, but as mistaken. Perhaps it's the result of confusing Holmes's claim that law is distinct from morality, that the "rights of man" in a moral sense are not to be confused with a person's legal rights under the Constitution,[119] and that "considerations of social advantage" often determine legal decisions,[120] with the quite different claim that there *are no* moral values. But that obviously *isn't* Holmes's position: he writes that he "take[s] for granted that no hearer of mine will misinterpret what I have to say for the language of cynicism";[121] he describes the law as "the witness and deposit of our moral life,"[122] and its evolution as representing progress "from barbarism to civilization."[123] Granted, Holmes doesn't believe that what's morally right or good is something that a judge (or anyone else) can know a priori, or with certainty. This, however, isn't moral skepticism; it is moral fallibilism.[124]

Holmes had opened a 1918 essay critical of natural-law theory with a marvelously ironic analogy: "[i]t is not enough for the knight of romance that you agree that his lady is a very nice girl—if you do not admit that she is the best that God ever made or will make, you must fight."[125] Not surprisingly, the antipathy was mutual: proponents of the natural-law approach abhorred Holmes's insistence on the distinctness of law and morality, and decried what they took to be his blindness to absolute moral values.[126] In 1941, quoting a letter to John Wu in which Holmes had deplored "unchecked propagation," and "the continuance of the unfit," Francis Lucey associated Holmes with just about everything natural-law theorists deplored: utilitarianism, pragmatism, realism, social Darwinism—and Nazism.[127]

Yes, Holmes sympathized with the eugenics movement, as his ruling for the Supreme Court in *Buck v. Bell* (1927)—that Carrie Buck's constitutional rights were not violated when the state of Virginia ordered that she be sterilized—reveals.[128] But this really shouldn't surprise us: Holmes was a man of his time, and in 1927 enthusiasm for what was perceived as the progressive potential of eugenics programs was just about world-wide.[129] More to the present purpose, though: while Lucey acknowledges Holmes's "pragmatism," he conflates pragmatism in its specialized philosophical sense with pragmatism in the everyday sense of "concern for expediency rather than principle." Concern for expediency over principle surely *can* lead to fascism;[130] but pragmatism in this sense is quite different from the philosophical pragmatism one sees in Holmes.

And what about Westbrook Pegler's description of Holmes as a "cynical brutalitarian"? Well, it's overheated journalistic bombast, that's for sure. Still, it's worth taking a moment to disentangle the two elements of Pegler's coinage: "utilitarian" and "brutal." It's true that Holmes focuses on the consequences of legal decisions; but it obviously doesn't follow that he accepts the utilitarian view that the morally best action is what conduces to the greatest happiness of the greatest number. It's also true that he doesn't seem greatly troubled about the price paid by those whom a generally beneficial law harms; but this is evidence less of his "brutality" than of his awareness of the value to everyone of living under a functioning legal system, and his understanding that a judge's job is to apply the law impartially to everyone, regardless of where his own sympathies might lie.[131]

Of course, as this last comment reveals, there are real tensions in Holmes's thinking: e.g., between his conception of a judge's task, not as making law, but as applying it, and his recognition that judicial interpretations do, in fact, shape the law; between his insistence on the distinctness of law and morality, and his conviction that the history of law is a history of moral progress; between his talk of the "inevitable" evolution of law, and his recognition of contingency and conception of law as experiment; and so on. But whether these tensions can be resolved and, more generally, whether, or in what respects, Holmes's view of the law is defensible are questions beyond the scope of the present paper. I'm certainly more inclined to Frank's than to Lucey's assessment of the value of Holmes's thinking; and in other articles I have developed and argued for a kind of neo-classical legal pragmatism of my own.[132] But even a half-way adequate assessment of Holmes's legal philosophy would require, at the least, a whole other paper.[133]

## NOTES



1. John Dewey, "Justice Holmes and the Liberal Mind," in *Mr. Justice Holmes*, ed. Felix Frankfurter (New York: Coward McCann, 1931), 33. See also Benjamin Cardozo, introduction to *Mr. Justice Holmes*, 11.

2. See, e.g., Karl N. Llewellyn, "Some Realism about Realism: Responding to Dean Pound," *Harvard Law Review* 44, no. 8 (June 1931): 1222–64, 1227 n.18; Lon Fuller, "American Legal Realism," *University of Pennsylvania Law Review and American Law Register*, 82, no. 5 (1934): 429–62, 429; and, more recently, Louise Weinberg, "Holmes's Failure," *Michigan Law Review* 96 (December 1997): 691–723, 692. For a critical perspective, see Brian Z. Tamanaha, "Understanding Legal Realism," *Texas Law Review* 87 (2009): 731–85.

3. See, e.g., Robert Cooter, "Models of Morality in Law and Economics: Self-Control and Self-Improvement for the Bad Man of Holmes," *Boston University Law Review* 78 (1998): 903–30; Richard A. Posner, "Savigny, Holmes, and the Law and Economics of Possession," *Virginia Law Review* 535 (2000): 535–67.

4. See, e.g., Albert W. Alschuler, *Law without Values: The Life, Work, and Legacy of Justice Holmes* (Chicago: University of Chicago Press, 2000).

5. Francis E. Lucey, "Jurisprudence and the Future Social Order," *Social Science* 16 (1941): 211–17, 214.

6. Westbrook Pegler, "Fair Enough," *Boston American*, December 18, 1950, 34, 45.

7. Max H. Fisch, "Justice Holmes, the Prediction Theory of Law, and Pragmatism" (1942), in *Peirce, Semeiotic, and Pragmatism: Essays by Max Fisch*, eds. Kenneth Laine Ketner and Christian J. W. Kloesel (Bloomington: Indiana University Press, 1988), 6. See also Philip P. Wiener, *Evolution and the Founders of Pragmatism* (Philadelphia: University of Pennsylvania Press, [1949] 1975), which includes a chapter on Holmes.

8. Here, I must confine myself to these three: but of course a full treatment of the history of pragmatism would also require reference at least to George Herbert Mead and to such radical pragmatists as F. C. S. Schiller in England and Giovanni Papini in Italy. See generally Cornelis de Waal, *On Pragmatism* (Belmont, CA: Wadsworth, 2005); Susan Haack, "Pragmatism, Old and New," in *Pragmatism, Old and New: Selected Writings*, eds. Susan Haack and Robert E. Lane (Amherst, NY: Prometheus Books, 2006), 25–67; Susan Haack, "The Pragmatist Tradition: Lessons for Legal Theorists," *Washington University Law Review* 95, no. 5 (2018): 1049–82.

9. Charles Sanders Peirce, *Collected Papers*, eds. Charles Hartshorne, Paul Weiss, and (vols. 7 and 8) Arthur Burks (Cambridge, MA: Harvard University Press, 1931–58), 5.12 (c. 1906).

10. William James to Oliver Wendell Holmes Jr., January 3, 1868, in *Letters of William James*, ed. Henry James (William James's son) (Boston: Atlantic Monthly Press, 1920), 1:126.

11. Sheldon Novick, "A Brief Biography of Justice Holmes," in *The Collected Works of Justice Holmes*, ed. Sheldon Novick (Chicago: University of Chicago Press, 1995), 1:8.

12. Ibid., 9–10. James Kent, *Commentaries on American Law*, ed. Oliver Wendell Holmes Jr., 12th ed. (Boston: Little, Brown, and Company, 1873).

13. See Peirce, *Collected Papers*, 5.12 (c. 1906); see also Max Fisch, "Was There a Metaphysical Club in Cambridge?" in *Studies in the Philosophy of Charles Sanders Peirce*, Edward C. Moore and Richard Robin (eds.) (Amherst, MA: University of Massachusetts Press, 1964), 3–23 (concluding that independent evidence suggests that Peirce's recollections are pretty accurate).

14. Peirce, *Collected Papers*, 5.12 (c. 1906). Peirce tells us that it was Green who urged the importance of Alexander Bain's definition of belief as that upon which a man is prepared to act, "of which pragmatism is scarce more than a corollary."

15. Ibid.

16. Novick, "A Brief Biography of Justice Holmes," 10. The law firm—later known as Shattuck, Holmes, and Monroe—had a busy practice in commercial and shipping law.

17. William James to Oliver Wendell Holmes Jr., January 3, 1868, in *Letters of William James*, ed. Henry James (William James's son) (Boston: Atlantic Monthly Press, 1920), 126.

18. I rely on Fisch, "Justice Holmes, the Prediction Theory of Law, and Pragmatism," 22.

19. Oliver Wendell Holmes Jr., *The Common Law*, in *Collected Works*, ed. Sheldon Novick, (Chicago: University of Chicago Press, [1881] 1995), 3:109–324.

20. Novick, "A Brief Biography of Justice Holmes," 11.

21. Novick, "A Brief Biography of Justice Holmes," 17.

22. John Dewey, *Experience and Nature* (Carbondale, IL: Southern Illinois University Press, [1925] 2008).

23. Oliver Wendell Holmes Jr. to Frederick Pollock, May 15, 1931, in *The Holmes-Pollock Letters: The Correspondence of Mr. Justice Holmes and Sir Frederick Pollock*, 1872-1932, ed. Mark DeWolfe Howe (Cambridge, MA: Harvard University Press, 1941), 2:287.

24. A doctrine Holmes described as "an amusing humbug." Oliver Wendell Holmes Jr. to Frederick Pollock, June 17, 1908, *The Holmes-Pollock Letters: The Correspondence of Mr. Justice Holmes and Sir Frederick Pollock*, 1872-1932, ibid., 1:139.

25. *Chance, Love, and Logic*, ed. Morris R. Cohen (Lincoln, NE: University of Nebraska Press, [1923] 1988).

26. "The Holmes-Cohen Correspondence," ed. Felix S. Cohen, *Journal of the History of Ideas* 9, no. 1 (1948): 3–52, 34.

27. Oliver Wendell Holmes Jr. to Charles Hartshorne, August 25, 1927; my source is Fisch, "Was There a Metaphysical Club in Cambridge?," 10–11.

28. Peirce, *Collected Papers*, 5.12 (c. 1906); William James, *Pragmatism: A New Name for Some Old Ways of Thinking*, Frederick Burkhardt and Fredson Bowers (eds.) (Cambridge, MA: Harvard University Press, [1907] 1975), 31.

29. Peirce, *Collected Papers*, 5.388–410 (1878).

30. The headings "The Pragmatic Maxim," "Applications of the Pragmatic Maxim" in the version of this paper that appears in the *Collected Papers* were supplied by the editors, and don't appear in the original.

31. Peirce, *Collected Papers*, 5.13 (c. 1906). At that time, by the way, the ordinary-language meaning of "pragmatist" was "busybody," or "conceited, self-seeking person," and the meaning of "pragmatism," correspondingly, "officious meddlesomeness," or "conceit." See *Oxford English Dictionary*, s.v. "pragmatist," accessed January 26, 2018, http://www.oed.com/view/Entry/149296?redirectedFrom=pragmatist#eid.

32. William James, "Philosophical Conceptions and Practical Results" (1898), in *Pragmatism*, eds. Frederick H. Burkhardt and Fredson Bowers (Cambridge, MA: Harvard University Press, [1907] 1975), 257–70.

33. See, e.g. Peirce, *Collected Papers*, 5.12 (c. 1906).

34. In "Philosophical Conceptions and Practical Results," 269, James comments that philosophy "can perfectly well *outflank*" Kant (my italics).

35. James's *Pragmatism* is dedicated to "the Memory of John Stuart Mill[,] from whom I first learned the pragmatic openness of mind. . . ."

36. See, e.g., John Dewey, "From Absolutism to Experimentalism," in *Contemporary American Philosophy*, George P. Adams and William Pepperall Montague (eds.) (New York: Macmillan, 1930), 2:13–27; Jane M. Dewey, "Biography of John Dewey," in *The Philosophy of John Dewey*, ed. Paul Arthur Schilpp (La Salle, IL: Open Court, 1939), 17.

37. James, "Philosophical Conceptions and Practical Results," 259.

38. This partly explains why not only his readers, but even James himself had difficulty disentangling his pragmatism from his doctrine of the Will to Believe.

39. Peirce's neologism "pragmaticism," introduced in 1905, was intended to refer to the doctrines and theories that he developed using the pragmatic method. Peirce, *Collected Papers*, 5.414 (1905). On Peirce's realism, see ibid., 5.470 (c. 1906); Rosa María Perez Teran Mayorga, *From Realism to Realicism* (Lanham, MD: Lexington Books, 2007).

40. See, e.g., James, *Pragmatism*, 32.

41. The year after the publication of James's "The Will to Believe" we find Peirce writing pointedly of "the will to learn." William James, "The Will to Believe" in *The Will to Believe and Other Essays in Popular Philosophy*, Frederick H. Burkhardt and Fredson Bowers (eds.) (Cambridge, MA: Harvard University Press, [1896] [1897] 1979), 13–33. Peirce, *Collected Papers*, 5.583 (1898).

42. John Dewey, "The Practical Character of Reality," in *Philosophy and Civilization* (New York: Minton, Balch and Co., [1908 under the title, "Does Reality Possess Practical Character?"] 1934), 36–55. Peirce, *Collected Papers*, 5.555 (c. 1906).

43. See, e.g., Peirce, *Collected Papers*, 5.407 (1878). James, *Pragmatism*, 95–114. John Dewey, "A Short Catechism Concerning Truth," in *The Influence of Darwin on Philosophy and*

*Other Essays in Contemporary Thought* (New York: Henry Holt and Company, 1910), 154–68; "The Problem of Truth" in *The Essential Dewey*, Larry A. Hickman and Thomas M. Alexander (eds.) (Bloomington, IN: Indiana University Press, [1911] 1998), 2:101–130.

44. James saw ethics as trying to discover what arrangements and rules would satisfy the most demands; Dewey, who writes in terms, not of what is desired, but of what is desirable, saw it as seeking to discover, rather, what arrangements and rules genuinely conduce to human flourishing. William James, "The Moral Philosopher and the Moral Life," in *The Will to Believe and Other Essays in Popular Philosophy*, Frederick Burkhardt and Fredson Bowers (eds.) (Cambridge, MA: Harvard University Press, [1891] [1897] 1979), 141–62; John Dewey, "The Construction of Good," in *The Quest for Certainty: A Study of the Relation of Knowledge and Action* (New York: Minton, Balch, 1929), 254–85.

45. This list is adapted from an earlier paper of mine, "Pragmatism, Law, and Morality: The Lessons of *Buck v. Bell*," *European Journal of Pragmatism and American Philosophy* III, no. 2 (2011): 65–87, 68–72.

46. Holmes's Civil War letters give one a sense both of his initially romantic, boyish enthusiasm, and of the grim realities of the war. *Touched with Fire: Civil War Letters and Diary of Oliver Wendell Holmes, Jr., 1861–1864*, ed. Mark de Wolfe Howe (Cambridge, MA: Harvard University Press, 1946).

47. Fisch, "Holmes, the Prediction Theory of Law, and Pragmatism," 8.

48. Ibid.

49. Oliver Wendell Holmes Jr., "The Path of the Law," in *The Collected Works of Justice Holmes*, ed. Sheldon Novick (Chicago: University of Chicago Press, 1995), 3:391.

50. Peirce, *Collected Papers*, 5.400 (1878).

51. James, *Pragmatism*, 30.

52. Fisch, "Justice Holmes, the Prediction Theory of the Law, and Pragmatism," 12.

53. Peirce, *Collected Papers*, 5.311 (1868).

54. Holmes, "The Path of the Law," 394.

55. As is Holmes's advice to his audience to think of an attorney as advising a "bad man," a client who simply doesn't *care* what's right, only what's legal.

56. James, *Pragmatism*, 95.

57. Holmes, "The Path of the Law," 403.

58. Peirce, *Collected Papers*, 5.383 (1877).

59. James, *Pragmatism*, 52 (he refers, of course, to words like "the Absolute," which sound impressive, but don't really explain anything).

60. Southern Pacific v. Jensen, 244 U.S. 205, 222 (1917) (Holmes dissenting).

61. Fisch, "Justice Holmes, the Prediction Theory of Law, and Pragmatism," 8. Fisch didn't mean this to suggest that the pragmatists were hostile to logic as such; he knew, of course, that Peirce was one of the pioneers of what is now called "modern logic."

62. Holmes, *The Common Law*, 115.

63. Dewey, interestingly enough, will later make the same point specifically with respect to legal concepts. John Dewey, "Logical Method and Law," *Cornell Law Quarterly* 10 (1924): 17–27, 20. See also Susan Haack, "The Growth of Meaning and the Limits of Formalism, in Science and Law," *Análisis filosófico*, XXIX, no. 1 (May 2009): 5–29.

64. Christopher Columbus Langdell, *A Selection of Cases on the Law of Contracts* (Boston: Little, Brown, & Co, second edition, 1879).

65. Oliver Wendell Holmes Jr., Review of Langdell (1880), in *The Collected Works of Justice Holmes*, ed. Sheldon Novick (Chicago: University of Chicago Press, [1880] 1995), 3:102–04.

66. Holmes, *The Common Law*, 117. See also Edward Levi, *Introduction to Legal Reasoning* (Chicago: University of Chicago Press, 1949); Susan Haack, "On Logic in the Law: 'Something, but not All,'" *Ratio Juris* 20, no. 1 (2007): 1–31.

67. Holmes, *The Common Law*, 115–34.

68. Peirce, *Collected Papers*, 2.302 (c. 1895). See also ibid., 7.587 (c. 1867).

69. Gompers v. United States, 233 U.S. 604, 610 (1914).

70. Missouri v. Holland, 252 U.S. 416, 433 (1920).

71. Holmes, "The Path of the Law," 397.

72. Oliver Wendell Holmes Jr., "Natural Law," in *The Collected Works of Justice Holmes*, ed. Sheldon Novick (Chicago: University of Chicago Press, [1918] 1995), 3:446.
73. Peirce, *Collected Papers*, 1.14 (c. 1897).
74. Ibid., 1.13 (c. 1897).
75. Ibid., 1.31 (1903).
76. James, "The Will to Believe," 17.
77. Oliver Wendell Holmes Jr., "Law and the Court," in *The Collected Works of Justice Holmes*, ed. Sheldon Novick (Chicago: University of Chicago Press, [1913] 1995), 3:507.
78. Abrams v. U.S., 250 U.S. 616, 624 (1919) (Holmes dissenting).
79. Dewey, "Justice Holmes and the Liberal Mind," 33.
80. Holmes, "The Path of the Law," 399.
81. Ibid., 400.
82. Peirce, *Collected Papers*, 6.102 ff. (1892).
83. John Dewey, "The Influence of Darwinism on Philosophy," in *The Influence of Darwin on Philosophy and Other Essays in Contemporary Thought* (New York: Henry Holt and Company, [1908] 1910), 1–19.
84. Holmes, "The Path of the Law," 398.
85. See Susan Haack, "The Evolution of Legal Systems: Response to Helena Baldina, Andreas Bruns, and Johannes Müller-Salo," in *Susan Haack: Reintegrating Philosophy*, Julia Göhner and Eva-Maria Jung (eds.) (Berlin: Springer, 2016), 195–202; Haack, "The Pragmatist Tradition: Lessons for Legal Theorists."
86. Lochner v. New York, 198 U.S. 45, 76 (1905) (Holmes dissenting).
87. Truax v. Corrigan, 257 U.S. 312, 344 (1921) (Holmes dissenting).
88. The "wedding-cake case" before the U.S. Supreme Court as I write this illustrates the point, since it will require weighing the right of baker James Phillips to refuse, on religious grounds, to make a wedding cake for a gay couple against the rights of the couple concerned not to suffer discrimination because of their sexual orientation. Masterpiece Cakeshop v. Colo. Civil Rights Comm'n, 584 U.S. ____, 138 S. Ct. 1719 (2018).
89. James, "The Moral Philosopher and the Moral Life," 141–62.
90. Oliver Wendell Holmes Jr., "The Law," in *The Collected Works of Justice Holmes*, ed. Sheldon Novick (Chicago: University of Chicago Press, [1885] 1995), 3:469.
91. James, "The Moral Philosopher and the Moral Life," 153.
92. See, e.g., Holmes's ruling in United Zinc and Chemical Co. v. Britt, 258 U.S. 268 (1922) (which is preoccupied with repudiating the legal doctrine of "attractive nuisance," and pays little attention to any dangers to unwary children such as those who had died because of their attraction to United Zinc's pool of poisonous chemicals).
93. This usage is, however, very old; according to the *Oxford English Dictionary*, its earliest occurrence is in a c. 1500 translation by John Blount of Nicholas Upton's *De Studio Militari*. See *Oxford English Dictionary*, s.v. "rule of law," accessed January 26, 2018, http://www.oed.com/view/Entry/277614?redirectedFrom=rule+of+law#eid.
94. Holmes, "The Path of the Law," 392.
95. Peirce, *Collected Papers*, 6.35–65 (1892).
96. Holmes, "The Path of the Law," 402.
97. Ibid., 399.
98. Holmes, "The Path of the Law," 404. Dewey will say something strikingly similar many years later. John Dewey, "My Philosophy of Law," in *My Philosophy of Law* (Boston: Boston Law Book Co., 1941), 84.
99. Holmes, *The Common Law*, 115.
100. Oliver Wendell Holmes Jr., "Learning and Science," in *The Collected Works of Justice Holmes*, ed. Sheldon Novick (Chicago: University of Chicago Press, [1895] 1995), 3:492.
101. Peirce, *Collected Papers*, 7.51 (n.d.). Eventually, Peirce writes, some will succeed, by climbing on the corpse of another who has fallen, "who has to ordinary apprehension failed, but has in truth succeeded by virtue of the lessons of his failure."
102. See, e.g., Alexandra O. Cohen et al., "When Does a Juvenile Become an Adult: Implications for Law and Policy," *Temple Law Review* 88 (2016): 769–88 (surveying the various ages

specified in different legal contexts as the point at which a juvenile becomes an adult, and summarizing recent scientific work on the maturation of the human brain).

103. See, e.g., Hall v. Florida, 572 U.S. ___, 134 S. Ct. 1986, 2000–01 (2014) (holding that a Florida statute foreclosing any further evidence of a defendant's mental disability if he or she scores above 70 on an IQ test is unconstitutional as applied).

104. See, e.g., Fraina v. United States, 255 F. 28 (2d Cir. 1918) (distinguishing a genuinely religious objection to war from one based on "idealism"); but compare United States. v. Seeger, 380 U.S. 163 (1965) (adopting a much broader conception of religion).

105. Rideout v. Knox, 148 Mass. 368, 19 N.E. 390, 392 (1889).

106. Truax v. Corrigan 257 U.S. at 342 (Holmes dissenting).

107. Jerome Frank, *Law and the Modern Mind* (New York: Coward-McCann, 1930), 6.

108. Ibid., 253.

109. Peirce, *Collected Papers*, 5.464 (c. 1906).

110. Karl Llewellyn, *Bramble Bush: Our Law and Its Study* (New York: Oceana, 1930), 5.

111. Peirce, *Collected Papers*, 4.445 (1905); ibid., 5.514 (c. 1905); ibid., 6.498 (c. 1906); ibid., 6.500 (c. 1906).

112. Karl Llewellyn, "A Realistic Jurisprudence—The Next Step," *Columbia Law Review* 30, no. 4 (1930): 431–65, 448.

113. Dewey, "Justice Holmes and the Liberal Mind," 35.

114. *New York Times*, March 6, 1935.

115. The full story is long and complex. See, e.g., Robin L. West, "Liberalism Rediscovered: A Pragmatic Definition of the Liberal Vision," *University of Pittsburgh Law Review* 46 (1985): 673–738; Laura Kalman, *The Strange Career of Legal Liberalism* (New Haven: Yale University Press, 1996); Edmund Fawcett, *Liberalism: the Life of an Idea* (Princeton, NJ: Princeton University Press, 2014).

116. Lochner, 198 U.S. at 75.

117. Raich v. Gonzales, 525 U.S. 1, 18 (2005) (Thomas dissenting) (arguing that "[o]ur federalist system . . . allows California . . . to decide for themselves how to safeguard the health and welfare of their citizens").

118. This, from Holmes, "The Path of the Law," 397, is about as ambitious a claim for the role of economics as I have found: "Why is a man at liberty to set up a business which he knows will ruin his neighbor? It is because the public good is supposed to be best subserved by free competition."

119. Holmes, "The Path of the Law," 395.

120. Ibid., 398.

121. Ibid., 392.

122. Ibid.

123. Holmes, *The Common Law*, 135. As I argued in Susan Haack, "On Legal Pragmatism: Where Does 'The Path of the Law' Lead Us?," *American Journal of Jurisprudence* 50 (2005): 71–105, 92–95, this is too optimistic; as the example of Nazi law reveals, a legal system may evolve in morally regressive, as well as morally progressive, ways.

124. As I argued in some detail in "Pragmatism, Law, and Morality."

125. Holmes, "Natural Law," 445.

126. See, e.g., Lucey, "Jurisprudence and the Future Social Order"; John Ford, "The Fundamentals of Holmes's Juristic Philosophy," *Fordham Law Review* 11 (1942): 255–78; Paul Gregg, "The Pragmatism of Mr. Justice Holmes," *Georgetown Law Journal* 31 (1943): 262–95. These criticisms were popularized by Ben W. Palmer in "Hobbes, Holmes, and Hitler," *American Bar Association Journal* 31 (1945): 569–73.

127. Lucey, "Jurisprudence and the Future Social Order," 214 (citing Oliver Wendell Holmes Jr. to John C. Wu, 21 July 1925, in *Justice Oliver Wendell Holmes: His Book Notices and Uncollected Letters and Papers*, ed. Harry C. Shriver (New York: Central Book Co., 1936), 181.

128. Buck v. Bell, 274 U.S. 200 (1927). See also Haack, "Pragmatism, Law, and Morality."

129. It is also worth noting that the Supreme Court's decision in *Buck* was 8-1; and that there was no written dissent.

130. Of course, Lucey is by no means alone in this confusion. In "Fascism's Indelible Mark on History," *Sunday Times* (London), April 11, 1926, 16, André Révesz reports Benito Mussolini's answer to a question about the most important influences on his character: Georges Sorel was the most important, followed by Friedrich Nietzsche and William James: "James taught me that an action should be judged . . . by its results. . . . I learnt of James that faith in action, that ardent will to live and fight to which Fascism owes a great part of its success."

131. In "Law and the Court" Holmes writes that "it is a misfortune if a judge reads his . . . sympathy for one side or the other" into the law (508), and describes the Court as "trying to do good work, with no thought but that of solving a problem according to the rules by which one is bound" (505).

132. See Haack, "On Legal Pragmatism," 71–105; Susan Haack, "The Pluralistic Universe of Law," 453–80; Susan Haack, "The Pragmatist Tradition: Lessons for Legal Theorists."

133. My thanks to Mark Migotti for helpful comments on draft versions, to Nicholas Mignanelli for help in finding relevant materials, checking the format of references, etc., and to Bianca Anderson for word-processing help.

## BIBLIOGRAPHY

Alschuler, Albert W. *Law without Values: The Life, Work, and Legacy of Justice Holmes.* Chicago: University of Chicago Press, 2000.

Cardozo, Benjamin. "Introduction: Mr. Justice Holmes." In *Mr. Justice Holmes*, edited by Felix Frankfurter, 1–20. New York: Coward McCann, 1931.

Cohen, Alexandra O. et al., "When Does a Juvenile Become an Adult: Implications for Law and Policy." *Temple Law Review* 88 (2016): 769–88.

Cohen, Felix S., ed. "The Holmes-Cohen Correspondence." *Journal of the History of Ideas* 9, no. 1 (1948): 3–52.

Cohen, Morris R., ed. *Chance, Love, and Logic.* Lincoln, NE: University of Nebraska Press, [1923] 1988.

Cooter, Robert. "Models of Morality in Law and Economics: Self-Control and Self-Improvement for the Bad Man of Holmes." *Boston University Law Review* 78 (1998): 903–930.

Dewey, Jane M. "Biography of John Dewey." In *The Philosophy of John Dewey*, edited by Paul Arthur Schilpp, 3–45. La Salle, IL: Open Court, 1939.

Dewey, John. "The Influence of Darwinism on Philosophy." In *The Influence of Darwin on Philosophy*, 1–19. New York: Henry Holt and Company, [1908] 1910.

———. "The Practical Character of Reality." In *Philosophy and Civilization*, 36–55. New York: Minton, Balch and Co., [1908 under the title, "Does Reality Possess Practical Character?"] 1934.

———. *The Influence of Darwin on Philosophy and Other Essays in ContemporaryThought.* New York: Henry Holt and Company, 1910.

———. "A Short Catechism Concerning Truth." In *The Influence of Darwin on Philosophy*, 154–68. New York: Henry Holt and Company, 1910.

———. "The Problem of Truth." In *The Essential Dewey*, edited by Larry A. Hickman and Thomas M. Alexander, 2:101–30. Bloomington, IN: Indiana University Press, [1911] 1998.

———. *Experience and Nature.* Carbondale, IL: Southern IllinoisUniversity Press, [1925] 2008.

———. "The Construction of Good." In *The Quest for Certainty: A Study of the Relation of Knowledge and Action*, 254–85. New York: Minton, Balch, 1929.

———. "From Absolutism to Experimentalism." In *Contemporary American Philosophy*, edited by George P. Adams and William Pepperall Montague, 2:13–27. New York: Macmillan, 1930.

———. "Justice Holmes and the Liberal Mind." In *Mr. Justice Holmes*, edited by Felix Frankfurter, 33–45. New York: Coward McCann.

———. "My Philosophy of Law." In *My Philosophy of Law*, 71–85. Boston: Boston Law Book Co., 1941.

Fawcett, Edmund. *Liberalism: The Life of an Idea*. Princeton, NJ: Princeton University Press, 2014.

Fisch, Max H. "Justice Holmes, The Prediction Theory of Law, and Pragmatism." In *Peirce, Semeiotic, and Pragmatism: Essays by Max Fisch*, edited by Kenneth Laine Ketner and Christian J. W. Kloesel, 6–18. Bloomington: Indiana University Press, 1988.

———. "Was There a Metaphysical Club in Cambridge?" In *Studies in the Philosophy of Charles Sanders Peirce*, edited by Edward C. Moore and Richard Robin, 3–23. Amherst, MA: University of Massachusetts Press, 1964.

Ford, John. "The Fundamentals of Holmes's Juristic Philosophy." *Fordham Law Review* 11 (1942): 255–78.

Frank, Jerome. *Law and the Modern Mind*. New York: Coward-McCann, 1930.

Frankfurter, Felix, ed. *Mr. Justice Holmes*. New York: Coward McCann, 1931.

Fuller, Lon. "American Legal Realism." *University of Pennsylvania Law Review and American Law Register* 82, no. 5 (1934): 429–62.

Gregg, Paul. "The Pragmatism of Mr. Justice Holmes." *Georgetown Law Journal* 31 (1943): 262–95.

Haack, Susan. "On Legal Pragmatism: Where Does 'The Path of the Law' Lead Us?"*American Journal of Jurisprudence* 50 (2005): 71–105.

———. "Pragmatism, Old and New." In *Pragmatism, Old and New: Selected Writings*, edited by Susan Haack and Robert E. Lane, 25–67. Amherst, NY: Prometheus Books, 2006.

———. "On Logic in the Law: 'Something, but Not All.'" *Ratio Juris* 20, no. 1 (2007): 1–31.

———. "The Pluralistic Universe of Law: Towards a Neo-classical Legal Pragmatism." *Ratio Juris* 21, no. 4 (2008): 453–80.

———. "Pragmatism, Law, and Morality: The Lessons of *Buck v. Bell*." *European Journal of Pragmatism and American Philosophy* III, no. 2 (2011): 65–87.

———. "The Evolution of Legal Systems: Response to Helena Baldina, Andreas Bruns, and Johannes Müller-Salo." In *Susan Haack: Reintegrating Philosophy*, edited by Julia Göhner and Eva-Maria Jung, 195–202. Berlin: Springer, 2016.

———. "The Pragmatist Tradition: Lessons for Legal Theorists." *Washington University Law Review* 95, no. 5 (2018): 1049–82.

Hartshorne, Charles, Paul Weiss, and Arthur Burks, eds., see Peirce, Charles Sanders, *Collected Papers*.

Holmes, Oliver Wendell Jr. "Langdell's Law of Contracts and Ansons's English Law of Contract." In *Collected Works*, edited by Sheldon Novick, 3:102–04. Chicago: University of Chicago Press, [1880] 1995.

———. *The Common Law*. In *Collected Works*, edited by Sheldon Novick, 3:109–324. Chicago: University of Chicago Press, [1881] 1995.

———. "The Law." In *Collected Works*, edited by Sheldon Novick, 3:468–70. Chicago: University of Chicago Press, [1885] 1995.

———. "Learning and Science." In *Collected Works*, edited by Sheldon Novick, 3:491–92. Chicago: University of Chicago Press, [1895] 1995.

———. "The Path of the Law." In *Collected Works*, edited by Sheldon Novick, 3:391–406. Chicago: University of Chicago Press, [1897] 1995.

———. "Law and the Court." In *Collected Works*, edited by Sheldon Novick, 3:505–08. Chicago: University of Chicago Press, [1913] 1995.

———. "Natural Law." In *Collected Works*, edited by Sheldon Novick, 3:445–48. Chicago: University of Chicago Press, [1918] 1995.

———. *Touched with Fire: Civil War Letters and Diary of Oliver Wendell Holmes, Jr., 1861-1864*. Edited by Mark de Wolfe Howe. Cambridge, MA: Harvard University Press, 1946.

———. *The Collected Works of Justice Holmes*. Edited by Sheldon Novick. Chicago: University of Chicago Press, 1995.

———. and Frederick Pollock. *The Holmes-Pollock Letters: The Correspondence of Mr. Justice Holmes and Sir Frederick Pollock*, 1872-1932. Edited by Mark DeWolfe Howe. Cambridge, MA: Harvard University Press, 1941.

James, Henry (William James's son). *Letters of William James*. Boston: Atlantic Monthly Press, 1920.

James, William. "The Moral Philosopher and the Moral Life." In *The Will to Believe and Other Essays in Popular Philosophy*, edited by Frederick H. Burkhardt and Fredson Bowers, 141–62. Cambridge, MA: Harvard University Press, [1891] 1979.

———. "Philosophical Conceptions and Practical Results." In *Pragmatism: A New Name for Some Old Ways of Thinking* (1907), edited by Frederick Burkhardt and Fredson Bowers, 257–70. Cambridge, MA: Harvard University Press, [1898] 1975.

———. "The Will to Believe." In *The Will to Believe and Other Essays in Popular Philosophy*, edited by Frederick H. Burkhardt and Fredson Bowers, 13–33. Cambridge, MA: Harvard University Press, [1896] [1897] 1979.

———. *The Will to Believe and Other Essays in Popular Philosophy*. Edited by Frederick H. Burkhardt and Fredson Bowers. Cambridge, MA: Harvard University Press, [1897] 1979.

———. *Pragmatism: A New Name for Some Old Ways of Thinking*. Edited by Frederick Burkhardt and Fredson Bowers. Cambridge, MA: Harvard University Press, [1907] 1975.

Kalman, Laura. *The Strange Career of Legal Liberalism*. New Haven: Yale University Press, 1996.

Kent, James. *Commentaries on American Law*. Edited by Oliver Wendell Holmes Jr. Boston: Little, Brown, and Company, 1873.

Langdell, Christopher Columbus. *A Selection of Cases on the Law of Contracts*. Boston: Little, Brown, & Co, 1879.

Levi, Edward. *Introduction to Legal Reasoning*. Chicago: University of Chicago Press,1949.

Llewellyn, Karl N. *Bramble Bush: Our Law and Its Study*. New York: Oceana, 1930.

———. "A Realistic Jurisprudence—The Next Step." *Columbia Law Review* 30, no. 4 (1930): 431–65.

———. "Some Realism about Realism: Responding to Dean Pound." *Harvard Law Review* 44, no. 8 (June 1931): 1222–64.

Lucey, Francis E. "Jurisprudence and the Future Social Order." *Social Science* 16 (1941): 211–17.

Mayorga, Rosa María Perez Teran. *From Realism to Realicism*. Lanham, MD: Lexington Books, 2007.

Novick, Sheldon. "A Brief Biography of Justice Holmes." In *The Collected Works of Justice Holmes*, edited by Sheldon Novick, 1:8–17. Chicago: University of Chicago Press, 1995.

———, ed., see Holmes, Oliver Wendell Jr., *The Collected Works of Justice Holmes*.

Palmer, Ben W. "Hobbes, Holmes, and Hitler." *American Bar Association Journal* 31 (1945): 569–73.

Pegler, Westbrook. "Fair Enough." *Boston American*, December 18, 1950.

Peirce, Charles Sanders. *Collected Papers*. Edited by Charles Hartshorne, Paul Weiss, and (vols.7 and 8) Arthur Burks. Cambridge, MA: Harvard University Press, 1931–58. References to Peirce's *Collected Papers* are by volume and paragraph number.

Posner, Richard A. "Savigny, Holmes, and the Law and Economics of Possession." *Virginia Law Review* 535 (2000): 535–67.

Révesz, André. "Fascism's Indelible Mark on History." *Sunday Times* (London), April 11, 1926.

Shriver, Harry C., ed. *Justice Oliver Wendell Holmes: His Book Notices and Uncollected Letters and Papers*. New York: Central Book Co., 1936.

Tamanaha, Brain Z. "Understanding Legal Realism." *Texas Law Review* 87 (2009): 731–85.

de Waal, Cornelis. *On Pragmatism*. Belmont, CA: Wadsworth, 2005.

Weinberg, Louise. "Holmes's Failure." *Michigan Law Review* 96 (December 1997): 691–723.

West, Robin L. "Liberalism Rediscovered: A Pragmatic Definition of the Liberal Vision." *University of Pittsburgh Law Review* 46 (1985): 673–738.

Wiener, Philip P. *Evolution and the Founders of Pragmatism*. Philadelphia: University of Pennsylvania Press, [1949] 1975.

# Index

# Author Biographies

**Brian E. Butler** is the Thomas Howerton Professor of Humanities and a member of the Philosophy Department at the University of North Carolina, Asheville. He also serves as Co-chair of the Black Mountain College Museum + Arts Center. He has advanced degrees in art, philosophy, and law. He is the editor of *Democratic Experimentalism* (Rodopi, 2012) and co-editor of *The Real Metaphysical Club: All the Philosophers, Their Debates, and Selected Writings from 1868 to 1885* (SUNY Press, 2017). His book *The Democratic Constitution* (Chicago, 2017) develops a democratic theory of constitutional interpretation based upon philosophical pragmatism.

**Raff Donelson** is Assistant Professor of Law and Philosophy at Louisiana State University. His philosophical interests include metaethics and the philosophy of law, while his legal doctrinal work focuses on constitutional protections for criminals and those accused of lawbreaking. His writing has been featured in *Contemporary Pragmatism*, *The Ohio State Journal of Criminal Law*, *UMKC Law Review*, and the *Washington University Jurisprudence Review*.

**Susan Haack** is Distinguished Professor in the Humanities, Cooper Senior Scholar in Arts and Sciences, Professor of Philosophy and Professor of Law at the University of Miami, where she teaches both in the College of Arts and Sciences and in the School of Law. Her books include *Philosophy of Logics*, *Deviant Logic, Fuzzy Logic: Beyond the Formalism*, *Manifesto of a Passionate Moderate*, *Defending Science—Within Reason*, *Pragmatism, Old and New*, *Putting Philosophy to Work*, *Evidence Matters: Science, Proof, and Truth in the Law*, and *Scientism and its Discontents*; and she has also published more than 200 articles in a wide variety of fora. Her work has appeared in 15 languages, and has been the subject of two volumes of essays—*Susan Haack: A Lady of Distinctions* and *Susan Haack: Reintegrating Philosophy*—and a special issue of *Estudios filosóficos*. (Another volume of essays on her work is now in preparation.) Haack has given more than 700 external lectures all around the world—in 30 countries so far. She has received awards for excellence in teaching, in research, and in writing. In 2011, she was awarded the degree of Doctor Honoris Causa by Petri Andreis University, and in 2016, the Ulysses Medal (its highest honor) from University College, Dublin in 2016. In 2020, she is to receive the Premio internacional de cultura jurídica from the University of Girona.

**Frederic Kellogg** was born in Boston, Massachusetts, in 1942. He was a federal prosecutor and served on the staff of U.S. Attorney General Elliot Richardson who resigned in 1973 in the "Saturday Night Massacre." He practiced as a criminal and public interest lawyer and served in the 1980s as General Counsel of the National Endowment for the Arts. He has published two books on Justice Oliver Wendell Holmes Jr. He received the Doctor of Juridical Science from George Washington University in 1983, has taught jurisprudence as a Fulbright Scholar in Poland (1996) and Brazil (2008), and was a MacCormick Fellow at the University of Edinburgh for Fall 2009. He is currently a Visiting Professor at the Federal University of Pernambuco in Recife, Brazil. Kellogg was awarded an honorary doctorate in 2002 from Bridgewater State University in Bridgewater, Massachusetts.

**Alexander Lian** is an independent scholar and a solo practitioner concentrating in commercial litigation. He lives and works in Miami, Florida. He is a graduate of Vanderbilt University (M.A., J.D.). His scholarship focuses on the development of American intellectual and cultural life, and the intersection of law with philosophy and history, especially in reference to Oliver Wendell Holmes. He has an avid interest in legal education. He has contributed pieces to *The New Oxford Review* and *Litigation Ethics*. He is the author of the forthcoming book, *Stereoscopic Law: Oliver Wendell Holmes and Legal Education*, to be published by Cambridge University Press.

**Allen Mendenhall** is Associate Dean at Thomas Goode Jones School of Law and Executive Director of the Blackstone & Burke Center for Law & Liberty. Visit his website at AllenMendenhall.com. He is the author of, most recently, *The Southern Philosopher: Collected Essays of John William Corrington* (University of North Georgia Press, 2017), *Of Bees and Boys: Lines from a Southern Lawyer* (Red Dirt Press, 2017), and *Oliver Wendell Holmes Jr., Pragmatism, and the Jurisprudence of Agon: Aesthetic Dissent and the Common Law* (Bucknell University Press, 2017). He has published hundreds of articles and reviews in various outlets, including *The Journal Jurispru-*

*dence, The Texas Review of Law & Politics, Canadian Journal of Law & Jurisprudence, The Wall Street Journal, Los Angeles Review of Books, The South Carolina Review, Academic Questions, Pacific Standard,Modern Age, Newsweek, Pleiades: A Journal of New Writing, The Federalist, The Hill, The Washington Times, The Georgetown Journal of Law & Modern Critical Race Perspectives, Southern Humanities Review, PEER English, The Indiana Law Journal Supplement, British Journal of American Legal Studies, The Salisbury Review, Quarterly Journal of Austrian Economics, Elon Law Review, The Michigan State Journal of International Law, Libertarian Papers*, and *The American Conservative*.

**Seth Vannatta** is Professor and Chair of the Department of Philosophy and Religious Studies at Morgan State University in Baltimore, Maryland. He is the author of *Conservatism and Pragmatism in Law, Politics, and Ethics*, (Palgrave, 2014) and articles on American Pragmatism, philosophy of law, philosophy of education, and philosophy of popular culture. His articles have appeared in *The Pluralist, Contemporary Pragmatism, Education and Culture, The Transactions of the Charles Sanders Peirce Society, Humanitas, Anamnesis, UMKC Law Review, Southwest Philosophy Review*, and others. He has edited two volumes on philosophy and popular culture: *Chuck Klosterman and Philosophy: The Real and the Cereal* (Open Court, 2012) and *The Wire and Philosophy: This America, Man* (Open Court, 2013). Seth is a member of the America Philosophical Association and the Society for the Advancement of American Philosophy.

**Catharine Wells** is Professor of Law at Boston College Law School. She was educated at Wellesley College (B.A.), the University of California at Berkeley (M.A and Ph.D. in philosophy) and the Harvard Law School (J.D.). Prior to entering law teaching, she served as an Assistant Attorney General for the Commonwealth of Massachusetts and Director of the Division of Public Charities within that office. Professor Wells has written extensively in the fields of jurisprudence and legal theory. Her main focus has been on the application of pragmatic principles to various questions in contemporary legal theory and on the influence of Peirce and James on the jurist, Oliver Wendell Holmes Jr. Her publications include: *A Pragmatic Approach to Improving Tort Law*; *Why Pragmatism Works For Me*; *Pragmatism, Honesty, and Integrity*; *Legal Innovation within the Wider Intellectual Tradition: The Pragmatism of Oliver Wendell Holmes*; *Situated Decision Making*; and *Improving One's Situation: Some Pragmatic Reflections on the Art of Judging*. She has also written a number of articles on the experience of women and minorities in legal education.

**Sarah H. Woolwine** teaches philosophy at the University of Central Oklahoma. She publishes primarily in feminist philosophy, philosophy of disability and Continental philosophy. Currently, she is writing a book on ableism and hermeneutical injustice. She has published articles in the *Southwest Philosophy Review*, *Res Philosophica*, and *The Journal of Speculative Philosophy*.

www.ingramcontent.com/pod-product-compliance
Lightning Source LLC
LaVergne TN
LVHW090358210926
848480LV00002B/380
* 9 7 8 1 4 9 8 5 6 1 2 6 6 *